Bullying

Bullying

A Handbook for Educators and Parents

Ian Rivers, Neil Duncan, and Valerie E. Besag

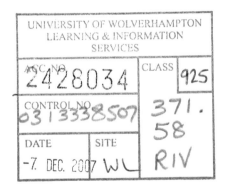
HANDBOOKS FOR EDUCATORS AND PARENTS
James T. Sears, Series Editor

Westport, Connecticut
London

Library of Congress Cataloging-in-Publication Data

Rivers, Ian.
  Bullying : a handbook for educators and parents / Ian Rivers, Neil Duncan, and
Valerie E. Besag.
    p.   cm.—(Handbooks for educators and parents, ISSN 1554–6039)
  Includes bibliographical references and index.
  ISBN 978–0–313–33850–2 (alk. paper)
  1. Bullying in schools—Handbooks, manuals, etc.   I. Duncan, Neil, 1956–   II.
Besag, Valerie E.   III. Title.
  LB3013.3.R58   2007
371.5′8—dc22   2007028079

British Library Cataloguing in Publication Data is available.

Library of Congress Catalog Card Number: 2007028079
ISBN-13: 978–0–313–33850–2
ISSN: 1554–6039

First published in 2007

Praeger Publishers, 88 Post Road West, Westport, CT 06881
An imprint of Greenwood Publishing Group, Inc.
www.praeger.com

Printed in the United States of America

The paper used in this book complies with the
Permanent Paper Standard issued by the National
Information Standards Organization (Z39.48–1984).

10 9 8 7 6 5 4 3 2 1

Contents

PART IV: THE WAY AHEAD

Series Foreword

How can I advocate for my child? What are the best school practices in teaching diverse learners? What programs are most effective in enhancing learning? These simple but profoundly important questions are at the heart of this book series.

This handbook is a practical guide for parents/families and a standard reference source for educators and libraries. The entire series provides an overview of contemporary research, theories, practices, policy issues, and instructional approaches on a variety of timely and important educational topics. It also gives straightforward recommendations for evaluating curriculum and advocating for children in schools.

Ian Rivers, Neil Duncan, and Val Besag cogently examine one of the most pernicious aspects of growing up: bullying. In a time not so long ago, this phenomenon of childhood insults, innuendo, scuffling, jokes, and rumors was considered a rite of passage—occasionally experienced by many children but routinely endured by just a few. Bullying was condoned if not embraced by adults who viewed it as a *schoolboy* practice which was either harmless or served a useful function of toughening up lads and building character of fortitude and, perhaps, empathy for the downtrodden. But as early the mid-nineteenth century, Thomas Hughes both challenged and embraced these notions. In *Tom Brown's Schooldays* his semiautobiographical hero empathizes with the victims of the cruel schoolyard bully Flashman but also understands and complies with the code of masculinity.

Discussion about bullying, however, remained the province of novelists and was not seriously undertaken as a research topic or a school issue until the late twentieth century. Among the earliest scholarly analysis of school bullying was Val Besag's *Bullies and Victims in Schools* (1989), but public concerns were not elevated until a range of shootings marred America's schoolscape. And, even then, the sexualized and gendered components of bullying were ignored in favor of psychological analyses or point-counterpoint debates over gun control. Here, Neil Duncan's book *Sexual Bullying: Gender Conflict and Pupil Culture in Secondary Schools* (2001) was particularly valuable as has been the empirical research of Ian Rivers (Rivers, 2001a, 2001b; Rivers and Cowie, 2006) on the prevalence and impact of homophobic bullying.

In *Bullying*, this trio of scholars offers a research overview of the multiple forms and facets of bullying, provides specific strategies for educators, and spells out avenues of action for concerned parents. Ultimately, as they and others have underscored, bullying is not simply a matter between the bully and the bullied but one that concerns us all. It is, after all, the onlookers who empower the bully by their gaze of complacency or action of complicity and society, encasing the rigidly gendered and heterosexualized atmosphere, which allows for the combustive power of repeated aggression of one human being over another to occur.

REFERENCES

Besag, V. (1989). *Bullies and Victims in Schools*. London: Open University Press.

Duncan, N. (2001). *Sexual Bullying: Gender Conflict and Pupil Culture in Secondary Schools*. London: Routledge.

Rivers, I. (2001a). Retrospective reports of school bullying: Stability of recall and its implications for research. *British Journal of Developmental Psychology*, 19, 129–142.

Rivers, I. (2001b). The bullying of sexual minorities at school: Its nature and long-term correlates. *Educational and Child Psychology*, 18(1), 32–46.

Rivers, I., and Cowie, H. (2006). Bullying and homophobia at UK schools: A perspective on factors affecting resilience and recovery. *Journal of Gay and Lesbian Issues in Education*, 3(4), 23–36.

Preface

Bullying is perhaps one of the most difficult issues we face today as parents and educators. While there is general recognition that all children have the right to an education safe from the fear of harassment, it is proving increasingly difficult for us adults to keep pace with changes in language, fashion, and technology that our children and young people value and place store by. Our failure to move in synchrony with young people often results in periods of time when we are baffled by new words and phrases, fail to appreciate the social significance of a particular baseball cap, schoolbag, t-shirt, or pair of sneakers, or find it difficult to understand the power a threatening e-mail or text message has over an individual. It is only with the passage of time, and the willingness of some young people to come forward, that we begin to fully understand the significance of those things that once we did not understand. We begin to appreciate the damage that can be caused by a name or label, the pain associated with memories of teasing because parents could not afford the right designer clothing, or the fear that a text message instilled.

In writing this handbook, we have endeavored to provide readers with those insights gleaned from our own research and educational practice with young people in schools. This book is designed to provide parents and educators with a framework to better understand the phenomenon we know as "bullying," and to provide some useful tips on how to spot it, deal with it, and work with a student to overcome the social, emotional, and educational challenges associated with it. We have written this handbook with the intention that it constitutes a starting point for reflective practice among educators, information and advice for parents, and a quick reference source for administrators.

There are four sections to this text and ten chapters, each chapter provides an overview of issues relevant to parents and educators who wish to work collectively to challenge bullying behavior.

PART I: GENERAL INTRODUCTION

In this part, we provide a review of research on bullying behavior, considering the different studies that have been conducted since the late 1960s and now provide us with a holistic view of the phenomenon from various cultural perspectives. We discuss the different types of victims and perpetrators that can be found within schools, providing case studies to demonstrate the dynamic and complex world of aggressive behavior.

PART II: ADVICE FOR EDUCATORS

In this part we discuss a number of issues associated with the ethos and culture of the school. Particular attention is paid to dynamics of the classroom and the playground, and the way in which stereotypes of masculinity and femininity are reinforced. Two chapters focus on the issue of sexuality: one on sexual bullying and the associated subculture of dominance; the other on homophobic bullying, a form of aggressive behavior increasingly prevalent in our schools and one that affects many more students than those who are perceived to be gay or lesbian. In this part we also focus upon issues associated with students who have special needs and pay particular attention to the legislation surrounding disability harassment. Finally, we provide an overview of current approaches to tackling bullying in schools. This is by no means an exhaustive list, but provides an overview of the different types of interventions that are available and have been shown to have an impact upon levels of bullying behavior.

PART III: ADVICE FOR PARENTS

This part consists of two chapters that have been written for the parents of students accused of bullying others, and those whose children are victims. The first chapter in this part addresses the long-term effects of bullying. It provides checklists of symptoms that have been found to be associated with bully or victim status in both elementary and secondary schools. The second chapter looks at ways in which parents can engage proactively with schools to ensure that their child is supported in finding a way out of bullying. It includes guidance relating to key pieces of legislation such as *The No Child Left Behind Act*, and offers a summary of state legislation, directives, and standards governing the teaching of social skills and antiviolence strategies in schools from grades K to 12.

PART IV: THE WAY AHEAD

The concluding part reviews what we have learned about bullying behavior, and provides parents and educators with some thoughts about their own practices if and when they encounter bullying. We ask key questions that every parent and educator should consider when determining the most appropriate method of challenging bullying in whatever form it takes, and consider the future of young people in public schools.

Acknowledgments

Invariably, we must acknowledge the support we have received from various colleagues in preparing this handbook. It is no mean feat for three British authors to write a book that will, we hope, be relevant to parents and educators working with a public school system very different from the one on which we have focused much of our professional lives. In drafting each chapter, we have relied upon our American friends and colleagues to challenge our ethnocentricity, and guide us in the use of language and examples that makes sense to a U.S. audience. We are particularly grateful to Mark Carter (Georgia State University) and Paul Poteat (University of Illinois, Urbana-Champaign) for their willingness to review many of the chapters of this handbook. We would also like to thank the National Association of State Boards of Education (NASBE) for their willingness to grant permission to reproduce some of their excellent guides and resources. We would also like to thank Dave Besag for his support in developing this book, and Viv Lever (York St. John University) for her suggestions on running a training event for educators and parents.

PART I

General Introduction

CHAPTER 1

Introduction: Bullying, What Is It?

EARLY RESEARCH ON BULLYING

History is littered with references to willful acts of aggression perpetrated against the innocent to placate those who claim greatness, or the majority who have sought a scapegoat upon whom they can transfer blame for their misfortune. Until the late 1960s and early 1970s, behaviors we today describe as "bullying" were viewed as being nothing more than one part of the fabric of human development—a rite of passage for those who survived, and a mark of shame for those who did not escape undamaged. It may be surprising to learn that it was not until 1972 when a Swedish physician named Heinemann recorded his observations of aggression among a group of children in a school playground that educators and researchers began to question the acceptability of such behavior.

Heinemann's (1972) observational study is, to all intents and purposes, the first investigation of bullying among schoolchildren—behavior he described as "mobbing." However, it was a fellow countryman, Dan Olweus, who systematically investigated the nature, frequency, and long-term effects of mobbing in Scandinavian schools, which culminated in a national study he conducted in Norway in 1983 (Olweus, 1985, 1987, 1991, 1993). Based upon survey data collated from 130,000 schoolchildren, Olweus found that 15% of those students attending elementary and secondary/junior high schools were involved in mobbing as either perpetrators or victims. In later years, an intensive study of 2,500 schoolchildren from Bergen, Norway, illustrated the fact that there are both age and gender differences in mobbing behavior. In addition to an age-related reduction in the frequency of mobbing, Olweus found that male students were much more likely to be victims of physical aggression and female students were much more likely to report name-calling, or being locked indoors.

DIFFERENT TYPES OF BULLYING BEHAVIOR

It was not until the early 1990s that research on bullying behavior began in earnest in the United Kingdom using English language versions of Olweus' survey instrument. Two studies, by Ahmad, Whitney, and Smith (1991), and Whitney and Smith (1993), extended the scope of the behaviors associated with bullying to include rumormongering, social isolation, and the destruction, loss, or theft of personal property. Through their work these researchers provided us with an opportunity to examine more closely those gender differences first described by Olweus in Bergen. However, it should be noted that such an extension in the practical definition of bullying also resulted in a fundamental inability to compare and contrast accurately the findings from the UK studies to those conducted in Norway. Similarly, outside Scandinavia, researchers used a different terminology when describing the aggression they studied. Both Heinemann and Olweus referred to such behavior as mobbing while in the English-speaking world it has been supplanted by the more familiar term "bullying."

In the early 1980s, in Finland, researchers Kaj Björkqvist, Kirsti Lagerspetz, and various colleagues began a series of studies exploring indirect bullying (social isolation and rumor mongering) among students (particularly girls) believing that any society that discouraged direct aggression particularly for females would, by implication, be responsible for the emergence of indirect forms of aggression among members of that sex. Several subsequent studies focused upon the exact nature of age and gender differences in students' use of *direct-physical aggression* (hitting, pushing, kicking), *direct-verbal aggression* (name-calling, labeling, threatening), and *indirect or relational aggression* (telling tales, spreading rumors, social isolation). Results showed that, while indirect or relational aggression was utilized by girls as young as eight years of age, it did not supplant direct aggression (physical and verbal) until a few years later—around eleven years of age. The Finnish researchers also found that levels of direct-physical aggression declined with age for both sexes, however, contrary to earlier research by Olweus, direct-verbal aggression increased steadily.

In 1994, Rivers and Smith (1994) compared survey data from 7,000 students to the findings of the Finnish researchers to determine whether or not a similar pattern of age and gender differences existed in the UK school population. In line with the findings from Finland, an age related decline in direct-physical and indirect bullying was found for both boys and girls; however, the UK researchers also found decline in direct-verbal bullying.

BULLYING IN U.S. SCHOOLS

In the United States, in a study of over 15,000 students attending public and private schools, Nansel, Overpeck, Pilla, Ruan, Simons-Morton, and

Scheidt (2001) found that 30% of sixth- through tenth-grade students said that they had moderate to frequent involvement in bullying at school with 13% reporting their role as perpetrators and 10.6% as victims. According to Nansel and colleagues, bullying occurred most frequently among students in grades 6–8 (middle school). They also found that those students who reported being victims of bullying behavior were also more likely to report having difficulty making friends and having poor interactions with classmates. Reports of loneliness were also common. More recently, a cross-national study of violence-related behaviors in adolescence has shown that rates of bullying in U.S. schools are similar to those reported in Ireland, Israel, Portugal, and Sweden (see Smith-Khuri et al., 2004) with as many as 40% of American students reporting some involvement in bullying (ranging from "once or twice" to "several times a week"). Comparable with data from other countries, in U.S. schools boys are much more likely to use direct-physical aggression than girls, and girls are much more likely to use indirect or relational methods of intimidation (Price, 2004). In terms of name-calling, Poteat and Espelage (2005) have found a strong correlation between bullying behavior and the use of homophobic epithets among American students, with words such as "gay" and "fag" taking prominence in the schoolyard and playground.

DEFINING BULLYING BEHAVIOR AND LEGISLATING AGAINST IT: THE U.S. CONTEXT

According to the National Conference of State Legislatures, the term "bullying" includes behaviors that constitute harassment, intimidation, taunting, and ridicule. Bullying can be motivated by hate or bias, ignorance or fear, it can be instilled through cultural norms, peer pressure, or in some cases the desire to retaliate against another perpetrator. Bullying includes initiation rituals, and it includes gendered or sexualized harassment.

Researchers have found it difficult to agree upon a single definition of bullying, however, most agree that there are common factors which should be taken into consideration. First of all, there should be a discernable pattern of behavior, which is repeated over time, with the intention of inflicting injury or discomfort on one or more students by one or more others. Secondly, there should be a perceptible imbalance of power between the perpetrator and the victim, thus allowing one student to domineer the other.

Currently twenty-four states have passed anti-bullying laws (see Limber and Small, 2003), and in those states bullying is a crime. The intention of these legislative efforts has been to attempt to define bullying and to ensure the establishment of policies at school and district levels that clearly indicate the unacceptability of such behavior. This task is made all the more difficult when state legislators have had to be mindful of federal laws that require schools and districts to consider individual circumstances (particularly where the perpetrator has special needs) rather than imposing blanket sanctions or penalties.

THE SOCIAL DYNAMICS OF BULLYING

Throughout the chapters of this book, reference will be made to the social dynamics of the classroom and playground, paying particular attention to the emergence of unofficial hierarchies that stratify and organize students into categories of social acceptance. Sometimes these categories will be determined by sex, sometimes by special needs, and sometimes, by race, culture, religious beliefs, and sexual orientation. The coherence of these categories of acceptance and rejection are fluid, and are dependent upon the makeup of the student body (in terms of ethnic mix, sex, socioeconomic status, and perceived adherence to group "norms"). An individual's identification with a category and her or his acceptance by members of that category of students is dependent upon her or his similarity to other members and dissimilarity to nonmembers. This is never an objective process as each individual member of a group not only categorizes others using the measure "How like me is this person?" but has, at some time, also been categorized and labeled as one who holds one or more ideals or values common to other members. Each group therefore seeks to ensure the purity of its ideals and beliefs by excluding those who hold or proffer alternative points of view. This is not survival of the fittest, rather it is survival of the purest and, as such, attitudes and beliefs have a tendency to become more rigid, and behaviors more extreme, as diversity is lost to uniformity. To understand how these categories arise, and how the loss of dissention and diversity breeds rigid and narrowly focused attitudes, it may be helpful to review some of the key theoretical models underpinning our understanding of bullying.

Perhaps one of the most pertinent social-psychological theories to emerge over the last forty years is social identity theory, first described in detail by Henri Tajfel in 1972. According to Tajfel, the emergence of a person's social identity is linked to her or his knowledge and understanding of belonging to a particular social group, and to the emotional significance and value membership of that group provides. Through his membership of a group, a student—John—not only acquires a social identity which defines his position within the social order of the playground, his membership can also promote the development of a positive or enhanced social identity, if his group is evaluated favorably relative to others. Hamner (1992) suggests that identification with a highly esteemed group confers two key benefits upon its members. Firstly, as already indicated, it assists in maintenance and promotion of self-esteem and social status; and, secondly, it has the potential to offer increased access to material resources at a cost to members of less highly esteemed groups. As Olweus (1993) has pointed out in his study of bullying behavior, perpetrators may have low social status, and can be isolates among their same-age peers, however, they may gain heightened social status and self-esteem outside their own peer group by bringing together an "in-group" consisting of younger confederates who are willing to participate in the bullying of members of their own peer group.

INDIVIDUAL RESPONSIBILITY AND BULLYING BEHAVIOR

Concomitant with social identity theory, which looks at the dynamics between categories or groups, researchers have also considered what happens within groups, and particularly within groups of perpetrators. Deindividuation theory, for example, seeks to provide an explanation for collective behaviors in an attempt to explain those forces that promote violence (Postmes and Spears, 1998). Festinger, Pepitone, and Newcomb (1952) proposed that, in hostile or volatile situations, a person's loss of individuality and her or his submergence into the crowd is a psychological defense mechanism that releases the individual from internalized moral constraints while at the same time reducing personal responsibility. Thus as the crowd becomes bigger and more volatile, those inhibitors that would prevent individual acts of aggression are released, and the individual is swept along giving license for more extreme acts of aggression while, at the same time, sharing less and less personal responsibility.

In terms of bullying behavior, deindividuation theory has two contributions to make. Firstly, deindividuation theory suggests that bullying perpetrated by groups rather than by individuals will be more aggressive because of the release from personal inhibition. Secondly, it seems likely that where an attitude, belief, or behavior is perceived to be a situational norm, bystanders will seek to identify with or participate in any bullying, goading the perpetrator on to ensure their own safety by retaining or augmenting their social status.

Status Establishment in Playground Subculture

So, the question arises, how is the status of each group determined? Is it by sheer force of strength or number, or is it something much more subtle? According to Ridgeway and Balkwell (1997), the process by which society arrives at a series of consensual beliefs about its order and the value of individuals and groups can be discerned by understanding the following:

- The distribution of resources
- The distribution of the population on individual-difference variables
- the relationship between these distributions

Basically, the distribution of resources and the distribution of the population on individual-difference characteristics constrain face-to-face encounters between those groups in one geographical location. As a result members of each group develop status beliefs about the individual-difference variables, determining a hierarchy of valued and unvalued traits. This lack of contact results in the development of group-centered status beliefs with each group enforcing its own beliefs about valued and unvalued traits through education. Consequently stereotypical representations denigrating the status of others emerge. Ridgeway and Balkwell (1997) indicated that where inter-action does occur between groups with nominal characteristics (e.g., based upon race or ethnicity) that also correlate with resource characteristics (e.g., wealth or poverty), estimations of "situational esteem and perceived com-petence" follow (p. 14). In other words, one race or culture with greater wealth will estimate its own worth as being greater than the other with less wealth. Think about your own class or school population, with which group of students and parents do the majority of economic resources reside?

Identifying Difference

Researchers have shown that children actively discriminate from a very early age. For example, Duveen and Lloyd (1986) found that three-year-olds actively discriminate between males and females, and Williams and Morland (1976) found that, by the age of four years children discriminate on the basis of race. Maras (1993) demonstrated that children not only make distinctions between themselves and others on the grounds of gender or race, but also upon criteria associated with the social desirability of minority groups. In her study, Maras asked a group of nine- to ten-year-olds to sort a selection of photographs of able-bodied and disabled children into categories, and she found one girl assembling three piles of photographs—"they're boys, they're girls, they're handicaps" (p. 140).

Findings such as those briefly described above indicate that discrimination serves a social purpose—maintaining both an individual's self-esteem, but also that of the group—and, as described below, discrimination is part of the school experiences of many students of color.

RACIAL BULLYING: SOCIAL DYNAMICS IN ACTION

In a qualitative study of racial prejudice among British schoolchildren, Davey (1983) asked a group of African-Caribbean, Indian, and White Eu-ropean children what color they would prefer to be: without exception they all replied that they would prefer to be white. The stigma women and men attach to a person's skin color can be seen clearly in the various pe-jorative terms used in everyday speech when referring to cultural minority groups. For example, among thirteen- to seventeen-year-old students, Cohn (1988) recorded sixty terms of abuse relating to people of color; among the under 13s, she recorded forty. Several recent studies of bullying have shown that, in terms of its nature at least, there are discernible differences in the school experiences of students of color when compared to those described as White European reinforcing the fact that race and ethnicity remain strong antecedents of bullying behavior (see, for example, Kelly and Cohn, 1988; Malik, 1990; Moran, Smith, Thompson, and Whitney, 1993; Boulton, 1995).

According to educationalists Troyna and Hatcher (1992), racially abusive name-calling is part of "the repertoire of children's discourse" (p. 35), and increases with age rather than decreases. As indicated previously, a key element underlying the reasons why some students bully their peers of color lies with the emergence of stereotypes that have developed about minority ethnic, cultural, and religious groups through a lack of contact. For example, Boulton (1995) looked at intragroup and intergroup bully/victim problems among 156 students (between the ages of eight and ten years), 53 of whom were described as "Asian" and 103 as "White." In this study, students were asked to nominate those peers whom they perceived to be "bullies" and those they perceived to be "victims." They were then asked to indicate the race/color of a preferred partner for a classroom activity using positive traits (e.g., "works hard," "friendly," and "clean") and negative traits (e.g., "lazy," "tells lies," and "dirty") to describe their decisions. Boulton found that White students reported more abuse about the color of their skin than Asian students, however, Asian students reported being socially excluded much more than White students.

In the United States, a study by Nansel et al. (2001) of 15,000 students revealed that Hispanic American youth are slightly more likely to report being involved in moderate to frequent bullying of peers, whereas Black youth are less likely to report being involved in such behavior. The issue of bullying among Hispanic American youth is one which has received a great deal of attention, and researchers have focused on the link between perceptions of neighborhood safety and youth culture, and its impact upon school engagement and behavior (Garcia-Reid, Reid, and Peterson, 2005). The research has shown that problems that occur outside of school (within the family, peer groups, or in the neighborhood) will impact upon the engagement of these youth in school, particularly where teachers have little or no understanding or experience of working with youth from cultures different than their own. Thus, bullying behaviors, perpetrated or experienced by youth of color, may not be addressed as effectively by educators who do not understand that these youth need to be reassured that the dangers they face outside the school will not manifest in the classrooms and hallways. Therefore, it is imperative that teachers cease to think of youth of color in terms of deficit, and focus on ways in which they culturally embed learning through an appreciation of the cultural diversity of the classroom.

ISLAMOPHOBIA AND BULLYING

Following 9/11, the invasion of Iraq, and the London bombings of July 7, 2005 we have seen evidence of intolerance toward Muslim students and their families. For example, following 9/11, one study conducted in the United Kingdom found that 28% of thirteen- to fifteen-year-olds reported that their attitudes toward Muslims had become more negative. Among older students attending college (nineteen years plus) 26% said that their attitudes toward Muslims had become more negative. While the majority of the 1,515 Caucasian students surveyed reported feeling uncomfortable with right-wing or racist views, nearly 10% of sixteen- to eighteen-year-olds indicated that they either *agreed* or *strongly agreed* with sentiments expressed by political movements with an overt anti-immigration, or anticultural diversity stance (see Brockett et al., in press).

CYBERBULLYING: ENTERING UNCHARTED WATERS

It is only in the last few years that we have begun to consider the role technology plays in bullying behavior. As young people redefine the way in which their social networks are structured, utilizing technology to pursue conversations that once would have occurred face-to-face, the phenomenon of "cyberbullying" has emerged. Cyberbullying can be defined at the abuse of Internet chat rooms, e-mail, cell phone, and text-messaging with the intention of embarrassing or otherwise hurting another person. Cyberbullying typically involves the sending of derogatory text messages or threatening e-mails, forwarding confidential e-mails to a third party in an attempt to publicly humiliate the sender, setting up derogatory Web sites and e-mailing others the URL inviting comments, and haranguing individuals in Internet chat rooms (Campbell, 2005). In one of the few published academic studies on the topic, Kowalski and colleagues (2005) sampled 3,767 American students and found that 25% of girls and 11% of boys had been the victims of electronic bullying in the past two months. In a British survey conducted by the National Children's Homes (NCH), 20% of 770 young people who responded had experienced some form of cyberbullying: 14% had been bullied by text message, 5% had been bullied in Internet chat rooms, and 4% by e-mail. In perhaps the only large-scale longitudinal study of cyberbullying conducted between 2002 and 2005 (over 11,000 students), Noret and Rivers (2006) found that while the number of boys who were bullied by threatening e-mail or text messages remained relatively stable over time (ranging from 12.4% in 2002 to 11.6% in 2005), girls reported almost a 50% increase over the four-year period (from 14.7% in 2002 to 21.4% in 2005). Although research is ongoing exploring the emotional consequences of this type of bullying behavior, in the United Kingdom reports of self-harming behavior and completed suicides related to malicious text-messaging and silent telephone calls have started to appear in the national press.

SUMMARY

In this chapter the phenomenon of bullying has been introduced. Beginning with a historical overview, it has considered the different types of bullying that exist in schools today, and how legislators have sought to introduce laws to combat it, despite a lack of clarity surrounding its definition. This chapter has also focused on the social dynamics of bullying, explaining how social scientists have understood the emergence of unofficial hierarchies and group competition in the playground with examples from research focusing on the victimization of students of color. Finally, a new form of bullying—cyberbullying—has been discussed, the implications of which we have yet to fully understand.

Tips for Parents

- Talk to your child about the different types of bullying that exist in schools today. Don't forget to include direct-physical behaviors such as hitting, kicking, punching, and tripping up, direct-verbal behaviors such as name-calling and labeling, and indirect or relational behaviors such as rumormongering and social isolation.

- Talk to your child about the use of cell phones and the Internet, and the fact that bullies can use text-messaging and e-mail to hurt others. Make sure your child knows that she/he can talk to you if they receive threatening text messages or e-mail. Think about equipping your home computer with a Net-Nanny.

- Find out if your state has anti-bullying laws.

- Talk to your child about the importance of valuing everyone at school. Make sure she/he understands that being different does not mean that a person is valued less.

Tips for Educators

- Remember that there are different forms of bullying behavior, and that name-calling or social isolation can be just as hurtful as a punch or kick.

✎ Remember that the most commonly used definition of bullying behavior does not include one-off incidents. There has to be a discernable pattern of behavior, repeated over time, and which has as its purpose the intention of inflicting physical, emotional, or psychological pain upon its victim.

✎ Think about the social dynamics of your local community, how might local prejudices relating to people of color affect your classroom?

✎ Consider talking to students about the value of diversity, and the ways in which the country has benefited from different cultures and populations.

✎ Remember that most bullying in U.S. schools occurs in grades 6–8.

✎ Check if your state has anti-bullying laws, and what they mean for you.

REFERENCES

Ahmad, Y., Whitney, I., and Smith, P. K. (1991). A survey service for schools on bully/victim problems. In P. K. Smith and D. A. Thompson (Eds.), *Practical Approaches to Bullying* (pp. 103–111). London, UK: David Fulton.

Boulton, M. J. (1995). Patterns of bully-victim problems in mixed race groups of children. *Social Development*, 4, 277–293.

Brockett, A. A., Noret, N., Harenwall, S., Baird, P. D., and Rivers, I. (in press). Adolescent attitudes in York towards Muslims and Islam. In S. C. H. Kim and P. Kollontai (Eds.), *Community Identity: Perspectives from Theology and Religious Studies*. London, UK: T & T Clark.

Campbell, M. (2005). Cyberbullying: An older problem in a new guise? *Australian Journal of Guidance and Counselling*, 15, 68–76.

Cohn, T. (1988). Sambo—a study in name-calling. In E. Kelly and T. Cohn (Eds.), *Racism in Schools: New Research Evidence* (pp. 29–63). Stoke-on-Trent, UK: Trentham.

Davey, A. G. (1983). *Learning to Be Prejudiced: Growing up in a Multiethnic Britain.* London, UK: Edward Arnold.

Duveen, G., and Lloyd, B. (1986). The significance of social identities. *British Journal of Social Psychology*, 25, 219–230.

Festinger, L., Pepitone, A., and Newcomb, T. (1952). Some consequences of deindividuation in a group. *Journal of Abnormal and Social Psychology*, 47, 382–389.

Garcia-Reid, P., Reid, R. J., and Peterson, N. A. (2005). School engagement among latino youth in an urban middle school context. *Education and Urban Society*, 37, 257–275.

Hamner, K. M. (1992). Gay-bashing: A social identity analysis of violence against lesbians and gay men. In G. M. Herek and K. T. Berrill (Eds.), *Hate Crimes: Confronting Violence against Lesbians and Gay Men* (pp. 179–190). Newbury Park, CA: Sage.

Heinemann, P. P. (1972). *Mobbning—Gruppvåld bland barn och vuxna.* Stockholm, Sweden: Naturoch Kultur.

Kelly, E., and Cohn, T. (1988). *Racism in Schools: New Research Evidence.* Stoke-on-Trent, UK: Trentham.

Kowalski, R., Limber, S. P., Scheck, A., Redfearn, M., Allen, J., Calloway, A., Farris, J., Finnegan, K., Keith, M., Kerr, S., Singer, L., Spearman, J., Tripp, L., and Vernon, L. (2005, August). Electronic bullying among school-aged children and youth. Poster presented at the annual meeting of the American Psychological Association, Washington, DC.

Limber, S. P., and Small, M. A. (2003). State laws and policies to address bullying in schools. *School Psychology Review, 32,* 445–455.

Malik, G. (1990). *Bullying: An Investigation of Race and Gender Aspects.* Unpublished M.Sc. thesis, University of Sheffield.

Maras, P. F. (1993). *The Integration of Children with Disabilities into the Mainstream.* Unpublished Ph.D. thesis, University of Kent at Canterbury.

Moran, S., Smith, P. K., Thompson, D., and Whitney, I. (1993). Ethnic differences in experiences of bullying in Asian and White Children. *British Journal of Educational Psychology, 63,* 431–440.

Nansel, T. R., Overpeck, M., Pilla, R. S., Ruan, W. J., Simons-Morton, B., and Scheidt, P. (2001). Bullying behavior among youth: Prevalence and association with psychosocial adjustment. *Journal of the American Medical Association, 285,* 2094–2100.

Noret, N., and Rivers, I. (2006, April). The prevalence of bullying by text message or email: Results of a four-year study. Presented at the British Psychological Society's Annual Conference, Cardiff.

Olweus, D. (1985). 80000 barn er innblandet i mobbing. *Norsk Skoleblad, 2,* 18–23.

———. (1987). Bully/victim problems among schoolchildren in Scandinavia. In J. P. Mykelbust and R. Ommundsen (Eds.), *Psykologprofesjonen mot år 2000* (pp. 395–413). Oslo, Norway: Universitetsforlaget.

———. (1991). Bully/victim problems among schoolchildren: Basic facts and effects of a school based intervention program. In D. Pepler and K. H. Rubin (Eds.), *The Development and Treatment of Childhood Aggression* (pp. 411–448). Hillsdale, NJ: Erlbaum.

———. (1993). *Bullying at School: What We Know and What We Can Do.* Oxford, UK: Blackwell.

Postmes, T., and Spears, R. (1998). Deindividuation and antinormative behavior: A meta-analysis. *Psychological Bulletin, 123,* 238–259.

Poteat, V. P., and Espelage, D. L. (2005). Exploring the relation between bullying and homophobic verbal content: The homophobic content agent target (HCAT) scale. *Violence and Victims, 20,* 513–528.

Price, D. A. (2004, September). No need to fear: Ending bullying in U.S. schools. Presented at International Policy and Research Conference on School Bullying and Violence, Stavanger, Norway.

Ridgeway, C. L., and Balkwell, J. W. (1997). Group processes and the diffusion of status beliefs. *Social Psychology Quarterly*, 60, 14–31.

Rivers, I., and Smith, P. K. (1994). Types of bullying behavior and their correlates. *Aggressive Behavior*, 20, 359–368.

Smith-Khuri, E., Iachan, R., Scheidt, P. C., Overpeck, M. D., Nic Gabhainn, S., Pickett, W., and Harel, Y. (2004). A cross-national study of violence-related behaviors in adolescents. *Archives of Pediatrics and Adolescent Medicine*, 158, 539–544.

Tajfel, H. (1972). La catégorisation sociale. In S. Moscovici (Ed.), *Introduction à la psychologie sociale* (pp. 272–302). Paris, France: Larousse.

Troyna, B., and Hatcher, R. (1992). *Racism in Children's Lives: A Study of Mainly-White Primary Schools*. London, UK: Routledge.

Whitney, I., and Smith, P. K. (1993). A survey of nature and extent of bullying in junior/middle and secondary schools. *Educational Research*, 35, 3–25.

Williams, J. E., and Morland, J. K. (1976). *Race, Color, and the Young Child*. Chapel Hill, NC: University of North Carolina Press.

CHAPTER 2

Understanding Bullies and Victims

In considering the issue of bullying, it is important to identify which children are perpetrators of bullying and which children are victims. The profile of both male and female bullies may come as a surprise to those who are unfamiliar with the current research on bullying. For example, boys who bully others are not necessarily the social, academic, or athletic failures as was once believed. Not all are loners who make life miserable for others to compensate for their own unhappiness. Undoubtedly, some boys do fit this profile. In recent years, there have been cases where such boys have killed others in revenge, as in the incident referred to in the film *Bowling for Columbine* by Michael Moore, but research shows that, most often, the reverse is the case.

GARY'S STORY

Gary was a young boy considered popular in the group. He was the leader and he took all the decisions. Gary was confident, quick-witted, and he had the enviable position of being the captain of the football team. Marty was not as confident as the other members of the group and he became the target for Gary's jokes. Many of these jokes were cruel although the other boys thought they were funny. Gary started to play tricks on Marty such as hiding his belongings. He took his cell phone and sold it for far less than it was worth. He threw the money at Marty saying it was a trashy phone and worth no more. Many of the other boys began to feel uncomfortable about this taunting but they said nothing and thought that Marty should stand up for himself. Marty was not able to do this and eventually left the school. Only later did the boys hear that he had tried to commit suicide. Only then did the boys in the group realize that they did not admire Gary. He was not popular but, as he was the most dominant, they had followed his lead. Marty did well in his new school but many in the group led by Gary experienced feelings of guilt that stayed with them for many years.

BOYS WHO BULLY

Dan Olweus wrote the first book on bullying, *Aggression in Schools: Bullies and Whipping Boys* (1978), in which he offered the following profile of boys who bully drawn from a large cohort study of students in Scandinavian schools.

Profile of the Male Bully

Socially confident

Socially competent

Good coordination skills

Good communication skills

Positive self-image

Olweus found the majority of these boys to be confident, assertive, energetic, and good communicators. Surprisingly, they were more popular among their peers than were their victims. As the title of the book suggests, this profile related only to boys. At this time, there was no published work on girls although some were in progress (Besag, 1989). Later research, such as that of Sutton and colleagues (1999), confirmed this profile. (The characteristics of girls who bully others are discussed later).

A boy possessing such a profile is far more likely than most to feel comfortable and confident in the company of his peers. It is difficult to discern any negative features in this profile as it would appear to indicate that male bullies are socially adept. These boys appear to posses an adequate range of social skills that allow them to manipulate the group and achieve their personal goals (Sutton, Smith, and Swettenham, 1999). Furthermore, many of these boys have well-developed leadership skills. We can see that many effective school leaders, sports captains, managers in industry, and those in an influential community or political role have these qualities. This poses the question, if these boys are socially skilled, why do they need to use negative behaviors such as bullying? The answer may lie in further exploration of social intelligence and its relationship with empathy (Kaukiainen et al., 1999). These boys may well be influential within their group, and be able to manipulate their peers due to their competent social understanding, yet they may be using their skills in a negative fashion. They are bullying, autocratic leaders rather than benign democratic ones. They are using their social awareness and skills to the advantage of their self regardless of any disadvantage to others. In other words, they are leading their group or gang for their own purposes rather than for the benefit of others.

Physical Prowess and the Competitive Spirit

Boys build up a hierarchy based on physical strength and prowess in their early years (Pellegrini, 1988). A boy knows from around the age of eight where he stands on this hierarchy. He knows whether he can strut around school with an air of confidence, able to take on all-comers, or whether it would be advisable for him to keep a low profile when in the presence of more aggressive peers. This relates to the finding that males would appear to have an inherent competitive spirit known as "The Young Male Syndrome" (Daly and Wilson, 1994). This leads them to continue to reaffirm their dominant position on this ladder of physical strength by testing out the ability of others and displaying their own prowess. They do this by roughhousing, fun fights, arm wrestling, and by using all manner of horseplay (Pellegrini, 1988).

Some form of play fighting seems to be an essential part of the interaction between young boys (Smith and Boulton, 1990; Pellegrini, 1988). Although these are games enjoyed for the fun they provide, they also demonstrate the skill and prowess of the combatants to all who witness them. Parents and teachers of young boys know they take any chance that comes their way to test out their physical skills against their peers. This can be in an informal manner by engaging in an impromptu wrestling match or a formal game of football. Their bullying behavior seems to be part of this need to demonstrate their ability to dominate others. Frequently, these displays occur in front of a peer audience as most bullying among males is part of their demonstration of physical strength, although hidden from adult eyes (Wachtel, 1973). This display behavior continues into young adulthood with these physical and verbal challenges identifiable in the barroom brawl of adult males. Many men admit to remaining wary of others in potentially aggressive situations. They surreptitiously weigh up the physical strength of their opponents before taking risks such as challenging the inappropriate behavior. They realize that often such behavior is employed solely to provoke other males into a fight they will lose in order to display the strength of the attackers (Archer, 2001).

Clearly, physical strength and power were essential attributes for males in the past. These were critical survival skills for them as they were the primary providers and protectors and may still be essential in some communities. This is the rationale suggested for why males, and some females, are more physically aggressive in areas of social deprivation than in more advantaged areas. In these areas, there is fierce competition for adequate resources and many are at risk of physical attack (Campbell and Muncer, 1987; Ness, 2004; Campbell, 2005). This means that these young people need to demonstrate in an obvious manner their ability to defend themselves. The youth in these areas, male and female, may need to offer a presence of strength, and possibly aggression, even if they are not combative by nature. In this way, they are warding off impending aggression from their peers in the way that animals fluff out their fur or use aggressive calls to deter marauders.

These shows of strength need not be physical in nature. Many men choose to use posturing or displays of wealth to confirm their position in the peer hierarchy. Some boys use "dozens" which is a ritualistic form of verbal competition to challenge and compete with others' steam (Labov, 1972; Goodwin, 1990). The male competitive spirit is in evidence whether shown by boys in an interest in play stations or later in adulthood by dominant behavior in the boardroom or by ostentatious displays of wealth. This may leave us with the suspicion that the need of young males to continue to reaffirm their dominant position in the peer hierarchy may be some form of an outdated and misplaced survival skill.

The Male "Bully" Role

The studies of Björkqvist, Österman, and Kaukianinen (1992) and Salmivalli et al. (1996) show the dynamics of the group supporting a male bully. He will be positioned central to the group and, unlike most girls who bully it is probable that he will be visible as the key player in the attack. He may be the one leading the physical assault or he may remain on the sidelines issuing instructions for the others to follow. Whatever his physical position, he will be the one in charge. There will be other boys in the role of "assistants" who enter into the attacks whether verbal or physical. In addition, there are "reinforcers" who remain on the sidelines but encourage the bullies and ensure all other than the target gain fun and entertainment from the attacks. A lot of bullying, among both boys and girls, contains an element of fun and entertainment for the attackers. The public humiliation of their victim adds spice to their attacks.

There may be a few "defenders" watching who would like to support the victim but, depending on a variety of factors, it may not be wise for these boys to make overt moves in this direction. Björkqvist et al. (1992) and Salmivalli et al. (1996) found many of these passive observers admitted that they would be hesitant to help a male victim, not only because of fear of reprisal, but because they see no need to alter the heritage of the dominant male leading the pack. In fact, many in the peer group admire the bullies as they consider that they are able to "handle themselves" effectively. Bullies gain many things from their bullying, but affirmation of their dominance is a major factor common to most bullying among boys. We can see this admiration of the male bully in the adult domain. How else could we explain the current phenomenon of dominant males who humiliate others on television yet who are among the most highly paid "entertainers"?

Families and Bullying among Males

Clearly, the role of adults is influential in forming the attitudes of the young. Boys brought up in families where there is an attitude of admiration for dominance over others will see no wrong in pushing others aside to achieve their own goals. Highly paid professional parents can encourage this attitude of achievement at all costs. High achievement in any sphere, academic, sport, or social, becomes the overriding goal.

Alan's Story. Alan was a boy who had such parents. They had well-paid professional employment but they wanted Alan to do even better. They wanted him to be the captain of the football team, the winner in the debating society, the lead actor in the school play, and to achieve the top marks in all exams. Alan made fun of those he considered less able or vulnerable in some way. He encouraged others to make these boys look foolish on every occasion.

Alan attended a school where the teachers encouraged this behavior by ignoring it. The influential adults in Alan's life were encouraging, even teaching him to be a bully. Such children may attain their goals, their achievements may be impressive, they may become highly influential members of society but, with this attitude, they will ignore the welfare of others. They will be autocratic rather than democratic leaders.

Summary Comments

In summary, many boys who bully others have good leadership skills: they are confident, good communicators, and often athletic—the latter being an attribute greatly admired by most boys. Their leadership skills are evident in that they are able to influence their followers, many of whom may have rejected guidance from parents and professionals. Like the Mafia godfather, they can read the social dynamics of the gang or group quickly and accurately. One effective way forward is to transfer these skills to other side of the fence. We need to aim to change the attitudes of these boys by making it more rewarding for them to use their leadership skills in a democratic, benign manner rather than in the autocratic, domineering mode of bullying behavior (Besag, 2002).

SUBCATEGORIES OF MALE BULLIES

Clearly, not all boys who bully others fit the profile outline above. There are several other categories of bullies (Besag, 2002).

Bully/Victims

These are boys who may be bullied at home or elsewhere and then use these techniques to bully others.

Tom's Story. Tom was a boy bullied by his older sister. She teased him about his height as he was small in stature for his age. She made him do all the chores that her parents assigned to her and she took his pocket money when she wanted to buy something special for herself. Tom soon learned that by domineering others it was possible to get what you wanted. He found that he could do the same with those younger or smaller than himself in school. Unwittingly, but effectively, his sister had taught him that bullying was an easy way of getting what you want.

Provocative Bullies

Some children do not understand even simple social behaviors. They provoke others and then wonder why they become the target of retaliation. There are several reasons for this. They may not have received training in understanding the feelings of others so they misjudge the effects of their provocation thinking they are just having fun. It may be that they have some difficulty in assimilating simple social skills due to an undiagnosed condition such as autism or Asperger's syndrome. Many such children escape diagnosis and flounder when faced with the need to interact with others during the school day.

A small minority of children provoke others due to a subconscious wish to receive the "punishment" they think they deserve. This is due to some psychological condition and such children require specialist assessment and support. There are boys who deliberately provoke others with the aim of getting them to fight so that they have a valid excuse to retaliate. This is a covert way of gaining permission to attack their target.

Adam's Story. Adam had coped as a young boy attending a small school but floundered on transferring to the senior school. He could not cope with the hundreds of people milling around in the building. He did not have the opportunity to build up a relationship with a specific teacher and many of his peers found him strange as he did not appear to want friends and he refused any overtures to join in their games. As he managed his work, his teachers did not think there was a problem. His father became angry when Adam showed no interest in sports or in going to any neighborhood clubs. His father was disappointed in him and his mother was confused. Eventually, it became clear that Adam was taunting the other boys. He would snatch their belongings and run away. Other children would become annoyed and give chase. The staff in school could not get him to stop and his behavior persisted and escalated to such an extent that he was putting himself at risk. His teachers and parents decided to ask a specialist psychologist for advice who found that Adam had significant difficulty in understanding the mores of social behavior. He found it extremely difficult to understand and communicate with his peers. He did want friends and had thought the chasing game was the way to make contact. With the support of his parents and teachers, he gradually made reasonable progress in all areas of his life.

The Anxious Bully

Boys fitting this category most often have feelings of failure leading them to attack others they consider more successful. They are jealous of boys who appear successful and are compensating for their own feelings of inadequacy. It may be that these boys come from homes where there is little money to spare for the possessions so loved by the young such as expensive trainers, mobile phones, or play stations. Unknowingly, they translate their unhappiness into anger that leads them to attack those they view as more fortunate.

BOYS WHO ARE VICTIMS

The profile of the male victim is less clear. It is important to emphasize that any boy may become a victim of bullying should he find himself in the presence of the wrong people, in the wrong place at the wrong time. However, the boys most at risk of becoming a victim have a profile that is the mirror image of that of the bully. Compared to their attackers, these boys will be less physically dominant and confident. They will be less socially skilled and have less facility and fluency with language. If such a boy has a powerful physical presence, he is unlikely to be challenged by the aggressors. If he has a confident presence despite his stature, it is less likely that he will come under attack. Should he possess good linguistic skills, he may be able to deflect the bullies with witticisms or humor. A boy lacking all these skills is in a more vulnerable position than most.

Bobby's Story

Bobby was a boy who was hopeless at sports. The others boys laughed at his lack of success. He was good at his schoolwork and always did well in exams, but unfortunately his peer group did not admire these skills. He lived in a tough neighborhood where being able to defend yourself from attack was an essential life skill. Bobby found that he could remember jokes and could tell them well. He wanted to become an actor but knew that his peers would ridicule his ambition and this would make things worse for him. Bobby bought himself a joke book and learned some good jokes. He soon won friends as all enjoyed his humor. Eventually, he found the confidence to make up his own jokes and to produce impromptu witty comments. He became one of the most popular boys in the group. Many male comedians have disclosed that they honed their skills while at school in an attempt to deflect the bullies. If a boy is socially adept, these skills will enable him to be popular within the peer group where he will find support from among friends. A group of friends who will defend him is the best protective factor for a boy. This is not necessarily the case with girls for reasons given later.

SUBCATEGORIES OF MALE VICTIMS

Just as there are subcategories of bullies, so there are subcategories of victims (Besag, 2002).

The Target of Jokes

One of the more difficult bullying behaviors to address is one that is hidden in a joke or game. The bullies shout out an abusive name to the target and then claim it was just a joke. A game may hide deliberate intent to hurt but this is difficult to prove as these acts are subtle and powerful. Not only does the attacker make a successful attack, and gain satisfaction from this, they claim those who complain have no sense of humor thereby taking away any access to help or arbitration. These acts are common and successful in demeaning those under attack.

False Victims

Note needs to be made of a group of children who falsely claim to be victims of bullying. Many such children make these claims in a bid to gain adult attention. They may genuinely need the attention but care needs to be taken that those who claim to be the targets of others are actually being bullied.

Colluding Victims

It is puzzling why some boys remain in a group of friends where they seem to be the target of unpleasant jokes or cruel tricks couched in humor. Some boys routinely take on the roles no others will accept such as preparing the pitch for a game or cleaning the equipment. Such boys accept these roles as it gives them entry into a group of "friends." Once they find others who are more amenable they soon leave these bullies.

THE LANGUAGE OF BULLYING

It is often possible to discern who is the most dominant in a group of boys simply by listening to their use of language, the more forceful and confident using the most directives and commands. Both male and female bullies will tend to use more directive speech in their verbal communications than their peers. This defines their attitude of dominance. Most boys come straight to the point in discussion or dispute with their peers with little preamble but the bullies among them and those most confident or forceful give clear, decisive orders and commands (Besag, 2006). These boys are more likely to use forceful linguistic structures to direct the action. Examples of this are such phrases as "We will..." and "You must..." They use the language of command. They take control in the playground by taking the best parts in the games and other activities and by telling others what to do.

Peter's Story

Peter was a five-year-old boy whom his teachers considered popular with the other children. At playtimes, he would run out into the playground with the other boys. He would shout out direct instructions such as saying he would be the sheriff with the gun and then command that the other boys would be the men he was chasing. Within a couple of minutes, he would have "shot dead" all the other boys. They would then remain lying on the playground for the rest of the playtime while he ran around enjoying himself.

Gender Differences

There would appear to be a discernible gender difference in the use of language. We can see this distinction between directive speech and the language of barter and negotiation even more clearly when comparing the language of girls with that of boys. Most girls tend to use a different style of speech preferring the language of negotiation, barter, and persuasion (Tannen, 1992; Chung and Asher, 1996; Rose and Asher, 1999; Besag, 2006). By listening to their language when there is a difference of opinion, we can discern that girls do not use as much directive language as boys. Most girls use few directives; they more readily seek consensus by negotiation and bartering.

It has been found that girls are more likely than boys to feel sadness and guilt if they openly challenge their friends (Whitesell and Harter, 1996). This was so in the study described in Besag (2006). The conversations of girls are peppered with such phrases as "Shall we...?" or "What about...?" They seek consensus by asking "Who would like to be first?" or "Whose turn is it next?" The question mark is an essential element in the discussion. Girls prefer to negotiate around a conflict situation. If there is only one skipping rope, they take it in turns to use it, timing each other carefully, making it clear they have divided the time equally. Girls like things to be equable and it is important to them that they are seen to be so. Often turn-taking is arrived at amicably by the use of rhymes or songs. Traditional rhymes and songs are integral to the many skipping, chasing, and ball games popular with girls and seem to be enjoyed as much as the activity itself. The rhymes show in a decisive manner who will be first or take the next turn. Boys do not use these traditional rhymes as frequently as girls do, nor are they as integral to their games and other activities as in the case of girls. When decisions need to be taken by a group of boys, the most dominant is the one who most often will take the lead.

This supports the findings of Collins and Laursen (1992) who found this style of conversation more readily used by adult females than adult males. The gender distinction regarding cooperation and competition seems to continue into adulthood in that females seem to take a group-negotiated leadership style, whereas males tend to prefer a task and self-enhancing style (Buss, 1981; Tannen, 1992; Cross and Madson, 1997; Rose and Asher, 1999).

GIRL BULLIES AND VICTIMS

The profile of girl bullies and their victims remains unclear. This is because most girls do not bully in the same overt and clearly identifiable manner as most boys. Until recently, there has been little investigation into the bullying behavior of girls. The subtle and complex nature of their bullying has received scant attention, perhaps partly because the covert nature of girls' attacks necessitates subtle and time-consuming research which is expensive (Maccoby, 2002). When considering the bullying behavior of girls, it is necessary to look to causes other than the establishment and reaffirmation of a physical hierarchy that appears to be the rationale behind the bullying of most boys. Many girls do not appear to have the same competitive spirit as most boys although this may be because it usually takes a less evident form as explained later. Even boys who are not bullies are more likely to be involved in competitive games than are girls. It has been said that, "girls cooperate and boys compete" (Ahlgren, 1983). Girls tend to choose to play in a negotiated turn-taking manner (Crombie and Desjardins, 1993) whereas boys more often settle for the strongest or most dominant being first in line (Smith and Boulton, 1990; Coie and Dodge, 1998). Girls appear to play and interact cooperatively with their friends (Ahlgren, 1983; Hughes, 1988) but this judgment can be misleading.

Recent studies have identified a trend toward gender difference in preferred modes of aggression as indirect, rather than direct aggression, appears to be the preferred *modus operandi* of girls (Whitney and Smith, 1993; Arnold et al., 1999; Archer, 2001; Campbell, 2004). A gender difference in bullying behavior reflects this distinction. However, Maccoby (1999) and Thorne (1993) prefer to regard this as a spectrum of behavior found across both sexes. The less overt modes of aggression have been termed variously such as social aggression, relational aggression, and indirect aggression. Indirect aggression first used by Björkqvist et al. (1992) in the context of bullying, is the term used in this work.

Whereas boys use direct, physical means such as hitting and kicking, using their feet and fists in their attacks, girls more frequently use a range of indirect aggressions including social ostracism, name-calling, abusive notes and messages to assert and abuse their power. They use more gossip whispered in secret behind the back of the target than boys do (Besag, 2006). Boys use more obvious verbal abuse such as calling out abusive names in front of the peer group. There are more subtle gender differences. It is not essential that boys know their target as the bullying actions of boys are used primarily to confirm their power over their victim. Most are only interested in displaying their ability to demean and debase those more vulnerable in the most obvious manner. Once they achieve this aim, they often lose interest in the victim as long as he remains out of sight. Boys pick out the vulnerable in their sights regardless of who the target may be (Besag, 2006). This allows a victim to use avoidance, deflective and distracting strategies to escape the bullying. This appears not to be the case with girls as it would seem that they bully in a different manner and for different reasons (Besag, 2006).

In considering whether a profile of girls who bully exists, as in the case of boys, it is important to study closely their friendship relations. We have not been fully aware that it is within their friendships and acquaintanceships that most bullying among girls occurs. Just as boys form a hierarchy of physical strength to display their power, girls manipulate the friendships in the group. "Little Miss Popular" holds a great deal of power in her hands.

Carrie-Louise's Story

Carrie-Louise was a troubled girl who came from a family that was financially secure. Both her parents were well-paid professionals but they had to work long hours, sometimes on weekends, to retain their positions. Carrie-Louise had been quite happy in school but then her parents needed to move to another area because of her father's employment. Carrie-Louise did not know anyone in her new school. She wanted to make friends with a particular girl in the class whose name was Sarah, but Sarah already had a close friend named Anne. Carrie-Louise did all she could to destroy the friendship between Sarah and Anne. Carrie-Louise told Sarah that Anne had spread gossip and lies about her. In this way, she hoped Sarah would leave Anne and become her friend. She even stole Sarah's purse and made sure it was found in Anne's desk. Sarah did end her friendship with Anne and became the friend of Carrie-Louise. Eventually, the truth was discovered and Carrie-Louise admitted to what she had done. Her parents decided that they must spend more time with her and take her to clubs and activities outside school to help her to make new friends.

Sandra's Story

Sandra was to attend a prestigious college. She applied to one of the popular sorority groups although she knew it was difficult to gain entry. She spent a great deal of money her family could ill-afford on getting the right clothes and accessories to wear for the interview held by the senior girls.

She was so nervous that she was sick the night before the meeting. In the interview it soon became clear that she was not going to be accepted by the group. The girls on the interview committee asked Sandra about her father's work. She explained that he was a firefighter. The girls laughed and became very abusive to her. Sandra was very proud of her father who had won an award for bravery but the girls ignored her defense of her father and told her to leave the room. For some time afterwards, they taunted and scorned Sandra in public about her father's employment and her lack of money. She became anorexic and started to fail in her academic work. Luckily, she made friends with other girls and settled happily into college life.

THE RESEARCH STUDY

In comparison to boys, we know little about the subtle and complex social interactions between girls, especially bullying. Studies such as those of Björkqvist et al. (1992), Crick and Grotpeter (1995), Simmons (2002), and Artz (2005) have considered aggression among girls. Analysis of the dynamics in the friendship groups of girls has been carried out by Eder (1985, 1991), who proposes a structure for this in her Cycle of Popularity model, and Alder and Alder (1995), who offer their Clique Formation hypothesis. However, we are only now beginning to understand the powerful influence of the dynamics underpinning their friendship relations. In an aim to understand and analyze girls' bullying, a weekly activity club for twenty girls in one class was organized that ran for sixteen months over the lunch break. The girls were ten to eleven years old. Each session lasted an hour and was videotaped with permission from the girls, parents, and school staff. This gave sixteen hours of material for analysis. Questionnaires about their friendship relations were given to the girls at the start of each of the first three semesters and a semistructured interview was held with the girls in the final semester of the study. This interview tapped into the wider constructs they held about their friendships and those of other girls in the class. Embedded in the interview were the same questions as were in the questionnaires. The girls went on a residential field trip in the final term and semistructured interviews were held with the adults who accompanied them on the trip. The class teacher kept a diary of any aggressive incidents that occurred throughout the study and these entries were discussed regularly with her. The information gained from all the aspects of the study was collated and cross-checked. Details of the study can be found in Besag (2006). It was hoped that the study would go some way in explaining how and why girls bully and offer profiles of girls involved in bullying whether bullies or victims. In particular, it was hoped that the dynamics of any relationship between girls' friendships and bullying would be identified.

The results showed that girls, unlike boys, bully within their friendships and acquaintanceships, whereas boys appear to have little interest in who they challenge. The target of boy bullies is often outside the friendship group and unknown to them. In the case of girls it is often a once previously close friend of the target who instigates the bullying. Girls' friendships are often their most troublesome relations. Anyone who has had close involvement with young girls, as professionals or parents will be familiar with the troublesome, paradoxical nature of their friendships and the damaging effects of their negative peer interactions. Girls' friendships are primarily characterized by a "best friend" dyad (Lever, 1976; Maccoby, 1999; Simmons, 2002). The friendship bonds between these pairs are powerful yet they also appear fluid and fragile. Trouble erupts as these dyadic relationships are rarely static over time (Savin-Williams, 1980; Harris, 1995; Simmons, 2002) with the composition of the pair changing frequently, seemingly on a whim. These friendship bonds are less stable than those of boys (Pipher, 1994; Harris, 1995; Simmons, 2002; Wiseman, 2002). This fluctuation of favor appears to be at the root of the constant low-key bickering and repeated calls upon adults to resolve the quarrels and conflicts between girls. Previously supportive friends may not only exclude a target girl from the group, but call her names, spread gossip about her, and text her with abusive messages thus making her life a misery (Owens, Shute, and Slee, 2000; Simmons, 2002).

The disappointment of losing a close friend is exacerbated by the closeness of the bonds girls frequently build up in their personal relationships. There is an exclusive, almost claustrophobic atmosphere in some dyad relations. It is this dichotomy between the close relationships, where disclosures are elicited and shared, and the volatile nature of the relationships resulting in a breakup that leads to conflict. The frequent, seemingly low-key disputes between girls take up more teacher contact time and are more demanding to deal with than the occasional violent episode between boys. Unfortunately, the girls involved as well as adult observers, misinterpret these disputes and conflicts as simply squabbles and quarrels between friends. Subsequently, they have been taken less seriously than if they had been recognized accurately as bullying incidents with clearly identified bullies and victims.

As most of the quarrels and conflicts among girls appear related to their friendship groups (Besag, 2006), the victims are unable to escape the mesh of social relationships within which the bullies lurk. The aggressors know all about their target due to past friendly relationships. They know where their victim lives and how to contact them by telephone, text, and e-mail—all of which may be used to send abusive and threatening messages.

EMOTIONAL EFFECTS OF BULLYING

Social exclusion is a good predictor of problems such as depression, loneliness, anxiety, and reduction in self-worth (Gilbert, 1992; Boulton and Hawker, 1997). Extremes of low or high status in the group may leave a permanent mark on the personality (Coie, 1990). We have come to recognize these effects on boy victims of bullying but only recently understood the negative effects of the quarrels between girls. If we accept the range of indirect aggressions used by girls as forms of bullying, we can begin to unravel the negative effects of the process (Besag, 2006). Although aggression between girls is often less visible, and so more easily missed or misinterpreted than the overt modes more usually employed by boys, we now recognize that it can be as equally destructive (Boulton and Hawker, 1997). The psychological, emotional, and social facets integral to the covert modes of bullying make them more difficult to cope with than physical attacks as they primarily involve the manipulation of the emotions of the target. The strategies employed to exclude, ostracize, ridicule, or demoralize another girl may be more sophisticated than has been acknowledged. Active rejection, being passively neglected, and being ignored by others are three different concepts but all may cause extreme emotional distress in the lonely child. Verbal, social, and psychological forms of bullying can drive a child to suicide having equal potency to modes of physical aggression (Owens, Shute, and Slee, 2000, Social Care Institute of Excellence, 2005). Female victims of bullying score low on measures of self-perceived social acceptance compared to those not involved in bullying (Boulton and Smith, 1994). In a study carried out by Kupersmidt and Patterson (1991), rejected girls were found to be more than twice as likely, and neglected girls four times as likely, to report high levels of depression in preadolescence than other girls.

The Emotional Effects for Victims

The emotional effects of bullying among both boys and girls can cause a rapid downward spiral in self-esteem and confidence so that the young person becomes even more vulnerable and at greater risk (Besag, 1989). It is not clear whether bullies choose their victims because their vulnerability makes them easy targets, or if victims develop low self-esteem because of the bullying they experience. It would seem reasonable to propose that a combination of both factors may be present. Unfortunately, most boys appear not to seek emotional support from their friends and adults in the way girls do. This means that although the negative behaviors used among girls appear more harmful than the more direct attacks that take place among boys, the level of distress experienced by boys is probably equal to that of girls.

The powerful emotional effect of bullying on a victim is because these behaviors thrive on the target being in a situation equivalent to a hostage situation where one party is obviously the more powerful. The uncertainty of what will happen increases the power of the attacker while decreasing the power of the hostage leading to an increase in tension and distress. A combination of hope and despair confuses the cognitive processes making it one of the most powerful psychological mechanisms holding the victim passive in the abusive situation. According to Besag (2006), behaviors common to a bullying and hostage situation include

- Repetitive Threat
- Brainwashing
- Degradation
- Physical or Emotional Isolation
- Name-calling
- Rhymes and Rhythm
- Intermittent Attacks

The Downward Spiral. As the bullying relationship develops, the power, competence, and confidence of the attacker increases while the confidence and self-esteem of the victim decreases (Besag, 2002; 2006). Emotionally the effects of the abuse become more intense, and include the following key features:

- Powerlessness—the victim feels unable to fight or flee and so flounders
- Hopelessness—no help seems available
- Uncertainty—the attacks are unpredictable
- Trapped—the victim feels emotionally or physically trapped
- Guilt—the victim has no access to effective defense strategies
- Shame—the victim feels ashamed and denigrated by the nature of the abusive attack and by feeling unable to take effective defensive action
- Fear—of attack and possible reprisals should they seek help
- Anxiety—may lead to depression
- Loss of identity—due to denigrating name-calling

The Emotional Effects for the Bully

Although we have gleaned information about the emotional effects of bullying on the victim, we know less about the effect on the bully. The repercussions of bullying affect not only victims, but also the witnesses and bullies. Many aggressors experience negative effects if allowed to continue their bullying behavior. The bully learns it is possible to gain emotional, social, or monetary benefit from the bullying, so their modus operandi may become habitual. They learn they can use dominance for their own purposes, an attitude that can lead to a career of crime (Olweus, 1993). A significant number of young male bullies make at least two court appearances for antisocial behavior in early adulthood (Olweus, 1978). Social aggression is linked to later peer problems with an expectation of a negative outcome such as delinquency and antisocial behavior (Coie and Dodge, 1998). There are links to depression in girls who bully (Obeidallah and Earls, 1999) and a prediction of early pregnancy (Miller-Johnson et al., 2005).

LACK OF REPARATIVE WORK

There is now evidence of the emotional repercussion of bullying and retrospective reports show that these negative effects may last long into adulthood. There appears little overt rationale in the choice of a girl selected for rejection, or ridicule, so she is often left confused and bewildered (Munthe, 1989). She may never know why she was a victim or later allowed back into the group. As targets often find no reason for the attacks, they have no idea how to remedy the situation. In the case of boys, they may feel a deeper reluctance to admit they have been the victims of attacks and seek out any support available.

There continues to be a sad lack of appropriate support for the victims of bullying whether they are boys or girls. Once all self-esteem and confidence is lost, the victim is in a defenseless and precarious situation. Adults freed from a hostage situation often have recourse to reparative work with a psychologist or therapist. It is by no means certain that young victims, similarly emotionally or psychologically damaged by bullying, will have any such support.

Tips for Parents

✒ Talk about dominance, and the fallacy of admiring those who dominate others.

✒ Reward democratic, positive behavior.

✒ Stop sibling bullying when it occurs.

✒ Watch for signs of bullying behavior: among boys bullying tends to be more direct, concentrated on the physical hierarchy, and includes a spirit of competition. Bullying among girls is more indirect, focused more on their friends, and is "behind the backs" of the victim.

Tips for Educators

✒ Be aware that some students come from environments where aggressive behavior is critical to survival (particularly in areas of social deprivation). Think about ways in which you can introduce alternative strategies to counter hostile environments.

✎ Think about ways in which you can facilitate a discussion of the pros and cons of autocratic versus democratic authority.

✎ Do not ignore bullying behaviour when you see it.

✎ When you see bullying taking place, stop it, don't give the perpetrators an audience.

✎ Don't write off altercations between girls as merely a squabble, make sure all aggressive interactions are investigated.

REFERENCES

Ahlgren, A. (1983). Sex differences in the correlates of cooperative and competitive school attitudes. *Developmental Psychology*, 19, 881–888.

Alder, P. A., and Alder, P. (1995). Dynamics of inclusion and exclusion in preadolescent cliques. *Social Psychology Quarterly*, 58, 145–162.

Archer, J. (2001). Evolving theories of behaviour. *The Psychologist*, 14, 414–430.

Arnold, D. H., Homrok, S., Ortiz, C., and Stowe, R. M. (1999). Direct observation of peer rejection acts and their temporal relationship with aggressive acts. *Early Childhood Research Quarterly*, 2, 183–196.

Artz, S. (2005). To die for: Violent adolescent girls' search for male attention. In D. Pepler, K. Madsen, C. Webster, and K. Levene (Eds.), *The Development and Treatment of Girlhood Aggression* (pp. 137–159). Mahwah, NJ: Lawrence Erlbaum Associate Publishers.

Besag, V. E. (1989). *Bullies and Victims in Schools: A Guide to Understanding and Management*. Milton Keynes, UK: Open University Press.

———. (2002). *We Don't Have Bullies Here!* Newcastle upon Tyne, UK: Val Besag.

———. (2006). *Understanding Girls' Friendships, Fights and Feuds: A Practical Approach to Girls' Bullying*. Milton Keynes, UK: Open University Press.

Björkqvist, K., Österman, K., and Kaukianinen, A. (1992). The development of direct and indirect aggressive strategies in males and females. In P. Niemela and K. Björkqvist (Eds.), *Of Mice and Women: Aspects of Female Aggressiveness* (pp. 51–64). New York, NY: Academic Press.

Boulton, M. J., and Hawker, D. S. (1997). Non-physical forms of bullying among school pupils: A cause for concern. *Health Education*, 2, 61–64.

Boulton, M. J., and Smith, P. K. (1994). Bully/victim problems in middle-school children: Self perceived competence, peer perceptions and peer acceptance. *British Journal of Educational Psychology*, 62, 73–82.

Buss, D. M. (1981). Sex differences in the evaluation and performance of dominant acts. *Journal of Personality and Social Psychology*, 40, 147–154.

Campbell, A. (2004). *Women's Hour*. Broadcast, October 10.

———. (2005, November). Keynote lecture given to the Association of Educational Psychologists, Hilton Hotel, Gateshead.

Campbell A., and Muncer, S. (1987). Models of anger and aggression in the social talk of women and men. *Journal for the Theory of Social Behaviour*, 17, 489–512.

Chung, T. Y., and Asher, S. R. (1996). Children's goals and strategies in peer conflict situations. *Merrill Palmer Quarterly*, 42, 125–147.

Coie, J. D. (1990). Toward a theory of peer rejection. In S. R. Asher and J. D. Coie (Eds.), *Peer Rejection in Childhood* (pp. 365–401). Cambridge, UK: Cambridge University Press.

Coie, J. K., and Dodge, K. A. (1998). Aggression and antisocial behavior. In W. Damon and N. Eisenberg (Eds.), *Handbook of Child Psychology: Social, Emotional, and Personality Development*, 5th ed. Volume 3 (pp. 779–862). New York, NY: John Wiley & Sons.

Collins, W. A., and Laursen, B. (1992). Conflict and relationships during adolescence. In C. U. Shantz and W. W. Hartup (Eds.), *Conflict in Child and Adolescent Development* (pp. 216–241). New York, NY: Cambridge University Press.

Crick, N. R., and Grotpeter, J. K. (1995). Relational aggression, gender and social psychological adjustment. *Child Development*, 66, 710–722.

Crombie, G., and Desjardins, M. J. (1993, April). Predictors of gender: The relative importance of children's play, games and personality characteristics. Paper presented at the biennial meeting of the Society for Research in Child Development, New Orleans.

Cross, S. E., and Madson, L. (1997). Models of self: Self construals and gender. *Psychological Bulletin*, 122, 5–37.

Daly, M., and Wilson, M. (1994). Evolutionary psychology of male violence. In J. Archer (Ed.), *Male Violence* (pp. 253–288). London, UK: Routledge.

Eder, D. (1985). The cycle of popularity: Interpersonal relations among female adolescents. *Sociology of Education*, 58, 976–985.

———. (1991). The role of teasing in adolescent peer culture. *Sociological Studies of Child Development, Part 4*, 181–197.

Gilbert, P. (1992). *Depression: The Evolution of Powerlessness*. Hove, UK: Erlbaum.

Goodwin, M. H. (1990). *He-Said-She-Said: Talk as Social Organisation Among Black Children*. Bloomington, IN: Indiana University Press.

Harris, J. R. (1995). Where is the child's environment? A group theory of socialisation. *Psychological Review*, 97, 114–121.

Hughes, L. A. (1988). But that's not really mean: Competing in a cooperative mode. *Sex Roles*, 19, 669–687.

Kaukiainen, A., Björkqvist, K., Lagerspetz, K., Österman, K., Salmivalli, C., Rothberg, S., and Ahlbom, A. (1999). The relationships between social intelligence, empathy, and three types of aggression. *Aggressive Behavior*, 25, 81–89.

Kupersmidt, J. B., and Patterson, C. J. (1991). Childhood peer rejection, aggression, withdrawal, and perceived competence as predictors of self-reported behavior problems in preadolescence. *Journal of Abnormal Child Psychology*, 19, 427–449.

Labov, W. (1972). *Language in the Inner City: Studies in Black English Vernacular*. Philadelphia, PA: University of Philadelphia Press.

Lever, J. (1976). Sex differences in the games children play. *Social Problems*, 23, 478–487.

Maccoby, E. E. (1999). *The Two Sexes: Growing up Apart, Coming Together*. Cambridge, MA: Harvard University Press.

————. (2002). Gender and group process: A developmental perspective. *Current Directions in Psychological Science*, 11(22), 54–58.

Miller-Johnson, S., Moore, B. L., Underwood, M. K., and Coie, J. D. (2005). African-American girls and physical aggression: Does stability of childhood aggression predict later negative outcomes? In D. Pepler, K. Madsen, C. Webster, and K. Levene (Eds.), *The Development and Treatment of Girlhood Aggression* (pp. 75–95). Mahwah, NJ: Lawrence Erlbaum Associate Publishers.

Munthe, E. (1989). Bullying in Scandinavia. In E. Roland and E. Munthe (Eds.), *Bullying: An International Perspective* (pp. 66–78). London, UK: David Fulton Publishers.

Ness, C. D. (2004). Why girls fight: Female youth violence in the inner city. *The Annals of the American Academy*, 595, 32–48.

Obeidallah, D., and Earls, F. (1999). Adolescent girls: The role of depression in the development of delinquency (FS000244). National Institute of Justice, Washington, DC: U.S. Government Printing Office.

Olweus, D. (1978). *Aggression in Schools: Bullies and Whipping Boys*. Washington, DC: Hemisphere.

————. (1993). *Bullying at School: What We Know and What We Can Do*. Oxford, UK: Blackwell Publishers.

Owens, L. D., Shute, R., and Slee, P. (2000). Guess what I just heard!: Indirect aggression among teenage girls in Australia. *Aggressive Behavior*, 6, 67–83.

Pellegrini, A. D. (1988). Elementary-school children's rough and tumble play and social competence. *Developmental Psychology*, 24, 802–806.

Pipher, M. (1994). *Reviving Ophelia: Saving the Selves of Adolescent Girls*. London, UK: Random House.

Rose, A. J., and Asher, S. R. (1999). Children's goals and strategies in response to conflicts within a friendship. *Developmental Psychology*, 35, 69–79.

Salmivalli, C., Lagerspetz, K. M. J., Björkqvist, K., Österman, K., and Kaukiainen, A. (1996). Bullying as a group process: Participant roles and their relations to social status within the group. *Aggressive Behaviour*, 22, 1–15.

Savin-Williams, R. C. (1980). Social interactions of adolescent females in natural groups. In H. C. Foot, A. J. Chapman, and J. R. Smith (Eds.), *Friendship and Social Relations in Children* (pp. 343–364). Chichester, UK: John Wiley & Sons.

Simmons, R. (2002). *Odd Girl Out: The Hidden Culture of Aggression in Girls*. San Diego, CA: Harcourt Trade Publishing.

Smith, P. K., and Boulton, M. (1990). Rough and tumble play, aggression, and dominance: Perception and behaviour in children's encounters. *Human Development*, 33, 271–282.

Social Care Institute of Excellence (2005). Deliberate self-harm among children and adolescents: Who is at risk and how is it recognized? Retrieved 2007 from http://www.scie.org.uk/publications/ briefings/briefing16/index.asp.

Sutton, J., Smith, P. K., and Swettenham, J. (1999). Bullying and theory of mind: A critique of the "social skills deficit" view of anti-social behaviour. *Social Development*, 8, 117–127.

Tannen, D. (1992). *You Just Don't Understand: Woman and Men in Conversation*. New York, NY: William Morrow.

Thorne, B. (1993). *Gender Play: Girls and Boys in School*. Milton Keynes, UK: Open University Press.

Wachtel, P. L. (1973). Psychodynamics, behaviour therapy and the implacable experimenter: An inquiry into the consistency of personality. *Journal of Abnormal Psychology*, 83, 324–334.

Whitesell, N. R., and Harter, S. (1996). The interpersonal context of emotion: Anger with close friends and classmates. *Child Development*, 67, 1345–1359.

Whitney, I., and Smith, P. K. (1993). A survey of the nature and extent of bullying in junior/middle and secondary schools. *Educational Research*, 35, 3–25.

Wiseman, R. (2002). *Queen Bees and Wannabes: Helping Your Daughter Survive Cliques, Gossip, Boyfriends and Other Realities of Adolescence*. London, UK: Judy Piakus (Publishers) Limited.

CHAPTER 3

Institutional Factors in Bullying

The vast majority of what has been written on bullying in schools has focused on the individuals involved with students being considered "the problem" and adult intervention "the solution." Students are normally characterized as "victims," "bullies," and "bystanders" (with a number of other variations on this theme, e.g., "bully-victims"). This is largely due to the fact that those who investigate the issue have a professional background underpinned by training in psychology, where within-person variables are more central to their understanding of human behavior than social and cultural practices.

With the great amount of literature addressing bullying, and the vast quantity of thorough research generated by researchers and practitioners, one might have expected greater efficacy from those interventions and projects designed to reduce bullying in schools. However, despite the various books, intervention resources and programs available to schools the problem of bullying continues to plague us. While some anti-bullying interventions reported varying levels of reduction in bullying—the most dramatic being reported by Olweus and Alsaker (1991)—others, such as Munthe and Roland (1989) have actually reported increases in bullying. Thus, it would seem that factors outside the scope or interest of past, recent, and current research and its associated initiatives should be explored more fully, moving away from the person-centered focus to a more holistic or institutional level approach.

This chapter and the following one that looks at the issues of sexuality and gender in relation to bullying behavior take a rather different perspective. Instead of dwelling almost exclusively on the personalities and attributes of individuals, and seeking change in them, these chapters take a more sociological perspective wherein bullying is seen in terms of systems and cultures within institutions. Here, bullying is seen not as the sum of unpleasant behaviors that are owned by children, but the product of complex interactions within a system of social relationships that cannot be changed by simply removing bullies or reinforcing victims.

A SOCIOCULTURAL PERSPECTIVE ON BULLYING

Sociocultural perspectives (Horton, 2006; Duncan, forthcoming) bring another dimension of understanding to the issue of bullying, thereby complementing what we already understand from those that have researched it from primarily a psychological perspective. Sociologists and cultural theorists posit that changing behaviors that are entrenched is very hard to do, however making small but crucial changes to the social environment in which those behaviors take place is possible, and can have significant positive benefits. This approach takes a step back from "the problem child" approach and surveys the school, not as a collection of individuals, but as an institution with crisscrossing mores, values, expectations, and codes of behavior that need to be understood before work can be effected on those individuals who are of concern to parents, teachers, and administrators.

One reason why this perspective is less popular than other, more traditional or person-centered responses to bullying behavior is that it places the burden of change upon the adults (teachers, administrators, and parents) and the institutions (the schools, the districts, and the boards of educations), rather than upon the students. It is far easier to assimilate a commonsense notion of bullying as a series of overt or, indeed, covert behaviors acted out by individuals whose reasons for such behavior are grounded in the personalities or idiosyncrasies of their victims, rather than engage with the sometimes abstract and complex ideas that are associated with the sociocultural perspectives.

An Example of the Sociocultural Perspective in Action

Consider two places where large groups of people come together to work: the first is the Harley Davidson motorcycle assembly plant in Pennsylvania, the other is the Rolls Royce motor car assembly plant in Crewe, England. Each can rightly be considered an institution of worldwide renown creating, as they do, fine automotive products that their competitors envy. Pass through these institutions and you will observe similar patterns of tasks, of organization, and of communication. Less easily observed, but certainly experienced, is the dramatic difference in human relationships, and the spirit, or ethos, of the workplaces.

In the Harley Davidson workshops you might be unsurprised to note a competitive and macho attitude, with the employees taking a pride in physical ability within a "can-do" ethos. In the Rolls Royce workshop, you might encounter a more refined, almost aesthetic, sensibility, with an unhurried and almost disdainful air. These two institutions have a distinctly different set of unspoken values, of expectations about their colleagues, and this behavior is a reflection of the ethos of each.

In the one place, a mistake made by an operative might be met with catcalls and friendly put-downs, whilst in the other the mistake might be coldly "ignored" by colleagues as an embarrassing personal weakness. If you reflect upon your own workplace, and compare its tone or atmosphere to another work setting with which you are familiar, you may recall one being more suited to you than the other. There are many examples of this sort of thing that might occur to you, but the issue is the same: the ethos of an institution is hard to define and difficult to describe, but inescapable in its experience, and it has a palpable effect upon the behavior of its inhabitants.

So, if this can be true for institutions of work such as factories, it can also be true for institutions of learning such as schools where young people come into close contact with one another. Indeed, the sociocultural perspective may be even more pertinent to schools, as one of the primary functions of education is to socialize young people, and guide them into behaving in an appropriate way. But what is "the appropriate way"?

Inevitably, all schools have two sets of rules: an official code of behavior, and an unofficial set of mores or customs. All schools will have official sets of rules and will, like the two motor factories mentioned above, have visible similarities. However, all schools will also have a series of unofficial mores that will be subtle, but powerful, in their differences.

SCHOOLS: A SOCIOCULTURAL VIEW

Schools are uniquely compulsory, and straddle phases of development that are highly formative in the life of the individual. They also concentrate large groups of people (students, teachers, and administrators) in compressed spaces in a way that is rarely replicated in later life. Furthermore, schools assess, grade, and evaluate just about every aspect of a student's performance, thereby affecting self-appraisal and self-esteem. Schools are the only institutions we have that organize people on such a fine and inflexible age gradation. As children develop at different rates, one might be tempted to ask why. However, the fact that so few of us even consider this illustrates how pervasive the ideology of schooling is, and how institutionalized both adult and child inhabitants become.

Understanding the Sociocultural Perspective: Class Task for Teachers

Anyone doubting the efficacy of children's absorption of what is valued and important in their schooling should try this: ask a third grader to rank order her peers according to age, ability, and behavior. To be safe on the ethical dimension of this task, you would need to have the anonymous papers returned to you, and not share their results with the class. Most children will be able to carry out this task easily, demonstrating that even though teachers do not publicly rate their students, covert signals and attitudes toward each student are conveyed to other students who pick them up and then structure their own relations upon them.

The characteristics of our systems of schooling, and their impact upon student behavior are highly potent but, interestingly, they often go unrecognized by students or even the professional educators, because of their institutionalization or acculturation.

SCHOOL ETHOS

Just as any institution has its distinct ethos or character, schools vary in theirs from bustling and jovial to serious and repressed. The origins of the ethos may be linked to its establishment as a faith school, a result of pedagogic innovation, or a legacy drawn from a philanthropic will, but, regardless of origin, it is the portrayal of that ethos and its outcomes that are of central importance, especially when one of those outcomes is, in effect, bullying.

There are a number of important factors to consider in understanding how a school develops and maintains its ethos, thereby encouraging or discouraging bullying. Some of these factors are completely outside the school's control. For example, schools usually do not choose their location, and therefore are subject to their local environment, the socioeconomic status of their intake, and family mobility (e.g., migratory movements). These external factors, in turn, have an impact upon families' parenting styles and behavioral expectations. The size of a school is usually beyond the control of the faculty and staff, and this might be an important issue in nurturing a personalized relationship between faculty, staff, and students. Indeed, a number of important research projects have reported that, while small schools are not always better schools, size really can matter with respect to both academic and welfare issues. Having said that, for many years it has been a puzzle to researchers who study bullying why it is that ostensibly similar schools have such a variance in reported bullying rates? Clearly it cannot be simply because those schools have more "bullies" or "victims" by chance: a more plausible explanation may lie in the lives of the institutions themselves.

Of course, individual students bring their own unique personalities to their school, and these "within-student variables" make a difference to the atmosphere of the classroom and the school. Occasionally a student with a personality or conduct disorder, a medical or a psychiatric condition that affects behavior, can exert a negative force in a classroom or playground situation. But these are exceptional cases, and are dealt with elsewhere in this volume and in other books on bullying and general behavior problems (see, for example, Chapter 6 of this handbook). Students demonstrating these tendencies have a low impact on rates of bullying in schools and are just as likely to be bullied as they are to bully because they are disconnected from the general group and excluded from it. Sutton and Keogh (2000), deftly demonstrate how a "Machiavellian type" of bully succeeds in adapting the prevailing peer culture of a school for his or her own social success. Exceptionally aggressive individuals do present a challenge to schools, but this challenge is not central to the understanding of how bullying operates within institutions in the mainstream.

More commonly, bullying is an unwanted product of an overlooked complex set of features relating to the process of schooling, and schools as institutions. Schools are not the only milieu where bullying takes place, but the words *bullying* and *school* have a more powerful association than, say, bullying and *family*, or bullying and *hospital*, for the very reason that the two so often coexist.

Schools and Bullying

So what are the features of the school as an institution that might affect a student's chances of being bullied, or being enabled to bully others? One of the most important issues here is the mission of the school. This will no doubt vary with the ages of the students attending. For example, one might expect a shift in emphasis from student-centered development toward academic attainment as students increase in age. Nevertheless, the character of an organization emerges from spoken and unspoken beliefs and attitudes, and these can often be very clear if you know what to look for (Harrison and Stokes, 1992). Here is a real-life scenario that exemplifies how staff can convey a great deal about the institution's position on student-centeredness.

A Parent's View of a School's Student-Centeredness. It is "open-evening" for junior high children to visit local high schools with a view to choosing one for next year. The school year has only just begun and the high school has brought in its youngest students to demonstrate the sorts of activities available at the school to promote it as a first choice for the undecided visiting families. A father asks for some clarification from the senior teacher responsible for the new intake of students:

Parent: I've been told by a number of your students that they are expected to devote two hours per night to homework right from the start, and that another four hours of homework is set for each weekend. That seems a lot to me, as I teach in a similar school and we give much less than that to our first year students.

Teacher: No, the students have got that correct, we do set that amount.

Parent: Well, Alex has a number of other calls on his time, so that might be a problem. He has attended junior karate lessons for 3 years, and is almost at his black belt stage, that takes a couple of two-hour sessions per week. He plays soccer in his local team—that accounts for a few hours over the weekend, and he has been studying saxophone and piano which also accounts for about four hours a week. I'm worried that he will have to drop some of these long-term activities which my wife and I feel make him a well-rounded kid.

Teacher: Well, there are two things Clifton High is known for: its dress-code policy and its homework policy, so he'll have to comply with those. Any homework we set must be completed or the student faces sanctions.

So, explicitly stated as the two highest priorities of the school are what the students wear and how much work they do outside of school. Alex's father could hardly have been less impressed. The school's official handbook offered quite a different mission statement that stressed "support for individual achievement and realization of every student's potential." But when challenged, a key member of the school's faculty was preoccupied with wholly non-child-centered issues: homework and appearance. The underlying philosophy here is one of controlling pupils for the school's benefit. Students are expected to conform to the school's ideals rather than have their own legitimate and relevant interests taken into account.

From Alex's perspective, if he were to attend Clifton High the informal lesson he would have to learn is that the only things that are valued by the school are those ratified by the school. This example may be something of a diversion from the central topic of bullying, however, the attitudes of faculty and staff are absolutely vital if a school is to be a center of learning and maximizing students' potential rather than one of blind conformity to superficial rules. If the stance of a teacher toward a student is one of top-down, autocratic, nonempathic, undifferentiated rule-enforcement, then the student will almost certainly absorb that ethos into their own interpersonal relationships and enact it.

The exchange at Clifton High shows how an individual who believes he has authority or power over another can privilege officiousness over humanity. Whilst the teacher is correct in his expression of the rules, there is no regard for an alternative legitimate point of view. Not only is there a lack of engagement with the other party (in this case a parent), but the teacher effects closure of the matter by invoking the possibility of punitive action by referring to sanctions.

Compare the actual exchange with this possible alternative response to the issue of homework.

Teacher: Well, we do set a lot of homework, that is true. The reason we do that is to make sure all our students consolidate what they learn in class. We'd like Alex to continue his extra-curricular interests as they sound really good, but if things get a bit too pressured, he can see me to discuss matters.

This second, hypothetical response does everything that is needed to be done, in terms of addressing the parent's enquiry. It does not equivocate or show any weakness, but it asserts the school's position as one that has some rationalization—it is to support learning, as well as valuing the child's preexisting commitments and offering negotiation at a later stage. By doing this, the teacher and the school are clearly modeling *benevolent* power. Most parents and prospective students experiencing this latter exchange would come away with a feeling that they had been treated fairly, and fairness is a value that does not rest easily with bullying. However, in the actual response by the teacher, the impression given is one where there is no room for personal expression, creativity, or even learning beyond that learned through the imposition of sanctions and this approach is one that can nurture an ethos where bullying can thrive.

TEACHERS' POWER AND THE ETHOS OF THE SCHOOL

The attitudes of teachers are of key importance when ensuring that schools can effectively challenging bullying, and the ways in which some types of incidents arise and are resolved can be critical in the way that students pick up cues about how to behave in certain situations. More important, however, is the prevalence of low-key exchanges such as the Clifton High example that builds up a set of behavioral or attitudinal norms for the institution. Students, parents, and other educators will silently attend to the way that statements or behaviors go unchallenged, and will come to understand that, within the context of a particular school, the ethos will allow a person to be treated in a discourteous way so long as the perpetrator has some form of power that is licensed by the institution. License by the institution can mean many things, but if a trusted teacher or parent talks to students about the abuses of power within the school that are not challenged, it is likely that those students will be able to provide an extensive list of examples.

Professionals in education, whether principals, teachers, administrative or other staff, are subject to the same pressures of modern life as any other social group, especially when politicians put such store by performance appraisals and target attainment. SAT scores and Adequate Yearly Progress reports add to teachers' burdens, and stress can develop leading to aggression and perceived unfairness becoming means of basic survival amongst those who would never drop their high standards under reasonable conditions. The pressures placed upon teachers to facilitate the achievement of the very best grades for students as well as managing the behavior of more than twenty very different personalities can erode the best of intentions, and impel the use of disciplinary strategies that subconsciously encourage bullying.

Below are two examples of discipline strategies that illustrate this point.

Scenario 1: Mr. Short's Story

Mr. Short teaches science, but some of his 9th-grade class resist his authority. He feels that his legitimate requests for quiet and calm are not responded to with sufficient goodwill. He entreats the students to come to order, but this does not work with all the students, and he finds that it is only by raising his voice can he be assured of managing the whole class. One day he decides to deal with the small group of students that resist his authority by putting the whole class on report for not coming to order immediately. He reinforces his intent by delegating the whole class the responsibility for good order.

Discussion of Mr. Short's Actions. Mr. Short has operated entirely within his terms of reference as a teacher. Many teachers use such techniques to assist them in gaining an atmosphere conducive to learning. Inadvertently, however, it can be argued that he is unfairly burdening some members of the class with a job that he, with his age, training, and official position, has not been able to do himself. There are a number of possible outcomes associated with this strategy. Firstly, he may believe that the threat of being put on report will suddenly enable students to see how important his demand for discipline is, and that the noisy, troublesome students will decide to behave better in future. But how likely is this really? Secondly, he may hope that the noisy, troublesome students will not show signs of change so the quiet, compliant group, will exert their combined social influence and effect the required change. But, just how plausible is this outcome? Finally, and more likely, Mr. Short will face the fact that the troublesome students will continue to disrupt and, as a result, periodically the whole class will suffer sanctions. Resentment will grow among the two groups of students thereby setting up interpersonal conflict outside of the class, and he will continue to be frustrated and stressed.

By insensitivity or weak leadership, or simply through desperation, Mr. Short has disturbed social relations among the student peer group that may well correlate with other experiences they consider unfair and which subtly but powerfully contribute to a climate where the perception is that power can be misused to achieve personal goals without consideration for others.

Scenario 2: Prize-Giving Day at Westway High School

It is prize-giving day in Westway High School. A procession of students is called upon to rise, mount the stage, and receive rewards for their successes and endeavors over the past year. Mrs. Lopez, the principal, addresses the assembly after the prize giving:

> These young people have all deserved the highest praise from the school community as they have made us proud with their achievements. We should take note that some of these prize-winners have won several trophies and awards,

so an especial congratulation is due to them. Next year I would love to see some of our students who have not received any presentations this time to try really hard to join us on this stage too. Our prize-winners are beacons of excellence, exemplars to inspire all our students.

Discussion of Prize-Giving. This is good wholesome stuff, instilling pride in parents and teachers alike, and the principal's speech seems beyond reproach in its delivery. However, in the audience sit a dozen young people, award-winners, who shuffle uncomfortably and try not to catch the eye of some of their peers. They know, though the fact is unspoken, that they are at risk of being verbally abused or even beaten up because of the praise they have received from officialdom that is, the principal. They know, as the aggressors know, that they are symbols of success and approval by the official school regime: the same regime that visits punishments, sanctions, ridicule, and failure upon a minority of students who, for whatever reason, are a reverse image of the successful ones.

Of course, there are many schools where the huge majority of students have an alignment of values in harmony with the school's official values. The competition for recognition and approval from authority may be embraced by all, and those who do not achieve accept their failure gracefully perhaps, and with renewed effort that will be rewarded next time. The culture of such schools promotes internal angst over external demonstration.

In Westway High too there will be children who are neither embarrassed over their public praise, nor aware or concerned about the possible consequences at the hands of their peers. However, a critical mass of students *will be* aware, and *are* being schooled in an institution where an antiestablishment ethos is sufficiently strong that they have to worry about their personal safety if and when they are held up by staff as being valued in contrast to those who are not. It is these students—we may consider them "floating voters"—who are aware of the potential dangers of success who will finally determine the school's ethos as they are drawn either in the anti-school or pro-school direction.

This scenario is not well recognized by educators generally because most caring parents and dedicated professionals have been, evidenced by their position, high achieving pro-school students in their youth. Consequently, they do not identify with those attitudes that are outside of their experience. Neither is it easy for the young people directly involved in this type of culture to understand or explain what is happening, but numerous practitioners do have experience of resolving maladaptive behaviors in such contexts where the roots lie in this suppressed and distorted jealousy, which is perhaps more common than we might like to believe.

How do we encourage potentially successful students who would rather destroy or refuse to complete their work because they live in fear of being publicly praised, and because peer approval overrides staff approval? Many educators will be familiar with incidents in which students have faked illness or absented themselves from school in order to avoid a situation where they would be singled out for reward. How does the school in which you teach, or in which your children attend score on indicators of an antiestablishment ethos?

How Might the True Ethos of an Institution Be Revealed?

It is not simply a set of unrelated exchanges that set the tone or ethos of a school. The way the school is organized can make a big difference (and some of the responsibility for this rests on local or state legislation or regulation), however, a substantial change can be effected by attending to the operational emphases of those who are in charge. One example of this relates to the way in which schools privilege age in their operations: the older a student is, the more favored she/he becomes. In some schools, we can see this philosophy in action in the way that older students will be favored with lunchtime arrangements, or are given freedoms that younger students do not have. Why should this be encouraged? Is it a case of older students "paying their dues," thereby earning their privileges? This does not really hold true as it favors students according to nothing other than chronology rather than addressing issues such as merit or effort. In effect, rewarding age is simply an institutionalized form of control: a means of constructing an artificial hierarchy where those in power maintain their power through leasing aspects of it to subordinates in order to prevent outright rebellion (e.g., hall monitors). Such unchallenged norms are consonant with an institutional philosophy that older is better and "might is right."

HIERARCHIES AND BEHAVIOR

We must always acknowledge that the public school system works on the basis of hierarchies. Even at school level, a distinct hierarchy is present with principals, vice-principals, and other professional adults forming the top layers with the youngest children at the very bottom of the chain. The culture of deference by teachers to their superordinates is understood by students who, in turn, create a pecking order among their peer groups. Pecking orders can be found in the very best of schools, but in a school where social relationships are inflected with fear and injustice, perfect conditions for bullying to take hold are provided.

For example, the parent at Clifton High recalled his own elementary education in which his teacher used to allow the class to indulge in craft activities on Friday afternoons, but warned them that they must never let the principal know, as she (the teacher) would get into serious trouble for not following the timetable. This little entreaty by the elementary school teacher into collusion seems mild and innocuous, but was connected to a number of other beliefs that built up a picture of an unfriendly system where kindness would be seen as weakness by the principal whose view could not be challenged. It may also have been an attempt by the teacher to buy some favor from the class for her unsanctioned lenience. Whilst this teacher's behavior might seem natural and well intentioned, often the outcomes of such behavior are not welcome, and propagate a culture of corrupt power.

Power in Schools

Those who hold power in schools will recognize the principle that it should only be used with the utmost consideration for fairness and justice. But the question posed is *"how often is this the case?"* To all intents and purposes, bullying is interpersonal abuse of power, and in schools, this abuse can simultaneously be omnipresent and elusive.

Case Study: Raul and Mr. Klein. One of the authors of this handbook, Neil Duncan, worked with Raul, a very disaffected fourteen-year-old young man who had been in trouble for years in various schools, who offered a good example of the type of interpersonal abuse of power referred to above. At the point of this conversation, Raul had been ejected several times from the same teacher's class: both he and the teacher knew how perilously close he was to a third strike and expulsion from the school.

Raul:	It's (Mr.) Klein, he knows how to wind me up. He knows how to spark me off. He does it deliberately. The way he talks to you, it gets me mad, I just wanna hit him.
Neil Duncan:	Are you saying Mr. Klein is lying in his reports about your behavior?
Raul:	Nah, it's true, but it isn't the same, d'you know what I mean? It's the *way* he talks to me, putting me down. He'd never talk to me like that in front of my Mom, he wouldn't dare. He wouldn't talk to anyone on the street like that.
Neil Duncan:	Did he curse you? Did he call you names?
Raul:	Nah, you don't understand either. Forget it.

Despite this student's frustrated inarticulacy, Neil thought he knew what Raul meant, and felt, as Raul was one of his charges, that he should do something about it. Raul's story illustrated that, by slight inflections and emphases in speech, Mr. Klein can completely change the meaning of words, from praise to ridicule, from respect to contempt without overtly making offensive or inappropriate comments—a charge of provocation would be almost impossible to prove. Neil went to speak with Mr. Klein.

In his conversation with Mr. Klein, Neil explained that Raul was easily angered and easily provoked, and he also explained the serious consequences for Raul if he failed to remain in school. Although Neil sympathized with

Mr. Klein and the burden placed upon him by Raul's unruly behavior, Neil appealed to Mr. Klein's sense of fair play, and asked him to try a different approach to modify his behavior. Using Raul's mention of his mother, Neil asked Mr. Klein if he would simply try relating to Raul as if his mother was present as an observer.

Neil did not intend that Mr. Klein should go easy on Raul, but that he should try to maintain a professional form of respect, of authority with reasonableness. It happened that Mr. Klein responded well to this request, and things did improve between him and Raul, though ultimately Raul did prove too difficult for the school. For Neil this was an important episode, because he subsequently used that maxim "treat them as if their parents are in the room" with all of his classes of trainee teachers. Such training is far more palatable prior to, rather than after, critical incidents, as professionals may see such maxims as censure rather than support.

COMPETITION AND CONNECTEDNESS

In a truly collegiate or democratic institution, there is no place for a "do as I say, not as I do" mentality. Official rules should not demand compliance only from the lower ranks, but all should subscribe to them. It is never considered good practice to list only negatives in school rules, for example, a litany of "thou shalt nots." A positive and optimistic school should have a few general principles, such as treating everyone with respect, modeled vigorously by the staff themselves.

Most schools will have codes of conduct that mention treating people with respect, but the pressures of work, the upheavals of daily life, and the less welcome elements of human nature will always test that intention. When good intentions are tested to their limits, it often happens that good conduct rules become ones that are applicable to students only, thus resulting in lapses of judgment wherein unpleasant exchanges with students end with a desperate "because I say so!" statement.

What makes one school more prone to a bullying culture than another is the result of a complex matrix of factors that confound analysis because they are ever changing and they invariably avoid scrutiny. One element, however, that seems to have a strong influence is competitiveness. In most cases, competitiveness is a desirable thing.

Competition makes us try to reach our potential, to make the most of ourselves. Competition is positive when it is something we opt into, and promises a reward. Competition is not so attractive when it is compulsory and the rewards are not general, but result in the identification of winners and losers, and where a critical mass are constantly in fear of failure. Under those conditions teachers and students may lose their moral compass and find that they are working to hidden agendas that require coercion rather than persuasion and manipulation rather than honesty.

In recent years there has been mounting political pressure on schools to improve performance against a set of criteria over which educators have not been fully consulted. These performance achievements are used to compare schools with one another thereby drawing them into a competition that few really want. Hostile competition encourages alienation of others—one school becomes the enemy of another, breeding opposition. This is inimical to empathy and caring, two values that many parents hope schools promote in their children.

Concomitant with this competitive ethic is the expectation that "good" teachers have "good" classroom discipline. In other words, effective teachers can control their students. Exactly how a teacher manages this is often left to her or him as the only adult in a room. Techniques might include sarcasm, scapegoating, and turning a blind eye to student-on-student aggression if it suits her or his interests. There is no doubt that teacher-powered approaches such as assertive discipline are highly effective, but they have been heavily criticized for being too rigid and "top-down" compared to others (Curwin and Mendler, 1999). Inhabiting a top-down model of behavior management allows some students to pick up the ethic of controlling subordinates who then misapply it in relationships with weaker or more vulnerable peers. The result is an institutional ethos that makes it easier for bullying to occur.

In schools where the work ethic, or student performance, is valued more highly than child development, successful teachers are often those that adopt authoritarian modes of discipline in their classes. Further down the hierarchy students compete with one another for a different prize: peer-group social dominance based upon the reputation of being clever or physically powerful. If academic success is not forthcoming, those who can will seek these other forms of success and social esteem.

When children observe adults competing rather than collaborating, it is likely that they will absorb the ethic of esteeming winners and shunning losers. In order to compete, one must display some forms of aggression, either physical or relational. Our culture tends to do this in a very mild way in schools, with many checks and balances that reduce the risk of aggressive competitiveness that nourishes bullying. However, the principle is evident when we look at cultures where pressure to succeed academically and to conform to institutional ideals is more overt and has a greater intensity.

JAPANESE SCHOOLS: A REVEALING COMPARISON

One culture that has been explored using a sociological paradigm for bullying is that of Japan. Research there draws very strong links with some practices that are not (officially) favored in the West, such as teacher evaluation of student attitude, a powerful ethic for standardization and conformity to the group, personal accountability to the peer group, casual physical violence, and physical punishments from teachers to students (Yoneyama and Naito, 2003). One theory for excessively cruel and violent student-on-student bullying in Japanese schools is that, in addition to the above, schools are more commune-like, more of a closed institution than schools in the United States, Canada, or Western Europe. Japanese students, even at high school age, are taught in substantially less fluid groups, and are expected to carry out a wider range of activities in very close proximity with the same peers in the same room including cleaning and eating together. Allied with a very pronounced and impersonal hierarchical control structure, it is posited that in the lowest orders these factors fuel a desire for power of any sort, and interpersonal attacks on fellow students are the eruptions of this official disempowerment.

This example is given as illustrative of the need to examine our own school cultures to make sure that what goes on in our schools as a matter of course is likely to discourage bullying rather than encourage it, and that the human relationships we want are warm and empathic rather than cold and alienating. Our reliance on profiling individual children for predisposition toward bullying is as insufficient to understanding the problem as our individualized interventions are at solving it.

WHAT CAN BE DONE?

When an institution has produced a culture of bullying, its whole system is infected with negative thinking and entrenched sets of behaviors. As such, there are no quick fixes for the parents of its students, or for those educators and administrators hoping to effect change. It is a sad truth that sometimes the best a parent can do is to highlight what is going on to the superintendent or school board, and consider moving their child to another school (see Chapter 9 which offers guidance to parents who are concerned about bullying in their children's school). For teachers, challenging the system is often fraught with dangers linked to future employability, professional reputation, and poor references as well as broken friendships with colleagues, and a lot of soul-searching. Below, I offer some suggestions for identification, but action is only advisable under certain circumstances and should be carefully considered in the light of one's own position and the potential risks to it.

Are there times when you see or hear school staff talking to students in a way that you would not like your own children to be spoken to? If the answer is "*yes*," then consider the circumstances. You might come to the conclusion that here are unseen pressures, for example, a professional ethos that encourages this type of behavior to be displayed by the staff. If you can locate the source, you might be in a position to challenge it or work on altering it.

Are there areas in the school where you feel uncomfortable due to being seen as an outsider? If the answer is "*yes*," think about whether this zone is controlled by students or staff (there are departments where faculty dislike other colleagues entering, such as a lab during recess where teachers can gather to complain about managers or students). Often zealous guarding of such a zone is a sign of a siege mentality where the inhabitants have formed a resistant subculture to something they feel threatened by. After identifying it, understanding it is the next step in reconstructing it.

Does the immediate environment outside the school premises operate on a different set of values from the school itself? If the answer is "*yes*," is there a perceptible backlash to an oppressive regime that they have endured all day? For example, some schools are like pressure cookers, where anger and resentment are stored up all day and which are suddenly released as loud obscenities, aggression, vandalism, and similar antisocial behaviors after school. This can be an indicator of young people's a lack of opportunity to be listened to or to feel safe when inside the school environs.

Are the behavior, language, and demeanor of students on the school bus, in alignment with the expectations within the school? If the answer is "*yes*," then the behavior on school buses can indicate a release from the repressed atmosphere of the classroom or schoolyard. It is often on school buses that students expend their aggression on a captive set of victims. Freire (1972) refers to this phenomenon (downward pressure being vented on weaker peers) as "horizontal violence."

Are staff relationships cordial across faculties and departments? If the answer is "*no*," then your school may have built up a culture of interfaculty rivalry that has become distinctly unhealthy and has transmitted itself to the students. Examples might include resentment when being asked to support staff from other areas, an abandonment of substitute teachers to the wolves, negative, sarcastic comments about the value of other faculties, or their way of doing things. Under these conditions, it is impossible to preach pro-social behavior to the students whilst they can observe the antipathy between groups of staff.

Are there any minority groups (students of color, sexual minorities, students with special needs, or member of faith groups) that would not feel comfortably included in your school? If the answer is "yes," such infringements of human dignity are perhaps the clearest and easiest to contest as there is legislation that protects such individuals and groups. Proven examples of such practices can sometimes form a lever for change in other areas that are less overtly unjust.

IMPROVING SCHOOL ETHOS

So what can be done to improve matters in our schools? Ethos, culture, ideology, tone—call it what you will, but the atmosphere of a school is crucial to understanding why we have bullying. Much more research is required to develop instruments that can detect and measure those currently intangible factors that constitute the ethos of a school and so, until then, parents and educators, and other stakeholders in education, will have to rely on their own radar to render these things visible.

A useful starting point is for teachers to take the initiative and, during unstructured times during the school day, to take time out and enter or visit locations where students might not expect to see them. For example, if you are rarely in the refectory at lunchtime, try it. If you have never walked the corridors during lesson time, do it. If you do not usually visit the basketball court, go there. The new perspective you will get of the school by doing this will help you form a wider picture of your institution. Be reflective. Were you intimidated by being in a certain space at a certain time? If so, then why? Did you witness exchanges between adults and young people that concerned you? If so, then in what ways were you concerned?

One can also get a deeper picture of the school by analyzing the formal, public face of the institution. Is the promotional literature a celebration of individuality and uniqueness in its students, or does it dwell heavily on uniformity, conformity, and regulation? How often a school uses sanctions is difficult to determine, but comparisons can be made between the rates of school expulsions and the reasons for them.

Tips for Parents

- ✎ Talk to other parents, find out how they perceive the school's ethos. Does the school listen to parents or does it impose rules upon parents and their children?

- ✎ Listen to your child, how does she/he talk about school?

- ✎ Look at the school handbook and talk to teachers, find out what they truly value. If it is restrictive then consider whether or not your child will be able to reach her/his full potential at that school.

Tips for Educators

- ✎ Think about how you would characterize the official and unofficial ethos of your school. Does the school handbook reflect the way in which students are valued and supported on a daily basis?

- ✎ What attributes does your school value? Do those attributes set up competition between students? If so, how is that competition represented? Consider ways in which you might effect minor changes that value the contributions of all students.

- ✎ How do students talk about the school, is it positive or is it negative? There will always be some aspects of negativity following a poor grade, or the loss of a football game, but if the ethos is oppressive, the majority of comments you hear over time will be negative.

✎ Try addressing students as if their parents were present, setting up a relationship that is professional, respectful, and instructional.

REFERENCES

Curwin, R., and Mendler, A. (1999). *Discipline with Dignity*. Alexandria, VA: Association for Supervision and Curriculum Development.

Duncan, N. (forthcoming). Bullying in schools or bullying schools? In G. Richards and F. Armstrong (Eds.), *Key Issues for Teaching Assistants Working in Diverse and Inclusive Classrooms*. London, UK: Routledge.

Freire, P. (1972). *Pedagogy of the Oppressed*. New York, NY: Continuum.

Harrison, R., and Stokes, H. (1992). *Diagnosing Organization Instrument*. San Francisco, CA: Jossey-Bass/Pfeiffer.

Horton, P. (2006, January). Bullies and the bullied—the construction of a discourse of blame. Presented at the NYRIS 9 Conference, Södertörns Högskola, Stockholm, Sweden.

Munthe, E., and Roland, E. (1989). *Bullying: An International Perspective*. London, UK: David Fulton.

Olweus, D., and Alsaker, F. D. (1991). Assessing change in a cohort-longitudinal study with hierarchical data. In D. Magnusson, L. R. Bergman, G. Rudinger, and B. Torestad (Eds.), *Problems and Methods in Longitudinal Research: Stability and Change* (pp. 101–132). Cambridge, UK: Cambridge University Press.

Sutton, J., and Keogh, E. (2000). Social competition in school: Relationships with bullying, Machiavellianism and personality. *British Journal of Educational Psychology*, 70, 443–456.

Yoneyama, S., and Naito, A. (2003). Problems with the paradigm: The school as a factor in understanding bullying (with special reference to Japan). *British Journal of Sociology of Education*, 24 (3), 315–330.

PART II

Advice for Educators

CHAPTER 4

Gender, Sexuality, and Bullying in Schools

In all the literature referring to research into bullying in schools, much has been written about the frequency and types of bullying perpetrated against students in the hope that a better understanding of the motives of perpetrators and the experiences of their targets might provide us with greater clues about why certain children become bullies and why some become victims (Ma, Stewin, and Mah, 2001). However, it has to be acknowledged that we know more about victims and that considerably less is understood about why some students bully others. In Chapter 3, which focused on schools as institutions and their propensity to encourage or discourage bullying, the importance of a sociological perspective in understanding this problem was highlighted. In this chapter, the peer-group subculture is explored, with a view to better understanding the social relationships within peer-group subcultures and how they impact upon bullying behavior.

PEER RELATIONSHIPS: VOLATILITY AND VULNERABILITY

Most educators and parents are very aware of the importance that young people place in friendships. It would be difficult to live or work with children older than the age of eight without noticing the preoccupation they have with spending as much time as possible with peers (at school during lunch and recess, before and after school, and during vacations), prioritizing their friends' opinions above those of others in their lives (i.e., parents and teachers).

For some parents, such a preoccupation presents a major problem. For example, just how do the parents of Michael and Madison manage to get them to dress, eat, or play in the way they feel is best, when they are constantly compared, usually unfavorably, to Jacob's and Emily's parents?

Of course, what Michael and Madison's mom and dad may not appreciate is that Jacob and Emily are doing exactly the same, to the exasperation of their own parents. Nevertheless, the fact remains, whether we like it or not, that at certain points in their lives children will form very strong allegiances with young people from other families (as did we in our own younger days) that may well conflict with the aspirations and values of parents and teachers (Pellegrini and Blatchford, 2000).

Of course, the strength of these bonds fluctuate with time, and, while some young people forge lifelong friendships, most will make and break friendships frequently throughout this time. According to Val Besag, girls especially can have extreme emotions in relation to their friendships during this period, and can move from the elation of having a best friend to the slough of depression very quickly (see Besag, 2006). It is within the context of this volatility that vulnerabilities emerge which become a fertile ground for bullies and their cohorts.

IDENTITY CONSTRUCTION, ESTEEM, AND GROUP MEMBERSHIP

An important part of human development is the acquisition and construction of a personal identity. Identity can be described as a two-layered construction: there is the individual's sense of self (who am I?) and a social construction by others (who do they think I am?). The two parts of this identity are in dynamic flux, with one affecting and modifying the other almost continuously. It is generally accepted that a person's sense of self cannot develop in complete isolation from others (Kroger, 2007). We need "others" with which to compare ourselves. This is a crucial point: we need to define certain qualities we hold against someone or something different. In other words, it is hard to explain *light* unless you already know what *dark* is, and we sometimes strive to establish our own positive self against the negatives of others.

Self-Esteem and Social Esteem

Within the sphere of identity comes the concept of *self-esteem*. This concept, and its deployment has been at the centre of heated criticism in recent years, but in its simplest sense one might describe self-esteem as the value that a person places upon herself or himself. Others also place a value upon each individual, whether or not they do so knowingly. This value might be called *social esteem*, and while there will be a wide variation in how others esteem an individual, an aggregate will emerge with strong feelings from those prominent proximal others carrying more weight than the ambivalent feelings of more distant or less influential persons. (For another take on the same issues, see Hwang, 2000.)

For example, Li might despise Brian but rarely come into contact with him. The students that do come into contact with Brian generally think he's OK. We might posit that Brian's social esteem stock is reasonable. Li himself, however, has a high social esteem, so his view of Brian will carry more weight across a wider sphere than the views of Brian's close contacts.

Group Membership

For most young people, being part of a group becomes an organizing principle in day-to-day living. This need for belonging grows steadily and often becomes all-consuming in early teenage years when young people begin to reject family-based activities if it means severance from their friends.

Those young people to whom this situation does *not* apply are often seen as rejects or outcasts from the main groups that exist both within and without the school. According to Bierman (2004), there are a number of reasons why some students are excluded from peer groups: poor social skills, a dislike of intimacy, or coming from different religious, ethnic, or social background. Differences associated with disabilities among students are considered elsewhere (in Chapter 6), however, students who exist outside the mainstream peer group are invariably more vulnerable to bullying, but, as this chapter demonstrates, membership of a friendship group has its own difficulties associated with bullying behavior.

Self-Esteem and Social Esteem: The Commodities Market Place

In order to have self-esteem and social esteem, a student must have some criteria upon which that esteem is based. Like all economies, there are sought-after commodities that are competed for within the esteem portfolio. For example, a student might be amusing (a joker), or helpful, or physically strong—all of these attributes or commodities have a social value and attract others. These attributes or commodities are different from natural resources such as jewels or land, because they are infinite. Unlike gold or real estate, there is no end to the human attributes we value.

Although these attributes or commodities are not finite they are competed for as if they were, with some attributes ranking more highly than others. Thus, in schools, students perceive invisible tiers of social power with which they either conform or contest. A student cannot avoid being caught up in this competition because frequently her or his own position will come under threat from others wishing to take their place (see Duncan, 1999).

For some students, life in school becomes a struggle, enduring the constant jockeying for position, making alliances, sundering them, improving and consolidating, resisting and dominating within the network that exists within the institution.

GENDER AND SEXUALITY: FLASHPOINTS FOR BULLYING

If we accept that the competition for a socially esteemed identity commonly exists in all schools, what are the flashpoints for bullying? There is some evidence that one of the most contested areas is that of gender and sexuality. In other words, fights break out over issues of dominant forms of femininity and masculinity: what it means to be a male and female.

For some people today and, indeed, in years gone by the core of their identity has been located around religion. History tell us how being referred to as "ungodly" or "heretical" was one of the most serious assaults upon an individual's reputation. In the subculture of the school sexuality has become the means of undermining an individual's reputation, though issues such as race, caste, or social class remain salient.

A good social indicator of the predominance of sexuality as an issue that impacts upon personal reputation comes from the voracity with which the media follow stories with explicit sexual content, and the political mileage to be had in expressing outrage at the actions of individuals or groups who profess a view of sexuality that is different from the mainstream. Further support for this proposition resides in the empirical evidence demonstrating the exceptionally high level of sexualized or gendered language used by young people to attack others.

Consider, for example, the names or descriptors used by young people (and older people too, on occasion) in an offensive exchange. If you were to rank order them in terms of their "power" to hurt, it is likely that the most hurtful and unpleasant words and names used are those that are sexually loaded.

However, many of the words and phrases that are sexually loaded have a social dimension to them. Rather than simply being obscene nouns and adjectives, names such as "slut," "homo," or "faggot" are used to highlight a devalued socio-sexual role or position within the hierarchy. For example, one author, Neil Duncan, recalls discussing this point with a boy who had just vented a torrent of verbal abuse on a twelve-year-old girl, in which the words "whore" and "bitch" had featured prominently. The incident had been triggered by her refusal to lend him a pen. When asked why he had used those sexual terms, it was clear that, despite knowing what the words actually meant, the choice of words was purely in order to wound her for not complying with his demands. (The boy understood that the incident had nothing sexual about it). He argued, "If I'd called her stupid or mean, she wouldn't be bothered. But if I call her a whore, she'll hate that."

Sexualized Bullying: A Pervasive Ideology in School?

Many educators and some parents will recognize the mindset of the boy who was refused a pen by a female student, but the phenomenon associated with sexualized aggression is not well recognized as a pervasive ideology that underpins bullying behavior in schools. In an aggressive competition for position among peers the most hurtful weaponry will be deployed to attain the goal—and such weaponry is often rooted in sexuality.

There are two main explanations for the prominence of sexuality in the competition for social status among students. It must be noted that these explanations are generalizations, and are not applicable in every case, but would seem too common to the majority of urban communities, especially in public schools that are not selective of the highest achieving students. Firstly, nature propels most children into puberty around the 7–10th grades. At this time, the childish identity is being overtaken from the inside by an adult identity. As the body grows and changes shape, the individual ceases to be a child, and changes into a man or woman. Some of these changes are visible, some are not. Some are expected, some are not. Some are pleasant, but others are not.

It is widely acknowledged that we all go through some form of turmoil during puberty, but this knowledge needs to inform our understanding of bullying (which sometimes seems disconnected from nature as though it were an alien aberration that we should not expect!). The uncertainties of physical maturation linked with sexual awakening make puberty a very unsettling period. Here, there is a nexus between the sexual and the social, and it comes along at just the time most students are transferring from small familiar school settings to larger, more impersonal, institutions.

Secondly, and as noted above, a major factor that strengthens the preoccupation with sexuality comes from the exceptionally high profile it has in Western societies. Our mass media use sex as the main selling point in just about anything from cleaning products to cars (Reichert and Lambiase, 2005). If you cast your eyes over any newsstand, even puzzle books have some form of glamorous model on the cover. Women's magazines, whilst not displaying as much flesh as men's "adult" magazines, have cover callouts that refer to improving one's sex-life, achieving orgasm, and ways of attracting men. In addition, the media constantly refer to the lifestyles of popular celebrities in which their sexual conduct is scrutinized. The importance of being or not being a "babe," a "love-rat," a "cheat," a "player," and so on, is absorbed directly and indirectly by young people whose interest in sex and associated matters is not satisfied by personal experimentation (legally they are too young) or by vicarious formal sex education (limited by professional and public inhibitions and mores).

Sexuality becomes an issue at the very forefront of young people's minds, and schools, both as institutions and as architectural spaces, compress young people of the same ages together as no other institutions do raising their awareness of their own bodily changes in comparison to others: a situation that is both exhilarating and threatening (Ross Epp and Watkinson, 1996).

In effect a combination of biological changes in the human body (hormones and sexual maturation), the compression of large numbers of same-age students into one space (a school), the imposition of hierarchy, and the competition for status together with society's preoccupation with sexual behavior and mores can have a pervasive and profound effect on the behavior of young people. To understand this further, try the following task.

Class Task. Please note that the exercise below should only be undertaken with students of an appropriate age, and in the context of a school program such as civics or social studies.

Ask the class (and it helps to split boys from girls for this exercise) to think of all the words used to insult a girl (then repeat the exercise for boys). Be prepared for a lot of sexual expletives, and be ready to deal with students who deliberately try to shock. Bear in mind, however, that if those words are offensive, you need to know them before you can tackle them.

Once you have a range of words on the board, get the class to analyze them in this way

- Are there words that could be used against both boys and girls equally?
- Are there any words that have a racial content?
- Are there any words that have a sexual content?
- Are there any words that have a religious or ethnic content?
- Are there any words that have a social class content?
- Are there any words that have a disablist content?
- Are there any words that would only be used between students of a certain age?

Once you have grouped the words into categories (some will overlap, and you might even have some that do not fit anywhere), write them down on card strips and code them with letters from "a" though "z."

Split the class into groups of four, and instruct them to work together with each group ranking the insults from the most common heard in school (at the top) to the least common (at the bottom).

Make a note of the order of selection for each group. Then ask students to reorder the insults with the most offensive and hurtful at the top and the least offensive at the bottom. Note the order for each group.

Teachers and researchers have found that the students are always very engaged in this process, and take it as seriously as any other class activity. A discussion should ensue considering why certain categories of insults are more or less offensive, or more or less common. This information provides an insight into the moral codes used by students in their own hierarchies—something usually hidden from the adult world.

If the outcome is different from the general pattern of research findings, that is, sexualized aggression is *not* the most common and the most hurtful mode of verbal attack on students, then further discussion would be worthwhile to ascertain what personal attributes those students believed to be salient. Such a finding might occur in a school or community with specific racial or religious tensions, for example. However, if the findings echo the usual pattern, and sexuality and sexual reputation are the main targets for attacking a person's identity, then a discussion can follow exploring why that is the case, and in what ways teachers and administrators can address this issue ensuring the school is a safer and more comfortable place for all.

UNDERSTANDING THE STUDENT UNDERWORLD

For some students it is not enough to achieve a certain fixed level of self-esteem, it is vital that whatever level is achieved it must be higher than certain others. In other words, the goal is *norm*-referenced rather than *criterion*-referenced: its value is only relative to the other competitors in the field. The key fact here is that those with the highest need for social achievement must be aggressive in their acquisition and maintenance of social power by entering into a zero sum game: "I can only win if you lose."

In a social group where power is spread unevenly through the hierarchy, to keep or advance one's position one must disempower others. Such disempowerment often results from verbal attacks that are backed up by potential physical force. Students who represent particular ethnicities or religions, those who come from a higher or lower social class, live in poorer or more wealthy neighborhoods, demonstrate greater or lesser academic ability or sporting prowess are often targets of bullying. Nevertheless, underpinning these attributes is the almost universal division of gender, which is inevitably linked to sexuality (Connell, 1987).

SEXUAL BULLYING

Sexual bullying takes many forms, and is not only manifest in inappropriate touching or crude remarks (though these behaviors frequently show themselves as the more obvious forms). For example, many girls who have been victims of sexual bullying report having had their breasts grabbed through their clothes by rapacious boys at school. Such behavior might legitimately be described as sexual assault, but as an isolated occurrence it may not constitute sexual bullying. Sexual bullying is more systemic and psychologically invasive. Its driver is not so much about sexual release but, as noted earlier in this chapter, the attainment of social power through acquiring a high-status reputation.

It is important to realize that sexual reputation is based upon much more than sexual behavior. An individual's sexual reputation can be founded upon fabrication spread by mischief-makers (in fact the research evidence indicates this is usually the case). For male students, the most common and powerful attack on their integrity is to be labeled "homosexual." Indeed, the word that boys most hate to be used against them is "gay" (see Duncan,

1999). The proportion of young people who are *actually* gay is likely to be very small, however, if one compares even the most inflated number to the proportion of boys who are called "gay" or "faggot" it is clear that the use of the label greatly exceeds the status.

What is going on here is not the "outing" of gay people (the public unmasking of individuals thought to be homosexual). Instead a continuous effort is being made by the majority of boys to assert their own high-status sexual identity in comparison with a low-status "other" identity: they need to show others as weak and undesirable to make themselves appear strong and more desirable (Mac An Ghaill, 1994).

Hypermasculinity and Hegemony

In the field of gender studies, the attempt to enhance one's sexual identity is part of a culture of excessive machismo usually referred to as "hypermasculinity." In a hypermasculine culture, the goal for boys is to belong to that elite ideal group of males who hold social power. The "ideal" boys are physically big and strong, aggressive, and quick to assert dominance over weaker individuals. They are more inclined to manual skills, sports, or athletic success rather than artistic or academic ability. They are emotionally cold or, at the very least, contained. They are *users* of females rather than *partners* of females, and they are not just heterosexual, but homophobic in order to explicitly underline their own "normality." It is quite easy to see how such a mindset will lead to a culture of bullying in schools.

Some sociologists use the theoretical concept of hegemony to try to understand this culture and particularly why it starts and how it prevails. "Hegemony" in this sense is the way a society or community maintains the belief that there is no alternative to the way things are done. Investors in the *status quo* do just enough to keep things as they are, and develop a subtle common cause among themselves to prevent any revolutionary change. Of course there are always alternative ways of doing things, but in a powerful hegemony others are prevented from thinking about or enacting dramatic changes to the norm by a number of pressures—the final one being physical coercion.

Heteronormativity

Maintaining an attitude that assumes that everything is fine until it goes wrong allows subcultures to develop that can be difficult to eradicate and may cause harm to some children and young people. For example, heteronormative hegemony closes our minds to any alternative that children will grow up heterosexual; that heterosexuality is implicit in all relationships in the school community and, furthermore, that it is the right and proper way for things to be.

Case Study. A group of fourteen-year-old students in a UK public school are challenged by a teacher who overhears verbal abuse. The following exchange occurs.

Teacher: Why did you call Andy a faggot just then?

Jack: We were only joking with him.

Teacher: He wasn't laughing, he looked upset.

Jack: Well he's too sensitive, we were only joking, and he took it the wrong way.

Teacher: That doesn't answer my question—why did you just call him a faggot? Why not something else? Do you think he is gay?

Carlo: No, he's not gay, not really, he's just faggy. He's just ... well he ain't like us.

Teacher: Go on ...

Jack: Well, he aint into football and stuff. He's just, well, like ...

Carlo: He's different to the other guys, aint he? He hangs with the girls in the class, like faggy kinda thing.

Teacher: But you are calling him gay and faggot. Wouldn't that mean he'd be more likely to be hanging around with guys? Don't *you* hang out with the girls too?

Jack: We do, yeah, but it's different, he kinda likes to *talk* with them ...

Carlo: Yeah, it's hard ... but he just hangs out with them, but when we hang with the girls we like to have a laugh, messing with them, you know? We don't wanna talk girl talk.

As the case study reveals further probing by the teacher shows that when the perpetrators of this incident were calling Andy "gay" they had no real concept of homosexuality in mind, but sought to contrast their own macho values with those of Andy. Indeed, many boys of this age vigorously deny any possibility that one of their fellow students could really be gay—such is the power of heteronormativity.

NEIL DUNCAN'S EXPERIENCES OF RESEARCHING SEXUAL BULLYING

As an outcome of my research, I am sometimes asked to present my theories and findings to conferences of practitioners as well as academics. On one occasion, having advanced the perspectives outlined in this chapter on the hidden drivers of bullying in schools, I was challenged by an experienced teacher from a prestigious high school. "Why," he demanded to know, "should we change our whole-school practices and policies on behavior to protect a tiny minority of *possibly* homosexual children in our school?" He went on to state that in all his years of teaching, he had never known a single gay student.

In this case, the teacher missed the central tenet of my research. It was not a case of protecting one or two different kids, but a challenge to the oppressive culture that pervades many schools and promotes aggressive behavior among the majority. If students know that gay kids, or alleged gay kids, get a tough time, then *all* kids are going to try to display behaviors and attitudes that keep them safe by distancing themselves from those targets. In other words, boys are going to be aggressively hypermasculine and mean to those weaker students who are less able to defend themselves at school.

In a very memorable interview I conducted with a group of fifteen-year-old female high school students, the conversation captured perfectly a paradoxical type of this behavior perpetrated by boys toward girls. I asked the group what they felt about the male students in their class. Generally, the group agreed that each was fine on his own (words such as "polite," "sensitive," "funny," and "sweet" were used). They said that they could be chatting with a group of girls outside the school and if a guy joined them he would engage in the same discussion as an equal. However, if one of his male friends joined the discussion, the conversation would alter to include teasing and baiting with each boy showing off to his friend that he could be more rude and insensitive than the other.

In subsequent interviews with young women I have suggested this scenario and they have responded with ready recognition, often giving accounts of their own experiences. Usually they are very sanguine about the formula that can be represented as follows:

$$A \text{ (group of girls)} + B \text{ (one boy)} = (C) \text{ good company}$$
$$A \text{ (group of girls)} + D \text{ (two boys)} = (E) \text{ a pair of idiots}$$

Despite their recognition and analysis of this scenario, girls themselves are just as embroiled in gender-specific forms of bullying at school. Indeed, the gendered quality of girls' bullying behavior at school is perhaps less recognized than the gendered nature of bullying amongst boys. Indeed, bullying by boys is usually seen as the norm against which other bullying is measured or compared.

GIRLS' SEXUALTIES AND BULLYING

Just as there is a masculine hegemony among boys, so there is a feminine hegemony among girls. As with boys, the ideal-typical girl is a social construction and it can change from location to location. For example, in some schoolsgirls strive to be forceful, physical, and aggressive, echoing the "typical" boy. In other schools the "ideal" may be more traditionally feminine, with expressions of secrecy, intimacy, and emotionality. There are many other variants of femininity and no form of femininity is necessarily better than any other. However, the "ideal" form of femininity, the dominant form, has a palpable effect upon the types of bullying expected in schools. It is not certain what factors decide the type of dominant gender identity in any community, but whatever identity is dominant it can be easily detected by faculty and staff trained to listen to informed students.

In any school where there are female students there will be a social hierarchy with a group of "popular" girls holding great influence over their peers (Duncan, 2004). They may be liked (or not openly disliked), they might be feared socially or physically, but their presence is felt by all, and transgressing their fashion codes, friendship codes, or dating codes can result in very strong negative consequences. Clearly, where the hegemonic femininity is physical and masculine, the forms of bullying will be fairly obvious and in some respects it will be easier for school staff to take action. However, if the hegemonic femininity is more traditional (involving close personal friendships and emotionality), the forms of bullying amongst girls are much more covert and subtle, and difficult to detect.

Just as boys openly attack other boys' sexuality, girls can do this too. Between boys, the mode is usually homosexuality, or some other presumed form of male inferiority, however, girls target the sexual morality and sexual desirability of their peers. On occasions they are labeled "lesbian," but much more common is the term "whore" or "ho." The majority of names and labels used by female students about their peers center on pathological promiscuity, lesbianism, dirtiness, and incapability of getting a date, pleasing him, or having a boyfriend.

What Girls Do

Quite often, attacks perpetrated against girls by girls are not as obvious as those perpetrated by boys against boys. Within this particular group, very subtle and cryptic messages are sent to other girls about modifying their behavior. These messages can be verbal or literary (including e-mail and cell phone text messages), but may also be conveyed via body language, group exclusion, and selective attending and responding. Among girls, the link between sexuality and gender in bullying is less obvious, but it is present. If one were to ask young people "what do boys fight about?" a variety of answers such as sporting allegiances, who can run faster, and even simply who is the better fighter would come to the fore. Ask what girls fight about and the answer is nearly always "boys."

Long before they have their first date or boyfriend, girls are involved in activities that relate to getting a date or a boyfriend. Read any magazine for adolescent girls and the pages are filled with advice with the aim of attracting boys. Girls' friendship talk is heavily boy-centered with a propensity for the sharing of secrets, confidences, fantasies, and hopes among friends. (For a detailed examination of these issues see Holland et al., 2004).

Body Shape, Weight, and Fashion

Issues such as body shape, weight, or fashion may appear to be far removed from gendered bullying, but in fact they are closely linked. Just as boys are under a great deal of pressure to be successful at sports, and to be strong and athletic in order to achieve the masculine ideal; so girls are under pressure to conform to a physical ideal, and wear clothes that position them favorable in the social-sexual hierarchy. Girls vigorously check indicators of femininity, commenting willingly on others' appearance, hairstyle, makeup, and physique. Feminist scholars have long noted the internalization of male values in young women, but have paid less attention to the intrafemale competition for male attention which manifests itself through girls labeling their peers as *too promiscuous* or *not hot enough* for even the slightest deviance from "perfection" (which has itself been created and managed by those students that teachers) will be perceive by the most "popular" girls in the class or grade.

Class Task. To explore the relevant mores and values female students have in your school try the following exercise:

Suppose that you have parachuted to another school, similar to your own, and your mission is to find the most socially powerful girls in this school and report back to your commander. You must do this without asking the question "who are the most popular girls, or who are the most influential girls in the school." Before you undertake the mission, you must make a list of identifying features that will help you to spot these girls.

Depending on the group of girls in the activity (i.e., their age and ability) you may need to prompt them with some characteristics such as "loud," "hangs out with older guys," or "smokes cigarettes." The results of such an exercise can be very revealing providing you with an insight into the type of peer culture predominant in the school, and the type of girl that is esteemed by others. However, it is important to validate the results with the girls, so that they are quite explicit about why those characteristics or behaviors would be likely to indicate powerful girls.

A telling outcome from one of the studies conducted by Neil Duncan showed that the word "virgin" was used as a slur against modest girls. When thirteen-year-old girls are using terms such as "virgin" as an insult, it says something very powerful about the peer culture and its values, and may be a serious cause for concern.

Cliques and Groups: Being "In" and Being "Out"

Nearly all girls are aware of the clique in their school that holds most power when it comes to identifying those girls who are "in" and those who are "out." It seems that, periodically, these cliques need to reaffirm their dominance by identifying one target for particularly harsh treatment which will act as a warning to others not to challenge the system and *status quo.* Identifying a solitary target for such treatment also performs the task of bringing the group closer together, reinforcing each individual's similarity to other members. Commonly the target of this aggression is one of the inner-circle who was expelled for some perceived transgression against group morality.

One of the most extreme transgressions among girl groups is to be thought disloyal to one's friends. Indeed, educators and parents of adolescent girls will probably have experienced the deep distress expressed by a student or a daughter who has been excluded or shunned by her former friendship group as a result of a rumor or suggestion that they have disclosed a secret, flirted with, or dated a particular boy who is the object of another's affection (regardless of reciprocation).

This approach to reinforcing systems and hierarchies among girls is particularly harsh. The girl who has been expelled from the group finds herself no longer in a position of power, and with few, if any, allies. Those who were once subject to her power will distance themselves from her for fear of incurring the further wrath of the dominant group, and, within the subculture of the school, attitudes such as "you gave it out, now you're getting it back" permeate.

After-Effects: Key Issues for Parents and Educators

Both parents and educators will be familiar with the petty jealousies inherent within girls' friendships. For many mothers and women teachers time has put a distance between their own experiences of friendship groups at school and those of their daughters and students. It may be tempting for harassed and busy parents and teachers to trivialize fall outs as an inevitability of growing up in the hope that the situation will resolve itself in time if left alone. In many cases that may well be true, but for some students it is not, and serious psychological difficulties emerge which can sometimes lead to self-harming behavior.

For those students who feel they can no longer face going to school and endure the insults or isolation at the hands of their peers, regular absenteeism is the first serious warning sign. While both boys and girls who are bullied by peers are likely to use school or class avoidance techniques, they are more prevalent among girls (Duncan, 2002). Whether or not it is openly refusing to go to school, feigning sickness to parents, doctors, or nurses, or class-selective truancy, parents and educators should be vigilant and look for patterns in this behavior—such a pattern may indicate flashpoints for bullying. A useful method of recording absenteeism or other incidents that are indicative of bullying is provided in Chapters 5 and 9 (see Tables 5.2 and 9.3).

A common effect of bullying is that the target's school grades decline which is not only due to a lack of concentration but also psychological disturbance, and the theft, defacing or destruction of equipment, homework, and school projects. A noticeable down turn in grades will be a sure sign that bullying is occurring in a school, especially if a son/daughter or student suggests moving schools would address the issue. In the case of sexual bullying, it is unlikely that most parents would be aware of any problems until related factors (absenteeism and failing grades) came to the fore. The decision to move a son or daughter to another school should not be made lightly, and in Chapter 9 some suggestions on ways of working with schools have been provided.

SUMMARY

This chapter has focused on a series of complex concepts and theories drawn from a variety of disciplines that provide a framework in which to better understand bullying behavior. Within this chapter, a set of conceptual tools and practical exercises have been provided that are intended to support investigation of bullying behavior and sexual bullying in particular which will assist educators in identifying the underlying hierarchies that permeate within student subculture. One should never underestimate the importance of the competition for high social esteem, gender identity, and sexual reputation particularly among high school students and through exercises such as those presented in this chapter and reflecting back students' attitudes, beliefs, and behaviors, it is possible to effect meaningful change.

Tips for Parents

- Do not underestimate the importance of social esteem in young people's lives.
- Look for the telltale signs of bullying, and watch for patterns in behavior.
- Do not be afraid to talk about sexuality with your children, ask them about their take on prominent media stories that involve sexual content.
- Ask them about the dynamics of the class or grade, ask about who is popular and who is unpopular and why.

Tips for Educators

- Use class exercises to understand the hierarchies and social systems used by students to determine popularity.

> ✎ If you have a civics program, use media coverage of stories to discuss social mores and beliefs about sexuality and sexual behavior.
>
> ✎ Be aware that changes in girls' relationships and friendship groups can be more subtle than changes in boys' relationships and friendship groups.

REFERENCES

Besag, V. (2006). *Understanding Girls' Friendships, Fights and Feuds: A Practical Approach to Girls' Bullying*. Milton Keynes, UK: Open University Press.

Bierman, K. L. (2004). *Peer Rejection: Developmental Processes and Intervention Strategies*. New York, NY: Guilford Press.

Connell, R. W. (1987). *Gender and Power: Society, the Person and Sexual Politics*. Cambridge, UK: Polity.

Duncan, N. (1999). *Sexual Bullying: Gender Conflict and Pupil Culture in Secondary Schools*. London, UK: Routledge.

———. (2002). Girls, bullying and school transfer. In V. Sunnari, J. Kangasvuo, and M. Heikkinen (Eds.), *Gendered and Sexualized Violence in Educational Environments*. Oulu, Finland: Femina Borealis.

———. (2004). It's important to be nice, but it's nicer to be important: Girls, popularity and sexual competition. *Sex Education*, 4, 137–152.

Holland, J., Ramazanoglu, C., Sharpe, S., and Thomson, R. (2004). *The Male in the Head: Young People, Heterosexuality and Power*. London, UK: Tufnell Press.

Hwang, P. O. (2000). *Other-esteem: Meaningful Life in a Multicultural Society*. Philadelphia, PA: Accelerated Development.

Kroger, J. (2007). *Identity Development: Adolescence through Adulthood*. Thousand Oaks, CA: Sage.

Ma, X., Stewin, L. L., and Mah, D. L. (2001). Bullying in school: Nature, effects and remedies. *Research Papers in Education*, 16, 247–270.

Mac An Ghaill, M. (1994). *The Making of Men: Masculinities, Sexualities and Schooling*. Buckingham, UK: Open University Press.

Pellegrini, A. D., and Blatchford, P. (2000). *The Child at School: Interactions with Peers and Teachers*. New York, NY: Oxford University Press.

Reichert, T., and Lambiase, J. (2005). *Sex in Consumer Culture: The Erotic Content of Media and Marketing*. Mahwah, NJ: Lawrence Erlbaum Associates.

Ross Epp, J., and Watkinson, A. M. (1996). *Systemic Violence: How Schools Hurt Children*. London, UK: Falmer Press.

CHAPTER 5

Homophobic Bullying

My aim in life was to keep as low a profile as possible ... to merge with the background. I suppose I had a few friendships, but they weren't particularly close. That's how it went on. There were flashes where, you know, merging into the background didn't actually work. So, that's how the five years [at school] passed I suppose.

—Rivers (1999, p. 377)

Alan is fifteen years old. He lives with his mom and dad, older sister and younger brother in a middle-class area of a medium-sized city in the Midwest. He is generally a B-average student, conscientious and tries his best. He excels in history, and has expressed an interest in an after-school theater class. He always does his homework which is always of a consistent standard. He gets through physical education classes with a C average. He is always well presented, helpful, quietly spoken, and tends not to draw attention to himself. One of his teachers has noticed that he tends to stand back in group exercises and rarely makes a contribution. Occasionally teachers have seen other boys and girls laugh when he answers a question in class, but he never reacts or complains. He has few friends, and does not congregate with classmates at recess, preferring to spend time with one or two students very much like him. No one expects Alan to fail a class or be held back. Everyone assumes he will go to college. Should the school or Alan's parents be concerned?

The difficulty in determining whether or not a teacher or parent should be concerned by Alan's behavior is of course that nothing has been said or done to bring him to their attention. As far as his teachers or his parents are concerned, he is doing fine. His grades are better than average, and he has some interests that allow him to shine. Yet there are some telltale signs (discussed later) that suggest that Alan may be a victim of homophobic bullying. This chapter explores the phenomenon of homophobic bullying and considers the reasons why Alan could be a victim of this particularly insidious form of aggression.

WHAT IS HOMOPHOBIC BULLYING

Homophobic bullying can be defined simply as any form of physical (e.g., hitting or kicking), emotional (e.g., spreading rumors or teasing), or social (e.g., being ignored) aggression perpetrated against an individual because of her or his actual or perceived sexual orientation, or because that individual's behavior is not typical of her or his sex. Homophobic bullying can be hard to identify. Name-calling is perhaps most frequently associated with it: names such as gay, fag, queer, dyke, and homo are the most often cited as a means of identification, though physical harm or emotional abuse (social isolation and rumor mongering) are also common. The gay activist Aaron Fricke once recalled an incident of bullying where fear was invoked by a simple look. He described the look he received from a classmate as, "an uninterrupted gaze that could melt steel" (Fricke, 1981). In front of his teacher and all his fellow students Aaron believed he was silently assaulted. The significance of the look, and its effect upon its victim went unrecorded. No words were said, no school behavior code or policy was broken and, at the time, no one knew or could offer him assistance. Yet, results from a UK study of homophobic bullying and its long-term effects suggests that being frightened by a look or stare is a very common phenomenon, experienced by over 50% of victims, and it is often a correlate of deliberate absenteeism or truancy (Rivers, 2000). For today's educators, tackling homophobic bullying has become a priority, but there are few guidelines and even fewer instructional classes on dealing with this issue effectively, particularly when the bullying is hidden from view. So, how do you draw up and enforce a policy that includes the prohibition of a certain look or stare?

RATES OF HOMOPHOBIC BULLYING

In a study conducted at Pennsylvania State University in the 1990s, Neil Pilkington and Anthony D'Augelli found that 30% of young gay men and 35% of young lesbians reported having being bullied or harassed in school by peers and 7% by teachers (Pilkington and D'Augelli, 1995). As early as 1992 Kevin Berrill suggested that, from the evidence collected by various state and national task forces and coalitions, estimates of homophobic bullying in U.S. schools ranged from 33% to 49% (Berril, 1992).

However, homophobic bullying does not just affect students who are gay and lesbian; it can also affect students who do not conform to gender stereotypes. Boys who do not share an interest in sports, or who take classes in the creative arts are likely to be victims of homophobic bullying. Similarly teenage boys who are physically underdeveloped in comparison to their peers and those who are less confident speaking out may also be labeled queer.

Among girls, those who like sports, or those who do not express an interest in boys may be labeled "lesbian." Girls who are overweight or girls who prefer to wear clothes that do not accentuate their developing figure can similarly be targeted for this type of bullying. Currently we do not know how many students in American public schools are called gay or lesbian because they do not conform to a stereotype. However, in one survey of 237,544 students in the state of California, the California Safe School Coalition working with academics at the University of California-Davis found that 7.5% of students in grades 7–11 (17815) reported being harassed or bullied because of their actual or perceived sexual orientation. The authors estimated that, in the state of California alone, some 200000 students were likely to be victims of this form of abuse (California Safe School Coalition and 4-H Center for Youth Development, University of California-Davis, 2004). Nationwide, based on the data drawn from school enrollments in the fall of 2002 by the National Center for Educational Statistics (www.nces.ed.gov), it is estimated that over 1.6 million students in public schools (grades 7–11) will be regularly subjected to harassment and bullying because of their actual or perceived sexual orientation. The best assessment we have of the frequency of homophobic name-calling comes from researchers at the University of Illinois (Poteat and Espelage, 2005) who found that 60% of students in middle school had been subjected to one or more homophobic epithets in the last week.

WHERE DOES HOMOPHOBIC BULLYING TAKE PLACE AND WHO ARE THE PERPETRATORS?

Homophobic bullying most frequently occurs during lunch and recess when young people are less likely to be supervised closely. However, it also occurs in the hallways and in the classrooms, sometimes with the passive collusion of teachers, many of whom are uncertain of how to deal with the issue of sexual orientation. Occasionally, as Pilkington and D'Augelli (1995) found, some teachers are active in the collusion, providing a safe environment where jokes and slurs go unchecked. For boys, this is typically the case on the sports field where masculine stereotypes are reinforced, and where comments by peers or sometimes by coaches and teachers are less likely to be tempered and more likely to be said in the heat of the moment.

Students frequently report that bullying takes place in transit to and from school, on the school bus, in the shopping malls, and even outside their homes. The combined effect of a lack of clear guidance on (1) challenging homophobic bullying and (2) the responsibilities of the school when students are harassed by others off campus means that little, if anything, is ever done to discipline perpetrators. One school district in California made an out-of-court settlement of over $1 million after a group of students began legal proceedings. One of the students filing the suit was so badly beaten up that he had to be taken to hospital, yet none of the perpetrators were disciplined even though a bus driver had been a witness to the incident.

Unlike other forms of bullying, homophobic bullying is generally perpetrated by groups of peers rather than by individuals. It is long term and systematic, typically beginning around the age of eleven and continues until a young person leaves school. While many researchers have reported a decrease in bullying with age, homophobic bullying seems to remain constant. It is most likely to be perpetrated by groups of boys and girls acting together, and is least likely to be perpetrated by an individual, especially a single male. In addition, it is also likely to be perpetrated by peers from the same grade as the victim and is rarely perpetrated by older or younger students. The fact that homophobic bullying is perpetrated by groups rather than by individuals is important in recognizing its signature in a school. Educational researchers Askew and Ross (1988) argued that such mobbing behavior reinforces each member of the group's own heterosexual identity and provides an opportunity for them to condemn those who are perceived to be gay or lesbian, drawing attention to their gender atypical behavior, and deflecting any scrutiny of a perpetrator's behavior.

TELLTALE SIGNS OF HOMOPHOBIC BULLYING IN SCHOOL

In the opening paragraphs of this chapter Alan's story is presented. To all intents and purposes he seems an able young man who has never been brought to the attention of the school. The question is posed: should the school or Alan's parents be concerned? The information provided suggests that he is an outsider, and does not conform to what may be typically expected of a fifteen-year-old young man in an urban high school. The fact that his expressed interests and observed abilities do not include physical education will, more than likely, single him out by peers as someone who perhaps is not going to be a team player. This perception seems to have spilled over into the classroom where his lack of sporting prowess has transformed into withdrawal and a perceptible reticence—especially when working as part of a group on academic projects. If his talents are sought out by members of his class, then the chances are that he will be exploited to ensure that others receive a good grade. The fact that those who make fun of him include both boys and girls is unusual, and, as noted earlier, this is often peculiar to homophobic bullying. In addition, Alan tends to associate with one or two similarly ostracized peers and, as a result, there is little or no interaction with other members of the class or grade and that perpetuates his isolation and the myth of his atypicality. If Alan's older sister and younger brother are also enrolled at the same school problems may be appearing within their class or grade, particularly for Alan's younger brother—he may be experiencing similar difficulties (guilty by association).

In reality, everything we know about Alan is circumstantial, there is no evidence that he is gay, and without proof of victimization a teacher or school administrator may feel powerless to intervene on his behalf. However, once perpetrators feel assured that their harassment will not be effectively challenged by the administration (i.e., there will be no disciplinary action) there may be a gradual escalation in Alan's victimization, which may also test the administration's will. Signs that there has been an escalation in Alan's victimization beyond isolation will include unexplained absences, perhaps a failure to hand in homework, occasionally disheveled appearances (following physical assault, or having objects or dirt thrown at him), a total withdrawal from making contributions to the class discussions (often as a result of a perceptible increase in the number of times he is ridiculed in class), and finally the appearance of graffiti which is sexualized in its content.

Sexualized graffiti is just one of a number of ways in which homophobic bullying takes physical form, and it is often a correlate or precursor of other physical forms of violence. For example, Pilkington and D'Augelli's (1995) study found that 18% of the gay and lesbian youth in their study had been physically assaulted, 9% had been assaulted at least once with a weapon, and 18% had been sexually assaulted.

In 2001, reflecting on the rise in gun-related crimes in school, the Illinois State Board of Education reported that, between 1996 and 1999, six of the eight perpetrators of gun violence had been regularly teased by peers, and four of them were specifically subjected to homophobic epithets. Of course, gun violence is an extreme reaction to bullying and victimization, however, data from the California Safe School Coalition suggests that students who are the victims of homophobic bullying are three times more likely to carry weapons to school than their peers. In addition, the level of connectedness with school and community was found to be weaker among those victims of homophobic bullying when compared to other students. Thus, for the victim of homophobic bullying, fears for personal safety may be combined with a lack of personal investment in the school system (its rules, administrators, teachers, and students), resulting in more extreme forms of behavior.

All of the available data suggest that when students perceive there is nowhere to turn for support their behavior will become all the more challenging. Grades may be affected, resulting from frequent absenteeism and, ultimately, there may be attempts to self-harm. Current estimates suggest that around 40% of gay and lesbian young people will attempt to take their own lives as a result of the intolerance they have experienced, particularly at school. Indeed in one study conducted in the United Kingdom, Rivers (2001) reports that of the 190 former victims of homophobic bullying surveyed, 53% had contemplated self-harm or suicide, 40% had attempted at least once, with three-quarters of those (30% of the total sample) attempting more than once. Typically, such incidents involved self-cutting and drug overdoses, and a small number have also attempted to hang themselves. Thus, schools should be alert to any students who are unexpectedly hospitalized. Reasons for the hospitalization may not always be clear, and there remains among many cultural and religious groups a belief that self-harm is something shameful and something that should not be talked about. Yet without the support of the families of victims, a school's administration may be powerless to address the bullying that goes on, and there is an onus upon both parties to find a way forward to support vulnerable students, and especially those who are bullied because of their actual or perceived sexual orientation. To assist teachers and administrators assess potential risk the checklist in Table 5.1 may be useful. It is not exhaustive, but it highlights key indices drawn from various studies conducted by the authors.

Teachers who believe that a student may be a victim of homophobic bullying should keep weekly records monitoring any changes in patterns of behavior, and provide opportunities for the student to discuss any difficulties she or he may be having. The chart in Table 5.2 is useful in recording patterns of behavior where a student fails to come forward, or where there is little evidence to support a suspicion. Remember homophobic bullying is not sporadic, it is long term, rarely opportunistic, and former victims often report that the bullying they experienced was systematic (located around particular classes, or periods). Therefore a pattern of behavior will emerge with time.

External Influences of Behavior

The fact that this form of bullying arises out of claims that a student is gay or lesbian means that perpetrators often feel that they have right on their side. Condemnation of homosexuality, particularly condemnation by individuals in positions of power or authority has been cited as a moral defense for collective action against individuals who are perceived to be gay and lesbian. In truth, there is no such moral defense, many religious communities have made supportive statements about the inclusion of lesbian, gay, bisexual, and transgender individuals in their congregations. Similarly, no school, district, or education board would approve of any circumstance in which it is appropriate for a child or young person to feel unsafe at school. Of course, personal beliefs about the acceptability or unacceptability of homosexuality and the right to express those beliefs are guaranteed under the First Amendment; however the Fourteenth Amendment makes it clear that all citizens are entitled to equal protection under the law. Therefore victims of bullying have the right of legal redress and have exercised that right successfully. Interestingly, such redress where there is evidence of violence or harassment, injury, or defamation has not taken into account the religious

Table 5.1.
Homophobic Bullying: Telltale Signs Checklist for Teachers

		Yes	No	Unsure
1.	Has the student increasingly become introverted or more introverted than usual?	☐	☐	☐
2.	Is she/he more likely to shy away from group activities in the classroom?	☐	☐	☐
3.	Is she/he laughed at when she/he makes contributions to group discussions?	☐	☐	☐
4.	Have you heard or thought you have heard sexualized comments about the student?	☐	☐	☐
5.	In your opinion, does the student dress or act in a manner that you feel is not typical of her/his sex?	☐	☐	☐
6.	Have you noticed her/him being teased by groups of students (both boys and girls)?	☐	☐	☐
7.	Has the student had any unexplained absences or has there been a rise in the number of absences recently?	☐	☐	☐
8.	Does the student often find reasons to stay in class during lunch and recess?	☐	☐	☐
9.	Have you or a colleague witnessed any incident where the student has been called names you associate with being lesbian/gay?	☐	☐	☐
10.	Have you or a colleague seen any graffiti which you believe relates to the student and her/his sexuality?	☐	☐	☐

Note: If you have answered "Yes" to all or most of the questions, then the student is more than likely to be a victim of homophobic bullying. What will you do next?

If you have answered "Yes" to some questions and "Unsure" to the remainder, then the student may be a victim of homophobic bullying. What will you do next?

beliefs of perpetrators, or indeed any other claim that resulted in inaction by school administrators.

BEING PREPARED TO TACKLE HOMOPHOBIC BULLYING

The shame that students feel when they are being bullied is magnified many times over when the type of bullying they are experiencing is homophobic. Regardless of whether or not a victim of homophobic bullying is gay or lesbian, most teenagers feel uncomfortable talking about sexuality, particularly homosexuality and its associated stigma, with parents or teachers. Yet, because homophobic bullying relies upon the collusion of peers, it is

Table 5.2.
Student Behavior Record

Student Name: _____ Class: _____

Date observation commenced: ___ / ___ / ___ Grade: _____

| Incident type | Day | Number of incidents per day/week | | | | | | | |
		Wk 1	Wk 2	Wk 3	Wk 4	Wk 5	Wk 6	Wk 7	Wk 8
Student becomes more introverted	Mon	—	—	—	—	—	—	—	—
	Tue	—	—	—	—	—	—	—	—
	Wed	—	—	—	—	—	—	—	—
	Thu	—	—	—	—	—	—	—	—
	Fri	—	—	—	—	—	—	—	—
Withdraws from class discussions	Mon	—	—	—	—	—	—	—	—
	Tue	—	—	—	—	—	—	—	—
	Wed	—	—	—	—	—	—	—	—
	Thu	—	—	—	—	—	—	—	—
	Fri	—	—	—	—	—	—	—	—
Laughed at by peers in class	Mon	—	—	—	—	—	—	—	—
	Tue	—	—	—	—	—	—	—	—
	Wed	—	—	—	—	—	—	—	—
	Thu	—	—	—	—	—	—	—	—
	Fri	—	—	—	—	—	—	—	—
Teased by groups of boys and girls	Mon	—	—	—	—	—	—	—	—
	Tue	—	—	—	—	—	—	—	—
	Wed	—	—	—	—	—	—	—	—
	Thu	—	—	—	—	—	—	—	—
	Fri	—	—	—	—	—	—	—	—

Table 5.2. (Continued)

Student Name: _____   Class: _____

Date observation commenced: ___/___/___   Grade: _____

| Incident type | Day | Number of incidents per day/week | | | | | | | |
		Wk 1	Wk 2	Wk 3	Wk 4	Wk 5	Wk 6	Wk 7	Wk 8
Absent from school	Mon	—	—	—	—	—	—	—	—
	Tue	—	—	—	—	—	—	—	—
	Wed	—	—	—	—	—	—	—	—
	Thu	—	—	—	—	—	—	—	—
	Fri	—	—	—	—	—	—	—	—
Homework missing or destroyed with no reason given	Mon	—	—	—	—	—	—	—	—
	Tue	—	—	—	—	—	—	—	—
	Wed	—	—	—	—	—	—	—	—
	Thu	—	—	—	—	—	—	—	—
	Fri	—	—	—	—	—	—	—	—
Avoids going out at lunch and recess	Mon	—	—	—	—	—	—	—	—
	Tue	—	—	—	—	—	—	—	—
	Wed	—	—	—	—	—	—	—	—
	Thu	—	—	—	—	—	—	—	—
	Fri	—	—	—	—	—	—	—	—
Overhear sexual comments about student	Mon	—	—	—	—	—	—	—	—
	Tue	—	—	—	—	—	—	—	—
	Wed	—	—	—	—	—	—	—	—
	Thu	—	—	—	—	—	—	—	—
	Fri	—	—	—	—	—	—	—	—

Note: Missing/vandalized homework is a good longitudinal indicator. This indicator should be used over a period of weeks and months rather than days. Most students who are victims of homophobic bullying tend to do their homework because they have few social outlets in the evenings and at weekends.

usually parents and teachers who first notice changes in students' behavior, and have to fit all of the pieces of the puzzle together before taking action.

In providing support to victims of homophobic bullying it is important that the school adopts a policy that clearly states that this form of victimization will not be tolerated. Such a statement should appear in the school's handbook for parents and its handbook for students to ensure that everyone knows who the appropriate contact person is (teacher or school counselor), and the process by which reports can be made to the school. It is also important that teachers and counselors feel confident in addressing this form of bullying, and have appropriate resources available to them (books, guides, and Web sites). A list of useful resources is provided at the end of this chapter.

What School Staff Can Do

The most important thing a teacher, counselor, or administrator can do is to be serious about tackling homophobic bullying. When an incident of homophobic bullying is observed or suspected, then it should be recorded. Schools should endeavor to ensure that all students know the protocols for reporting homophobic bullying, and it may be helpful to consider having an anonymous reporting scheme to build a picture of the bullying that may be happening. The localized nature of homophobic bullying means that any intervention can be enacted on a class-by-class basis rather than across the school. Consequently, class surveys may be a quick and useful way of assessing the student dynamic. Table 5.3 shows a short survey that provides all the information needed to obtain an overview of what is going on in a class.

The survey provides an entry point for a discussion about bullying and also an opportunity to reintroduce the school's antidiscrimination and behavior policy, to ensure that all students understand what is acceptable and unacceptable. Time permitting, the following two exercises may provide a means to actively engage students in developing an awareness of discrimination. Both exercises can be used from middle school onwards. The first exercise can be used for all forms of discrimination; the second exercise specifically addresses homophobia.

Exercise 1: Understanding Difference (40 minutes). The purpose of this exercise is to encourage students to take on the perspectives of others and to consider what it means to be different, and to obtain an understanding of what students consider "different" to be. The exercise is broken down into four tasks, and requires students to work in groups.

Class Task 1 (10 minutes). To begin, ask students to volunteer definitions of what it means to be different. The aim of this task is to reach a consensus about the definition. At the end of the task, the teacher should read out the consensus statement "We believe that being different means . . . ."

Group Task 1 (10 minutes). In groups of no more than six, students should consider the ways in which some people are identified as being

Table 5.3.
How's Our Class Doing?

1. Who are your friends in class? (name up to five people)
   (i)_____ (ii)_____
   (iii)_____ (iv)_____
   (v)_____
2. Who sits alone during lunch or recess? (name up to five people)
   (i)_____ (ii)_____
   (iii)_____ (iv)_____
   (v)_____
3. Does anyone in the class become upset because others hurt or tease them? (check one box)
   ☐ Yes ☐ No
4. Can you list 5 reasons why others in your class has been hurt or teased? (do not give any names)
   (i)_____ (ii)_____
   (iii)_____ (iv)_____
   (v)_____
5. How do you feel when you see someone being hurt of teased by others in the class? (write a short answer below)
6. Why do you think others in your class are hurt or teased? (write a short answer below)

"different" at school, and how they think those people are treated. Teachers provide two guiding questions:

- How many differences have you observed?
- In this school, how do we treat people who are different?

Group Task 2 (10 minutes). The second task involves each group reaching a consensus statement about supporting people who are different at school. Each group should then read out their statement.

Class Task 2 (10 minutes). In the last 10 minutes pupils should vote on the statement they wish to adopt as a class policy on supporting difference. This policy should then be reproduced and displayed.

Exercise 2: Homophobia (40 minutes). The purpose of this lesson is to get pupils to think about homophobia in terms of their own behavior. The exercise is broken down into four tasks, and requires students to work in groups.

Class Task 1 (Class 10 minutes). To begin the exercise, ask a series of questions about homophobia and why people are homophobic:

- What is homophobia?

- What does it mean to be homophobic?
- Why do you think people are homophobic?

Students' answers should to be recorded so they can be referred to at a later stage.

Group Task (15–20 minutes). In groups of no more than six, students should consider the questions below. No more than 5 minutes should be spent on each question.

- How many different ways do you think people express homophobia?
- In what ways are lesbians, gay men, and bisexual men and women different from heterosexuals?

Each group should report back their answers to the whole class.

Class Task 2 (10–15 minutes). Students should be reminded of the statement they adopted as a class policy on supporting difference and asked the question:

- Should gay and lesbian people be included in this statement? Once again a consensus should be reached, and if not included already, where appropriate the class policy should be amended and displayed.

Both exercises will help students gain a better understanding of what is and is not acceptable behavior in their school. Research has shown that where students have an input into the establishment of school behavior policies, they have a greater sense of connectedness to school, and a greater investment in adhering to those policies.

Finally, wherever possible, confidentiality should be guaranteed to students who disclose to staff members their sexual orientation and/or that they are victims of homophobic bullying. An assessment should be made of the advisability of informing parents as this may have a detrimental impact upon the student's home life. A useful way to think about such an assessment is to ask the following questions before contacting parents:

- What is the purpose of telling the student's parent(s)?
- Whom will this information benefit?
- Will there be any consequences of the disclosure, positive or negative?
- Can I continue to support this student if I disclose?
- What are my legal responsibilities, do I have a choice?

Although experience suggests that not telling parents is the safest option until some assessment of their likely reaction is made, this is not always possible and in counseling a student it is important that she or he is made aware of the circumstances where confidentiality cannot be guaranteed (e.g., where there is a threat of self-harm or suicide).

What Parents Can Do

Before their child enrolls in a school, parents should always ensue that the handbook provides sufficient information about disciplinary procedures and codes of conduct. Nondiscriminatory policies should include explicit reference to sexual orientation, and where it is not mentioned, parents are entitled to ask a school principal why it has been omitted. In several states, laws and regulations relating to discriminating on the grounds of sexual orientation have been introduced, and in many cases, these extend to elementary and secondary school. Some states have even introduced regulations on nondiscrimination and sexual orientation that specifically relate to elementary and secondary education (Alaska, California, Connecticut, Florida, Massachusetts, Pennsylvania, Rhode Island, Utah, Vermont, and Wisconsin).

First and foremost parents want to be assured that the school is a positive environment in which their son or daughter will be educated. A school that includes sexual orientation in its nondiscriminatory policy is a good starting point, but there are a number of indicators that provide insights into how the administration deals with bullying. Questions parents should consider asking administrators include the following:

- How are students made aware of the procedure for reporting bullying to a teacher?
- Was the school's behavior policy drawn up in consultation with parents and students?
- Do staff actively demonstrate continued vigilance?
- How have staff been trained to deal with incidents of bullying, and what did that training cover?
- How are incidents of bullying addressed?
- How would a case of homophobic bullying be addressed?
- What positive and nonpunitive interventions are used when bullying is found or suspected? How are these interventions delivered?
- How have recent incidents of bullying been addressed? What was the outcome?
- How does the school work with parents to tackle bullying?
- Are updates on bullying incidents regularly reported at school, district, and PTA/PTSA meetings?
- Who are the key people (by grade) to contact in the school when concerns about bullying arise?

For a school that has taken its responsibilities seriously, most of these questions will be featured in its handbook for parents and the student handbook.

Of course, policies do not prevent bullying, and have to be followed up by interventions and programs that allow young people to develop a healthy respect for one another. Though programs such as Steps to Respect (www.cfchildren.org) help students learn to take responsibility for their actions, not all will include homophobic bullying as a discrete area for enquiry, intervention, and education. Therefore encourage schools to seek advice from organizations such as GLSEN (Gay, Lesbian, Straight Education Network, www.glsen.org) which has resources and training programs to assist parents, teachers, and school administrators build a safe educational environment for gay, lesbian, and straight students.

Today, we estimate that as many as one-third of all gay and lesbian people will have been bullied at school, ostensibly on the grounds of their perceived sexual orientation (Rivers and Duncan, 2002). For the parents of gay and lesbian students or any student who is a victim of homophobic bullying, look out for the following indices:

- Introversion and withdrawal
- Unexplained sudden illnesses that require a day off from school (over time you will see a pattern)
- Stops going out with friends in the evenings or on weekends
- Friends stop calling
- Stops being invited or no longer wishes to go to parties and proms
- Notes from school asking about missing homework
- Greater irritability
- Unexplained cell phone calls (this particular form of harassment is on the increase)
- Graffiti on schoolbooks, bags, clothing
- Unexplained cuts and bruises

Parents who are concerned about their child's behavior and who have noticed some of the changes outlined above, should always endeavor to find out what has happened. Quite often a class teacher will also have observed these changes, particularly a student's interaction with her or his peers, and a good working relationship with teachers will assist parents in obtaining a holistic view of the difficulties their child may be experiencing.

For some school boards, the belief still holds that sexual orientation and homophobia are not issues that should be addressed within secondary education, and certainly not elementary education. For the parents of gay and lesbian students or those of any victims of homophobic bullying, the challenge lies not in changing the narrowly focused minds of some school board members, but in ensuring that the board acknowledges its duty of care, and its Fourteenth Amendment responsibilities. While the Constitution does not include the right to an education as one of its fundamental rights for all citizens (though some states have the right embedded in their own constitutions), it does require that all people be treated equally before the law. Therefore, the argument is not one about the appropriateness or lack thereof of talking about homosexuality in school, but about the rights of young people to be educated without fear of discrimination, and as the following section of this chapter demonstrates, in one case a school district's failure to protect a gay student resulted in an appeal court ruling in favor of the student citing the responsibilities laid down by the Fourteenth Amendment.

What the School, District, and Board of Education Can Do

School policies that specifically include references to sexual orientation are becoming more common, and require administrators and educators to be proactive in their enforcement. The implications of not enforcing a policy that ensures the protection of gay and lesbian students, or indeed any student who is subjected to homophobic bullying, are significant. In 1996, a Wisconsin school district paid damages of $900,000 after the 7th U.S. Circuit Court of Appeals ruled that the district had violated a student's rights to equal protection under the Fourteenth Amendment. As mentioned earlier in this chapter, in 2004 a Californian school district settled out of court, including legal fees estimated at $1.1 million, following a protracted case that involved a group of students who were taunted with sexual slurs and pornography, and, in one case, physically assaulted by peers. The district's case against the students' action rested on the belief that as public servants they were immune from court action because their legal obligation to protect students against homophobic abuse was unclear, and thus could not be enforced. Lawyers acting on behalf of the district also claimed that the efforts that it made to address the issues absolved the district of any liability. The 9th U.S. Court of Appeals disagreed with this view, and all three judges determined that the lack of action on the part of administrators to resolve the harassment experienced by the students could be construed as intentional discrimination (Illinois State Board of Education, 2001). Today, as mentioned earlier in this chapter, several states including Alaska, California, Connecticut, Florida, Massachusetts, Pennsylvania, Rhode Island, Utah, Vermont, and Wisconsin have adopted specific legislation or introduced regulations that prohibit discrimination on the grounds of sexual orientation in elementary and secondary education.

A school that is serious about tackling homophobic bullying has a nondiscrimination policy that includes actual or perceived sexual orientation. A model of good practice is provided by the New Jersey Department of Education (NJDOE) which requires schools to have a definition of harassment, intimidation, and bullying which is *no less inclusive* than the following:

Harassment, intimidation and bullying means any gesture or written verbal or physical act that is reasonably perceived as being motivated either by any actual or perceived characteristic, such as race, color, ancestry, national origin, gender, sexual orientation, gender identity and expression, or a mental, physical or sensory handicap, or by any other distinguishing characteristic, that take place on school property, at any school-sponsored function or on a school bus and that:

a. a reasonable person should know, under the circumstances, will have the effect of harming a student or damaging a student's property, or placing a student in reasonable fear of harm to his person or damage to his property; or

b. has the effect of insulting or demeaning any students or group of students in such a way as to cause substantial disruption in, or substantial interference with, the orderly operation of the school. (New Jersey Department of Education, 2006)

The NJDOE requires school administrators to develop and implement procedures that will not only ensure that perpetrators of bullying (students or members of staff) will face appropriate consequences for their actions, but that attempts will be made to remedy such behavior, taking into account personal (life skills deficiencies, social relationships, talents, traits, hobbies, strengths and weaknesses) and environmental factors (school culture, staff ability to prevent and manage inflammatory situations, community connectedness, neighborhood and family circumstances). Table 5.4 provides an eight-point guide to help administrators and teachers ensure that their school is prepared and able to tackle homophobic bullying. Each point is phrased as a question, and asks how an administrator or teacher might evidence their commitment to ending homophobic bullying. In addition to the inclusion of statements that refer to homophobic bullying or discrimination on the grounds of sexual orientation, questions address the frequency with which homophobic bullying appears on the agendas of meetings, how it is monitored and addressed (inherent within this is the requirement for the training of all school staff), and how procedures are enacted when an incident occurs.

A prepared school will be one that can answer "Yes" to every question, and takes pride in being able to celebrate diversity.

PROVIDING TRAINING FOR TEACHERS

Training is ultimately at the heart of any successful intervention, and the more administrators and teachers that are trained to deal with homophobic bullying the less likely it is to become a regular feature in the lives of young people at school. For a training day to work, it has to address the core concerns of those seeking training and equip them with the skills necessary

Table 5.4.
Challenging Homophobic Bullying in Your School: 8 Points for Demonstrating Good Practice

Question	Where can you locate this evidence?	Is this an action point for your school?
School administration		
1 Can you demonstrate that you challenge and respond to homophobic bullying as part of a school behavior policy?	• School nondiscrimination policy? • School handbook? • Student handbook? • Is homophobic bullying on the agendas of teachers' meetings?	☐ No (If not, why not?) ☐ Yes ☐ No (If not, why not?) ☐ Yes ☐ No (If not, why not?) ☐ Yes ☐ No (If not, why not?) ☐ Yes
2 Can you provide evidence of commitment to promoting inclusion and challenging homophobic bullying when it occurs?	• Is homophobic bullying on the agenda of PTA/PTSA meetings? • Is it an item on the agenda of school council meetings?	☐ No (If not, why not?) ☐ Yes ☐ No (If not, why not?) ☐ Yes
3 Can you demonstrate how homophobic bullying is monitored and addressed through surveys/audits and through student disciplinary procedures?	• Do you record incidents of homophobic bullying? • Do you conduct student surveys or hold student consultations on this issue? • Do you report back to students and parents on your activities to challenge all forms of bullying?	☐ No (If not, why not?) ☐ Yes ☐ No (If not, why not?) ☐ Yes ☐ No (If not, why not?) ☐ Yes
Curriculum and resources		
4 Do you have an opportunity to address homophobia and homophobic bullying within the curriculum?	• Do you promote debates on social issues among students? • Do you plan classes that deal with different forms of discrimination including homophobia?	☐ No (If not, why not?) ☐ Yes ☐ No (If not, why not?) ☐ Yes

5 Do you make resources available to teachers, parents, and students about homophobic bullying?

- Are those resources available in the library? ☐ No (If not, why not?) ☐ Yes
- Are those resources online and easily accessible? ☐ No (If not, why not?) ☐ Yes
- Are those resources permitted by the School Board? ☐ No (If not, why not?) ☐ Yes
- Have staff been trained to use resources? ☐ No (If not, why not?) ☐ Yes

Supporting students and parents

6 Do you provide an environment that supports students who are distressed as a result of homophobic bullying?

- Do you guarantee confidentiality on issues of sexual orientation? ☐ No (If not, why not?) ☐ Yes
- Have teachers, school counselors, and administrators received training on homophobic bullying and the appropriate way to support students (recognizing any legal limitations)? ☐ No (If not, why not?) ☐ Yes
- Does the school celebrate diversity, and demonstrate its commitment to equality (e.g., Posters)? ☐ No (If not, why not?) ☐ Yes
- Are procedures for reporting bullying clear and how do you ensure students understand them? ☐ No (If not, why not?) ☐ Yes

7 Do you provide parents with a means of raising concerns about all forms of bullying, including homophobic bullying?

- Does it appear in the school handbook? ☐ No (If not, why not?) ☐ Yes
- Does the PTA/PTSA have a role in supporting parents concerned about bullying? ☐ No (If not, why not?) ☐ Yes

8 Do you ensure that letters/communications to parents are nondiscriminatory (i.e., do not always assume that a student has two parents, or that her/his parents are heterosexual)?

Have you checked:

- School handbook? ☐ No (If not, why not?) ☐ Yes
- Student handbook? ☐ No (If not, why not?) ☐ Yes
- Student record system? ☐ No (If not, why not?) ☐ Yes

Figure 5.1.
Homophobia and Heterosexism

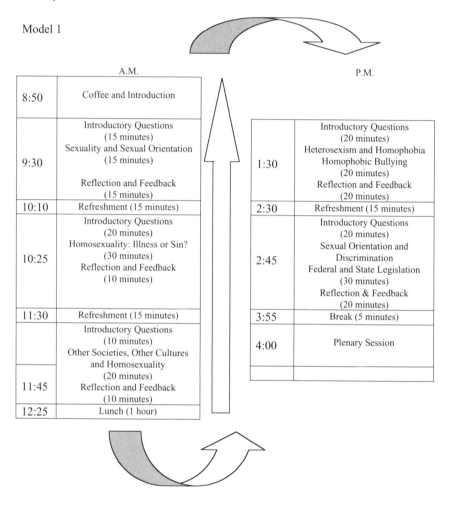

Model 1

A.M.		P.M.	
8:50	Coffee and Introduction		
9:30	Introductory Questions (15 minutes) Sexuality and Sexual Orientation (15 minutes) Reflection and Feedback (15 minutes)	1:30	Introductory Questions (20 minutes) Heterosexism and Homophobia Homophobic Bullying (20 minutes) Reflection and Feedback (20 minutes)
10:10	Refreshment (15 minutes)	2:30	Refreshment (15 minutes)
10:25	Introductory Questions (20 minutes) Homosexuality: Illness or Sin? (30 minutes) Reflection and Feedback (10 minutes)	2:45	Introductory Questions (20 minutes) Sexual Orientation and Discrimination Federal and State Legislation (30 minutes) Reflection & Feedback (20 minutes)
11:30	Refreshment (15 minutes)	3:55	Break (5 minutes)
11:45	Introductory Questions (10 minutes) Other Societies, Other Cultures and Homosexuality (20 minutes) Reflection and Feedback (10 minutes)	4:00	Plenary Session
12:25	Lunch (1 hour)		

to tackle homophobia. Figures 5.1 and 5.2 provide an overview of how a training day might look.

Figure 5.1 suggests a model that focuses upon understanding the different ways in which homosexuality is perceived by different faiths and different cultures. It then moves to consider the ways in which homophobia is expressed in schools, and provides opportunities for staff to ask questions, receive information and reflect upon current guidance when working with gay and lesbian young people and their families. This model works best when facilitators for the morning session include representatives of outside agencies such as gay and lesbian organizations and civil rights groups. Input

Figure 5.2.
Homophobic Bullying in Our School

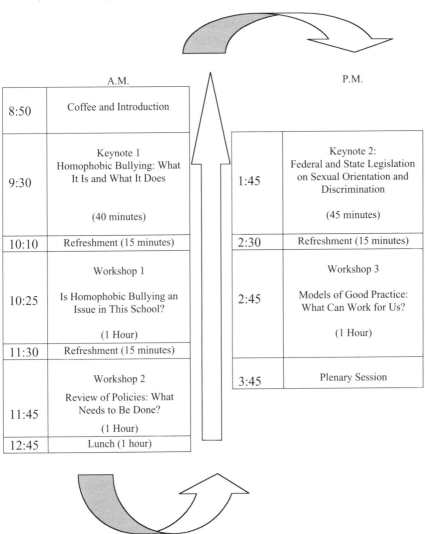

A.M.		P.M.	
8:50	Coffee and Introduction		
9:30	Keynote 1 Homophobic Bullying: What It Is and What It Does (40 minutes)	1:45	Keynote 2: Federal and State Legislation on Sexual Orientation and Discrimination (45 minutes)
10:10	Refreshment (15 minutes)	2:30	Refreshment (15 minutes)
10:25	Workshop 1 Is Homophobic Bullying an Issue in This School? (1 Hour)	2:45	Workshop 3 Models of Good Practice: What Can Work for Us? (1 Hour)
11:30	Refreshment (15 minutes)		
11:45	Workshop 2 Review of Policies: What Needs to Be Done? (1 Hour)	3:45	Plenary Session
12:45	Lunch (1 hour)		

on key federal and state legislation relating to sexual orientation discrimination and how it applies to schools should be available from the state board of education.

Figure 5.2 suggests a model that focuses upon issues associated directly with homophobia and homophobic bullying. It provides an overview of ways in which homophobic bullying manifests itself at school, its impact upon students, the school and the local community, and ways in which it can be challenged effectively. Basic information is provided via keynote presentations in the morning and afternoon followed by workshops addressing specific issues. With a little background research, this type of training day can be run by schools themselves, and requires facilitators to utilize the online resources suggested at the end of this chapter.

SUMMARY

Homophobic bullying occurs in all schools. It can be subtle, and yet has a devastating effect upon all of its victims. Failure to include sexual orientation in nondiscrimination policies gives tacit approval to this most pernicious form of abuse, and it is incumbent upon us all to challenge homophobia as well as all forms of discrimination in schools and ensure that young people are educated in a safe environment.

Tips for Parents

- Do not be afraid to ask specifically about the school's nondiscrimination policy. Does it include sexual orientation?
- Check if homophobic bullying is an issue the school feels confident in tackling.
- If you are concerned that your child is a victim of homophobic bullying, look for the telltale signs, and talk to her or his teacher.
- Contact you local GLSEN chapter, they will be able to offer you advice and information, http://www.glsen.org.
- Become active in the PTSA and make sure that questions are asked about homophobic bullying.

Tips for Educators

- Include sexual orientation in your nondiscrimination policy.
- Check the state board of education's regulations on sexual orientation discrimination.
- If you think homophobic bullying is a problem in your school contact your local GLSEN chapter, they will be able to offer you advice and information, http://www.glsen.org.
- Remember to keep records of any homophobic incidents you witness.

❧ Regularly audit your class/school, checking that homophobic bullying is being addressed adequately.

❧ Think about introducing a Gay-Straight Alliance in your school. Further information can be obtained from your local chapter of GLSEN, http://www.glsen.org.

ONLINE RESOURCES

Administrators' Guide to Handling Anti-Gay (LGBTQ) Harassment, http://www. safeschoolscoalition.org/guide_administrator_handleharass2005.pdf.

Citizens for Equal Protection, http://www.cfep-ne.org. A nonprofit organization advocating equity for Nebraska's gay, lesbian, bisexual, and transgender families.

Educators' Guide to Intervening in Anti-Gay (LGBTQ) Harassment, http://www. safeschoolscoalition.org/guide_educator_interveneharass2005NAT.pdf.

En Español: Guía Familiar para Manejar el Acoso Anti-Gay, http://www. safeschoolscoalition. org/guide_family_in_spanish.pdf.

Families' Guide to Handling Anti-Gay (LGBTQ) Harassment, http://www. safeschoolscoalition.org/guide_family_handleharass2005NAT.pdf.

Gay, Lesbian & Straight Education Network, http://www.glsen.org. GLSEN's aim is to ensure that every child learns to respect and accept all people, regardless of sexual orientation or gender, identity or expression.

Human Rights Campaign, http://www.hrc.org/worknet. Information on workplace policies and law surrounding sexual orientation and gender identity.

National Association for Multicultural Education Bullying Resources, http://www. nameorg.org/resources/Bullying.htm.

National Union of Teachers (NUT), http://www.chooselife.net/web/site/Resources/ Toolkit/TacklingHomophobicBullyingAnissueforeveryteacher.asp. Guidance that provides information and advice on supporting pupils who are lesbian, gay, bisexual, or transgender (LGBT) and on tackling homophobia within schools.

Silence Is Not Golden, http://www.silenceisnotgolden.org/educating.aspx. Resource page offering guidance on homophobic bullying.

Stand up for Us, http://www.wiredforhealth.gov.uk/cat.php?catid=1101.Tackles homophobic bullying.

Students' Guide to Surviving Anti-Gay Harassment and Physical or Sexual Assault, http://www.safeschoolscoalition.org/guide_student_surviveharass2005NAT. pdf.

REFERENCES

Askew, S., and Ross, C. (1988). *Boy's Don't Cry: Boys and Sexism in Education*. Milton Keynes, UK: Open University Press.

Berril, K. T. (1992). Anti-gay violence and victimization in the United States: An overview. In G. M. Herek and K. T. Berrill (Eds.), *Hate Crimes: Confronting*

Violence against Lesbians and Gay Men (pp. 19–45). Newbury Park, CA: Sage.

California Safe School Coalition & 4-H Center for Youth Development, University of California-Davis. (2004). *Safe Place to Learn: Consequences of Harassment Based on Actual or Perceived Sexual Orientation and Gender Non-conformity and Steps for Making Schools Safe.* San Francisco and Davis: Authors.

Fricke, A. (1981). *Confessions of a Rock Lobster.* Boston, MA: AlyCat Books.

Gay.com. US students receive compensation for homophobic bullying. January 7, 2004 [Online], http://uk.gay.com/headlines/5612. Accessed on October 2006.

Illinois State Board of Education. (2001). Bullying: Bad behavior is not just kids "neong bad." *Education Insight,* 1, 1–8.

New Jersey Department of Education. Model policy and guidance for prohibiting harassment, intimidation and bullying on school property, at school-sponsored functions and on school buses. Updated April 2006 [Online, October 2006], http://www.state.nj.us/njded/parents/bully.htm.

Pilkington, N. W., and D'Augelli, A. R. (1995). Victimization of lesbian, gay, and bisexual youth in community settings. *Journal of Community Psychology,* 23, 33–56.

Poteat, V. P., and Espelage, D. L. (2005). Exploring the relation between bullying and homophobic verbal content: The Homophobic Content Agent Target (HCAT) Scale. *Violence and Victims,* 20, 513–528.

Rivers, I. (1999). Psychosocial correlates and long-term implications of bullying at school for lesbians, gay men, and bisexual men and women. Unpublished Ph.D. thesis, Roehampton Institute London.

Rivers, I. (2000). School exclusion, absenteeism and sexual minority youth. *Support for Learning,* 15, 13–18.

———. (2001). The bullying of sexual minorities at school: Its nature and long-term correlates. *Educational and Child Psychology,* 18, 33–46.

Rivers, I., and Duncan, N. (2002). Understanding homophobic bullying in schools: Building a safe educational environment for all pupils. *Youth and Policy,* 75, 30–41.

CHAPTER 6

Special Needs and Bullying

Educationalists and researchers agree that students with special needs are at particular risk from bullying at school. Within the public school system, students who are disabled, or those who are perceptibly different from the mainstream (i.e., those who are overweight, those who require particular educational support, or those who have behavioral or emotional difficulties) are more likely to be targets of bullying than their able-bodied or less-different peers. Research has also shown that some students with special needs are also more likely to be perpetrators of bullying behavior, particularly where their special needs relate to emotional and behavioral difficulties (Unnever and Cornell, 2003). In a recent analysis of the data provided by the National Survey of Children's Health (NSCH, www.cdc.gov/nchs/about/major/slaits/nsch.htm), Van Cleave and Davis (2006) reviewed information on 102,353 children aged between zero and seventeen years. From the information provided by the survey, they were able to identify 12,488 children (mean age 12.1 years) with special health care needs (this group included children with attention-deficit/hyperactivity disorder, behavioral or conduct problems, anxiety, depression, developmental delay, physical impairment, and autism). The data showed that children with special health care needs were more than three times more likely to be victims of bullying than other children, and they were also more than three times more likely to report engaging in bullying behavior. In this chapter, we review the research currently available on bullying behavior among students with special needs, and consider what parents and educators can do to challenge such behavior and provide a supportive environment for this particularly vulnerable group within our schools.

RESEARCH FINDINGS

According to research conducted in the United Kingdom and the Republic of Ireland, children with moderate learning difficulties are four times more likely to be victims of bullying behavior than their peers (O'Moore and Hillery, 1989; Nabuzoka and Smith, 1993). Nabuzoka and Smith (1993) suggest that one of the reasons why children with special needs experience much more bullying than their nonspecial needs peers results from the fact that they have few social support networks, and are generally rated less popular by their classmates. For example, Martlew and Hodson (1991) found that students with special needs were more likely to be isolated by others during lunch and recess and had fewer friends with whom to associate. While these studies suggest that children with special needs, and specifically learning difficulties, are bullied much more frequently than students with no special needs, research focusing upon those students with physical or motor difficulties is open to interpretation.

In a very early study of bullying behavior, Olweus (1978) noted that 75% of those students he identified as victims of bullying had motor coordination problems (he described them as "clumsy children"). Subsequently, Anderson, Clarke, and Spain (1982), asked a group of 119 young people with motor disabilities to describe their experiences of attending both public and special schools (89 students had cerebral palsy and 30 suffered from spina bifida). According to Anderson and colleagues, students reported feeling unhappy and worried at school, and felt isolated by their peers. Few of those who were integrated into mainstream public schools said that they had developed friendships outside the classroom with able-bodied peers, and most reported that "watching television" was their primary recreational activity. Overall, 30% of students in mainstream public schools said that they were teased as a result of their motor difficulties (some said that able-bodied peers imitated their walk or gait at lunch and recess). Interestingly, within special schools, Anderson and colleagues found that 12% of participants said they had been bullied. The authors believed that, despite the high rates of bullying reported within the mainstream public school system, having a physical disability did not necessarily increase students' likelihood of being bullied by able-bodied peers, however, they recognized that when bullying occurred, it was the nature of the disability that attracted the perpetrator rather than the victim's behavior or personality. However, within special schools (where all the pupils suffered from some form of learning or motor disability) they argued that the converse was true: the disability had little or no significance, and perpetrators were attracted by the student's personality. These conclusions are contentious and they suggest that the disabled children may have overreacted when they were being teased by their able-bodied peers. However, Whitney, Smith, and Thompson (1994) found in their study of the experiences of 93 students with special needs (including children which physical disabilities, visual and hearing impairments) who were matched with 93 students with no special needs, that those with special needs experienced much more bullying in elementary/middle school (62% and 48% respectively) and secondary school (59% and 16% respectively).

In secondary school they found that students with special needs were almost three times more likely to be bullied regularly than peers with no special needs (30% and 11% respectively).

The findings of Whitney and her colleagues have been replicated several times over by researchers looking at various subgroups of students with special needs. For example, Judith Dawkins (1996) found that children with disabilities that affected their appearance, gait, or posture were more likely to be called names that related to the nature of their disability. Yude and colleagues found that children (aged nine to ten years) with Hemiplagia (paralysis down one side of the body) were more likely to be bullied by others and were rated less popular and had fewer friends than their peers (see Yude, Goodman, and McConachie, 1998). In one retrospective study, Hugh-Jones and Smith (1999) reported that 83% of adults who stammered reported having been bullied at school with 71% recalling having been bullied once a week or more.

More recently, various researchers have focused on the impact of obesity upon bullying behavior. In one study conducted in Canada, Janssen and colleagues (2004) found that overweight boys (between the ages of eleven and twelve years) and overweight girls (between the ages of eleven and sixteen years) were much more likely to report being socially isolated by peers, and that overweight girls were also more likely to report being bullied physically (being hit, kicked, punched, or tripped up). In the United Kingdom, Rivers (2005) reported that 28% of students surveyed between the ages of thirteen and sixteen years reported being bullied at school because of the weight, size, or body shape.

The wealth of evidence we now have does clearly suggest that students with special needs are vulnerable to bullying behavior, and are not overly sensitive. However, for some students "bullying" does not adequately describe their experiences at school; they face constant and regular harassment that has had a significant impact upon their educational achievement.

DISABILITY HARASSMENT

The U.S. Department of Education is clear on the illegality of bullying or harassment on the grounds of disability. Disability harassment is illegal under Section 504 of the 1973 Rehabilitation Act and under Title II of the 1990 Americans with Disabilities Act. Disability harassment constitutes any action that can be perceived to be "intimidation or abusive behavior toward a student based on disability that creates a hostile environment by interfering with or denying a student's participation in or receipt of services, or opportunities in the institution's program" (U.S. Department for Education, 2000).

In their letter dated July 25, 2000, to school principals, superintendents of school districts, presidents and chancellors of colleges and universities, the

Assistant Secretary for Civil Rights and the Assistant Secretary for Special Education and Rehabilitative Services identified the key responsibilities of States and school districts under Section 504, Title II and the 1997 Individuals with Disabilities Education Act (IDEA). These responsibilities include the following:

- Ensuring that a free appropriate public education (FAPE) is made available to eligible students with disabilities.
- Ensuring that state and local civil rights, child abuse and criminal law is not violated by failure to act when disability harassment occurs which could result in action being taken against the educational institution.

The letter also included examples of disability harassment that could lead to a hostile environment and, thus, put an educational institution at risk (they are reproduced here):

- Several students continually remark out loud to other students during class that a student with dyslexia is "retarded" or "deaf and dumb" and does not belong in the class; as a result, the harassed student has difficulty doing work in class and her/his grades decline.
- A student repeatedly places classroom furniture or other objects in the path of classmates who use wheelchairs, impeding the classmates' ability to enter the classroom.
- A teacher subjects a student to inappropriate physical restraint because of conduct related to his disability, with the result that the student tries to avoid school through increased absences.
- A school administrator repeatedly denies a student with a disability access to lunch, field trips, assemblies, and extracurricular activities.

Parents Reporting Harassment: Who to Write to

All schools have a duty to protect those students in their care from any form of harassment either by other students, or by school staff. Therefore, it is imperative that any behavior that raises concerns should be reported to the school immediately. In particular parents should do the following:

- Report incidents of harassment in writing to the following people:
  - the special education director
  - the school principal
  - the appropriate grade teacher
- If an incident involves a member of faculty or staff acting inappropriately or otherwise harassing a student, then the report should be circulated to the following key people:
  - the superintendent,
  - the school board,

- the school principal, and
- the special education director
- If an incident involves physical violence or a sexual assault, then the police should also be informed.

The law requires that action must be taken to challenge any form of bullying or harassment that impedes a student's access to education. School principals, faculty, and staff are aware of their responsibilities with respect to disability harassment, and failure to act will only prolong the suffering of a child or young person.

A Quick Guide for School Administrators

In addition to Section 504, Title II, and IDEA, school districts and those in the district's employ may be liable for federal antiharassment claims if standards have been developed that have established district liability when one student has suffered at the hand of another. A summary of state laws, directives, and standards is provided in Appendix 1 of Chapter 9. For such a claim to be pursued, the following would have to be established:

- that the harassment experienced by a student was based upon her/his disability;
- that the harassment was so severe that it denied the student educational benefit or access;
- personnel employed by the district and with authority to stop the harassment had knowledge of the actual harassment; and
- personnel employed by the district failed to act or acted with "deliberate indifference" to the harassment of the student.

Legal experts suggest that it is much easier for a student with special needs and her or his parents to prove denial of access and benefit to educational resources when compared to claims by other students and their parents. Issues such as a drop in grades, absences resulting from an expressed fear of harassment, or attempts to resolve the issue by keeping the student with special needs in the class during lunch or recess could constitute grounds for denial of access and benefit to education. It is important that administrators do not presume that solutions that have worked for students without special needs will necessarily work for those with special needs. If the intervention restricts the student's access to educational resources (on the sports field, during lunch or recess, or in physical education classes) then the school may still be liable.

DISCIPLINARY CODES OF PRACTICE: WHEN A STUDENT WITH SPECIAL NEEDS BULLIES OTHERS

Some students with emotional or behavioral difficulties, or conduct problems do bully other students. In elementary school, it is sometimes the case that students may not be aware that their playful behavior can hurt others. Sometimes students who are accused of bullying others believe that the aggressive behaviors they have witnessed among other students constitute the appropriate responses to difficult or challenging social interactions with peers. If a student has witnessed an argument that has been resolved through physical violence, then without appropriate guidance, that student may presume that any disagreement can be resolved through violence. Therefore, it is always important to establish why a student, and particularly a student with special needs, resorted to bullying tactics before deciding upon the appropriate action to take (U.S. Department for Education, Office of Special Education Programs, 2006).

Most students with special needs also have individualized educational plans (IEPs) which may be developed in collaboration with a number of supporting public agencies as well as parents and teachers. The purpose of an IEP is to allow each and every student the opportunity to achieve the very best she/he can by ensuring that she/he has equal access and benefit of educational resources. Where a student with special needs is accused of bullying another, it is imperative that all aspects of their educational experience are reviewed, and in 2004 changes were made to IDEA which require schools and those involved in the education of students with special needs to consider all possible explanations for behavior that violates school codes of conduct.

Individuals with Disabilities Education Act (IDEA)

On the December 3, 2004, President George W. Bush reauthorized the IDEA. The final regulations, which were published on August 14, 2006, included significant changes regarding discipline procedures for students with special needs associated with a disability. Those changes are summarized below.

Violations of School Code of Conduct

- School personnel should consider unique circumstances when deciding upon actions to be taken (i.e., change of school placement) relating to a student with special needs. For example, if a student is found to be carrying a weapon to school, it should not necessarily be assumed that the weapon is for offensive purposes, it may be carried as a means of defense.

- School personnel may remove a student to an alternative educational setting for not more than forty-five school days regardless of whether the behavior is believed to be a result or correlate of the student's special needs.

- School personnel can remove a student with special needs who violates the school's code of student conduct to an appropriate alternative educational setting, another setting, or suspend him or her, for not more than ten days.

- If the behavior that gave rise to the violation of the school code is determined not to be associated with the student's special needs, school personnel may then apply the relevant disciplinary sanction in the same manner and for the same duration as would be applied to students without special needs.

- Appropriate educational services should be provided during the absence or suspension from school by the appropriate public agency or agencies.
- If appropriate, the student should receive functional behavioral assessment, and behavioral intervention services to address the behavior violation so that it does not recur.

For further information on IDEA and school discipline go to http://idea.ed.gov/.

Consultation with Educators and Parents. On the day in which the decision is made to remove a student from a school the local education authority (LEA) must notify the parents of the decision. Within ten days a meeting should be held which includes parents, appropriate members of the LEA, and members of the IEP team to determine the following:

- If the student's conduct was caused by or had a direct relationship to her or his special needs.
- If the conduct in question was the direct result of the LEA's failure to implement the student's IEP.
- If it is determined that the conduct was a direct result of the failure to implement the student's IEP, then the situation must be remedied immediately.
- If the determination is made that the student's conduct was a manifestation of her or his special needs, a functional behavioral assessment should be conducted (unless the LEA had conducted a functional behavioral assessment before), and a behavioral intervention plan should be implemented or reviewed and modified as necessary.
- A parent of a student with special needs who disagrees with any decision taken to place that student elsewhere, or who challenges the belief that their child's conduct was not associated with her or his special needs, may appeal the decision by requesting a hearing.
- The LEA that believes that a student's current placement is likely to result in injury to her or him, or other students may similarly appeal the decision by requesting a hearing.

WHAT PARENTS CAN DO: LESSONS LEARNED FROM OTHER PARENTS

Very little has been written that provides a guide to parents on ways in which they can prepare their child with special needs for school. The following information has been synthesized from various blogs and Web sites written by the parents of children with special needs, and provides some useful tips on protecting a child with special needs from bullying behavior.

Suggestion 1: Talk about Bullying

It is important that parents are not afraid to raise the issue of bullying with their children. Bullying occurs in all schools, it can be overt (hitting, kicking, punching, name-calling, and teasing) but it can also be covert (rumormongering, social isolation, text-messaging, and e-mail threats). Define bullying behavior for your child, make sure that she/he understands how subtle it can be. Older children may already understand the fear, distrust, disgust, or even malice behind a look or stare, and may have become used to it. However, just because they are used to it does not mean it has to continue.

Suggestion 2: What to Wear

All young people are fashion conscious, and whether your child is able-bodied, disabled, a typical learner, or a learner with special needs, clothes are important. The right sorts of t-shirt, schoolbag, jeans, or footwear matter to young people, and this can be something that is easily forgotten. Increasingly we are seeing reports of fashion bullying as more and more designer labels hit the shops and malls.

Suggestion 3: Suggest Exit Strategies

It is important that students have an effective exit strategy when dealing with a bully. Well-rehearsed key phrases such as "stop bullying me" or "leave me alone" will help. Often, amid the fear and confusion that occurs when a child is being bullied, victims find themselves without the necessary verbal skills to challenge her or his aggressors, and having a few key phrases at hand will be helpful as the ability to respond shows strength. Walking or moving away from the bully in the direction of a teacher or member of staff is also a useful exit strategy, and one that will also usually bring to an end any altercation.

Suggestion 4: Watch and Listen to Your Child

Students entering a new school are particularly vulnerable as they have to find their own position within the student hierarchy. It is important that parents watch and listen to their children as they integrate into a new school. Are there any perceptible changes in behavior? Do they seem more withdrawn or sullen? Do they talk about the new friends they have made at school? Which classes do they like and dislike, why? Get a feel for how your child is coping at school. Do not be afraid to contact her or his teacher. Suggest to your child that she/he invites her/his new friends over one evening or weekend.

Suggestion 5: Friendships out of School

Various researchers have shown that even when a student has difficulty making friends at school, if they can develop friendships outside school they are less likely to experience many of the problems regularly associated with isolated or rejected children (depression, anxiety, low self-esteem, and poor social skills). Find out about the local groups that exist in your neighborhood for young people, and get your child involved.

Suggestion 6: Work with the School to Stop Bullying

Chapter 9 provides guidance to parents on what they can do to bully-proof their child's school. It is important that parents who have children with special needs get involved in school activities to prevent bullying to ensure that special needs are not forgotten. It is all too easy to presume that interventions and sanctions that work for students with no special needs will also work for those who have special needs. This is simply not the case. Some students may not understand that their behavior can be construed as bullying, and as indicated earlier in this chapter, they may be removed from school if their behavior is perceived to have broken the students' code of conduct. Parents need to ensure that the principal, faculty, and staff in the school where the child is placed understand fully the nature of her or his special needs, and consider those when addressing bullying behavior.

WHAT SCHOOLS CAN DO: SUGGESTIONS FROM PARENTS AND EDUCATORS

Schools act in the best interests of students, but occasionally students with special needs are forgotten, perhaps because they are few in number, or perhaps because the nature of their special needs means that they do not participate fully in the curriculum undertaken by peers with no special needs. In developing anti-bullying interventions, parents of children with special needs have identified areas where principals, school administrators, and teachers could improve practice. These have been synthesized into five suggestions.

Suggestion 1: Understanding "Difference" and Diversity

Not all disabilities or special needs are "seen," some are hidden, and it is important that all members of the school community understand that the world is made up of different people with diverse backgrounds, needs, beliefs, and aspirations. One size does not fit all. Parents of children with special needs have, in the past, found that where their child's disability or special need is not readily apparent teachers, school staff, and students have been less than tolerant. Sometimes such intolerance is a result of a simple lack of knowledge about the nature of a student's disability, but other times parents have reported overt insensitivity on the part of teachers, or collusion in the mimicry of a student with a stammer. Annual training days led by special education teachers and the parents of students with special needs can be an important source of information for colleagues who perhaps have not had much exposure to students with disabilities or special needs.

Suggestion 2: Social Skills Education

Introducing a social skills curriculum into the school can be a useful way of introducing issues such as respect of difference and diversity among the student population. A social skills curriculum should include discussions about being nice to other people, respecting other people's views, valuing others' contributions, understanding that different people have different skills and skill levels, but primarily it should incorporate an understanding of the idea that *all people are born equal.*

Suggestion 3: Rethinking Zero-Tolerance Policies

Although the reauthorization of IDEA provides for the power to remove a child with special needs from a school as a result of a breach of code of conduct, it is all too easy to ignore the fact that a student's behavior may be aggressively defensive rather than offensive. Take time to try and understand the reasons why the student did what she/he did. Was it born out of frustration? Is she/he having difficulties coping with the IEP? Try not to jump to conclusions, and consider alternatives before removing a student with special needs from a school for even a short time.

Suggestion 4: Staffing Levels

Ensure that there are adequate staffing levels to monitor activities in the school playgrounds, hallways, and classrooms during lunch and recess, and in between classes. Unstructured times are when most bullying takes place.

Suggestion 5: Incorporate Special Needs into Anti-Bullying Policies

In line with legislation, ensure that anti-bullying policies include reference to the sanctions the school will impose upon those who bully students with special needs. The policy should appear clearly in the student handbook, and be reinforced to parents. It is important that all members of the school community understand that disability harassment is illegal, and that sanctions will follow any and all incidents.

SUMMARY

Students with special needs require a great deal of support in schools, not only with their education, but also in ensuring that they are fully integrated into the student community. Bullying is a perennial problem and it is a problem that has been identified as affecting students with special needs especially. Section 504 of the 1973 Rehabilitation Act and Title II of the 1990 Americans with Disabilities Act clearly identifies disability harassment as an issue relevant to the schooling of young people with special needs. The reauthorization of IDEA in 2004, and the subsequent guidance surrounding the application of school disciplinary procedures with respect to students with disabilities and special needs, makes it clear that individual circumstances and the nature of a student's disability or special needs should be taken into consideration when deciding upon a course of action where there has been a breach in the code of conduct. It is incumbent upon all educators to be familiar with the legislation governing the support of students with special needs.

Tips for Parents

- Talk about bullying with your child, define it and make sure that they understand how subtle it can be.
- Do not let your child be a fashion victim.
- Suggest exit strategies, key phrases ("stop bullying me") and tactics (walking or moving toward a teacher) to prepare them to tackle bullying.
- Watch, listen, and talk to your child, look for any signs that she/he is having difficulty in school (see Chapters 8 and 9 for further guidance).
- Help your child develop friendships and activities out of school.
- Work with the school to stop bullying.

Tips for Educators

- Know the law and check your responsibilities under Section 504, Title II, and IDEA.
- Introduce social skills training to the school and include classes on understanding "difference" and diversity.

✎ Rethinking zero-tolerance policies on bullying when the perpetrator is a student with special needs.

✎ Ensure that staffing levels are sufficient to monitor all unstructured time in school.

✎ Incorporate references to students with special needs in antibullying policies.

REFERENCES

Anderson, E. M., Clarke, L., and Spain, B. (1982). *Disability in Adolescence*. London, UK: Methuen.

Dawkins, J. L. (1996). Bullying, physical disability and the paediatric patient. *Developmental Medicine and Child Neurology*, 38, 603–612.

Hugh-Jones, S., and Smith, P. K. (1999). Self-reports of short and long terms effects of bullying on children who stammer. *British Journal of Educational Psychology*, 69, 141–158.

Janssen, I., Craig, W. M., Boyce, W. F., and Pickett, W. (2004). Associations between overweight and obesity within bullying behaviors in school-aged children. *Pediatrics*, 113, 1187–1194.

Martlew, M., and Hodson, J. (1991). Children with mild learning difficulties in an integrated and in a special school: Comparisons of behaviour, teasing and teachers' attitudes. *British Journal of Educational Psychology*, 61, 355–372.

Nabuzoka, D., and Smith, P. K. (1993). Sociometric status and social behaviour of children with and without learning difficulties. *Journal of Child Psychology and Psychiatry*, 34, 1435–1448.

Olweus, D. (1978). *Aggression in Schools: Bullies and Whipping Boys*. New York, NY: John Wiley & Sons.

O'Moore, A. M., and Hillery, B. (1989). Bullying in Dublin schools. *Irish Journal of Psychology*, 10, 426–441.

Rivers, I. (2005, April). The dynamics and correlates of bullying: beyond the "victim" and "bully" status. Presented at the Centers for Disease Control and Prevention (CDC), Surveillance and Epidemiology Branch, Division of Violence Prevention (DVP), Atlanta, GA.

Unnever, J. D., and Cornell, D. G. (2003). Bullying, self-control, and ADHD. *Journal of Interpersonal Violence*, 18, 129–147.

U.S. Department of Education. (2000). Prohibited disability harassment: Reminder for responsibilities under Section 504 of the Rehabilitation Act of 1973 and Title II of the Americans with Disabilities Act [last updated March 11, 2005]. Retrieved from http://www.ed.gov/about/offices/list/ocr/docs/disabharassltr.html on February 25, 2007.

U.S. Department for Education, Office of Special Education Programs. (2006). Discipline [last updated October 5, 2006]. Retrieved from http://idea.ed.gov/explore/view/p/%2Croot%2Cdynamic%2CTopicalBrief%2C6%2C on February 25, 2007.

Van Cleave, J., and Davis, M. M. (2006). Bullying and peer victimization among children with special health care needs. *Pediatrics*, 118, 1212–1219.

Whitney, I., Smith, P. K., and Thompson, D. A. (1994). Bullying and children with special educational needs. In P. K. Smith and S. Sharp (Eds.), *School Bullying: Insights and Perspectives* (pp. 213–240). London, UK: Routledge.

Yude, C., Goodman, R., and McConachie, H. (1998). Peer problems of children with hemiplegia in mainstream primary schools. *Journal of Child Psychology and Psychiatry*, 39, 533–541.

CHAPTER 7

Challenging Bullying Behavior in Schools: Current Approaches

The most effective way of addressing any problem is to ensure that sound preventative work is in place. However, bullying like any other behavior will occur from time to time even with sound preventative practices established. It is essential to have a repertoire of effective responses at hand so that action can be taken before the emotional effects of bullying impinge too heavily on the victim and before aggressive attitudes become the established modus operandi of the bully.

Any response to bullying incidents needs to be multifaceted. Work done to support a victim is unlikely to be successful if, in parallel, we fail to address the behavior of all those who have been involved as bullies. In addition, the attitudes and behavior of those who witnessed the bullying will need to be considered. The Olweus Bullying Prevention Program is the most well-known intervention program available (see the appendix of this chapter for overview).

WORKING WITH VICTIMS

No one should have to endure bullying in any form. The primary response must be to ensure that the victim feels safe while knowing that there is to be a determined effort to stop the bullying.

Self-Confidence

Victims of bullying react in different ways. Some are able to stand up to the bullies; usually in such cases the bullying soon stops. Since not all are able to do this, we need to identify what makes it difficult for some to use effective personal coping strategies. Other than having a group of supportive friends, the most effective protective factor is the child's *apparent* self-confidence.

Those under attack who *appear* confident can escape the bullying even though they may be afraid. Some use humor. Some learn techniques that make it appear that they are ignoring the attacks. Others are able to deflect the bullies in some other way. Once the peer group identifies a child as vulnerable, the bullying could continue despite any alteration in the feature that was previously the focus of the bullying. Altering the focus of name-calling or taunts, such as pinning back ears, losing weight, or altering an accent, may not to be as successful as building up the child's self-esteem and confidence.

Ignoring Techniques

It is essential to learn how to stay calm when under attack. Adults often tell children to ignore the bullies, but this is a skill that must be taught and practiced. The following techniques can help the victim get out of a bullying situation and seek help without losing face. These techniques need rehearsal with parents, faculty, and staff at school or an older child so they become an automatic response when faced with bullies.

Fogging. Fogging is a technique whereby the victim deflects insults by saying well-rehearsed phrases.

- "You may think that, but I am happy with my weight."
- "I'm lucky. My Mom's a great cook."
- "I like my hair this way. It took a long time getting it to look like this."

Broken Record. Children can use this technique when faced with peers trying to get them to do something they do not want to do. When put under increasing pressure, the target just repeats the sentence like a broken record without giving any explanation. Giving an explanation or excuse for the refusal gives the persuaders a lever to use to wear the victim down.

- "No. I don't want to smoke, thank you."
- "No thank you. I don't want to try drugs."

Concentration Techniques. Concentration techniques deflect the mind, and subsequently the emotions, on something other than the bullies. The following mental exercises are examples of cognitive techniques that can take the mind off what is happening so that the victim gives the outward appearance of ignoring the bullies.

- Recite a multiplication table or the alphabet backward.
- Imagine you are in a clear plastic tube where no harm can come to you.
- Pretend to be a turtle and you can pull your head in your shell.
- Pretend to be wearing protective armor or a magic cloak.
- Imagine a favorite hero is by your side.

Negating the Power of the Bullies

Victims come to believe the hurtful things repeatedly said by the attackers.

- Explain that the bullies are seeking faults in their target rather than acknowledging their own.
- Ask victims to write down all the distressing and abusive comments and then destroy the paper in front of them. They have destroyed the negatives and can look forward to the positives.
- Ask the victim to write down all the good things they feel about themselves on special paper. This is most powerful if others volunteer to do this for them and frame the paper.

Desensitization

Everyone needs to be able to cope with criticism. The victim can get used to unkind remarks made by others by practicing in a benign situation with supportive adults or older friends.

Humor

The use of humor is a very effective strategy. It is best to have a few well-prepared sentences to say to the bullies. Supportive adults and friends can help them see the funny side of the taunts. It is better to laugh at yourself than have others laugh at you even though this is difficult and needs practice. This skill has gained many comedians financial reward as well as popularity.

Building Up Friendship Skills

Bullies do not pick on those protected by a strong alliance of friends. Children without such networks of friends may feel rejected and lonely. Feelings such as these erode confidence and self-esteem. The peer group may ignore or isolate a child through thoughtlessness rather than active rejection. Circle Time, Circle of Friends, and the Friendship Program are techniques used to raise awareness of the needs of others and develop friendship skills. All the techniques are in common use in British schools.

Circle Time. The teacher holds a weekly class meeting that brings emotional issues that affect group cohesion into the open and discuss them in a sensitive manner.

Circle of Friends. Canadian and British schools have used this structured approach successfully for many years. After a class meeting with the teacher, a small group of volunteers are selected to befriend the lonely child. The teacher meets this group regularly to guide and support the integration of the target child into a friendship group. This technique is applicable to children who are without the support and protection of friends either because of their own aggressive behavior or because of a lack of friendship skills.

Friendship Program. Many children need help to find friends. It is best if they seek out those with similar interests. They may need adult support to identify suitable social groups internal or external to school. It may be best to start with a gradual program of integration. The aim of the program is to integrate the young person, as soon as is comfortable, into the peer group. To push an isolated young person into a club or disco will only display their friendless state and social rejection to all. The following is only an outline and needs to be adapted according to individual needs and progress.

It is advisable to start with groups that include both young people and adults as older people are often welcoming, tolerant, and forgiving. Later children can gain social confidence by working alone but in communication with others. When more confident, the child can be introduced to groups where social interaction with peers can take place under supportive adult supervision. As social confidence grows, they can be eased into regular groups supervised by adults. Finally they may attempt entry to groups such as a public club or party (see Besag, 2006).

Adult Mentor

At school, each child needs an identified faculty or staff member with whom to discuss personal matters. This mentor should strive to make the student feel comfortable. Many children involved in a distressing bullying situation will not make an approach or speak to an adult unless they feel fully at ease.

Pupil Pursuit

Covert observation by an adult of the interactions in the playground or corridors can offer insights into the behavior of the target child, the aggressors, and the peer group. If appropriate, an older student could shadow the victim. It is essential that this be done covertly so that even the victim is unaware of this happening.

Multiagency Approach

An approach to an educational, social, or medical agency within the community could bring relevant skills into a restorative program. Any program, such as assertiveness training, a social skills program, language and communication training, a program addressing dyspraxia, or any other mode of support offered to the victim must be viewed in the context of helping the target child to develop useful skills. Victims should not feel they are being "cured." The bullying is not the fault of the victim.

Discussion Group

Older students can talk in supportive settings to younger students about bullying behavior. It may help them to know that many famous people have suffered bullying when they were young and that most people have come across bullying at some time.

Survey

Administering an anonymous survey such as the one illustrated in Chapter 5 could show victims that they are not alone. A survey of those about to leave school could reveal that many students come across bullying in some form in their school career. It could be useful for these older students to make a booklet of advice for younger students drawing on what they found helpful.

TALKING TO VICTIMS OF BULLYING

Many victims find it difficult to talk about bullying. Bullying is peer abuse. Talking about the bullying may be as painful an experience as any other disclosure. Acknowledge the courage of victims in seeking help.

When talking to a victim aim for the following:

- No interruptions.
- Equality in height of seating between interviewer and victim.
- Seats slightly askew rather than face-to-face as this can feel threatening.
- Openness of posture rather than sitting leaning forward with arms folded.
- Starting with what victim wants done.
- Seeking permission from the victim before taking any action.
- A calm approach.
- Speaking slowly giving the victim time to respond.
- A listening ear as this may be all that is required.

Stages in the Process of Talking to a Victim

Often young people do not want to face up to the problem of bullying hoping it will just go away. They deny that there is a problem or that they need help. If the victim denies the bullying at first, the following stages may be in evidence:

1. *Denial.* The victim denies any knowledge of bullying.

2. *Partial disclosures.* The victim says that there has been bullying but she/he has not been a target.
3. *Disclosure and acceptance of the problem.* The victim admits to having been bullied but does not want anything done.
4. The victim admits there has been bullying and wants something done.
5. Problem solving.

Problem Solving Approach

A problem solving approach is the most valuable mode to use in the long term as the victim finds the best way forward with support rather than relying on others to resolve the problem. This skill can solve a wide variety of problems encountered throughout life. It is important that the victim takes a full part in the problem solving. This empowers the victim and is an effective way of raising self-esteem. In addition, the victim will feel more confident when required to face problems in the future.

Solution-Focused Practice. Solution-focused practice is a problem solving approach used widely in schools but specific training is required by anyone wishing to use a solution-focused approach (De Shazer, 1985).

Restoring Confidence and Self-Esteem

Building lost self-esteem is an important part of a child's recovery and empowerment, but it is difficult to restore. If the child finds it too distressing to talk about the bullying, the best response is to ignore this defensive behavior and embark upon a *practical* plan of action, discussing the bullying as little as possible.

Mastering a New Skill. Learning a new skill often increases confidence and self-esteem and we all feel proud when we have passed a test. This is possible to achieve without any mention of the bullying. Ask the child to identify a skill to learn or improve.

Keeping a Diary. It is often constructive to provide the victim with a notebook in which to keep a record of the bullying incidents. This shows that you are taking the bullying seriously. An added advantage is that the pupil will realize that there are many occasions during the school day when they are not bullied and not all from the peer group are involved.

In addition, a diary can be kept recording only the positive things that happen. This helps the victim to keep the bullying in context.

What Can the Victim Do?

Self-Protective Strategies. The most important message we can give to children is that they must tell someone about the attacks. It is important that all faculty and staff, as well as parents, know how to at least access help for the child if they are not trained or knowledgeable in how to help the victim themselves. All children witnessing bullying should understand that it is their responsibility to alert staff. This can be done anonymously by

- putting a note a bully box placed in a quiet corner in school
- writing a letter from home
- asking parents to phone school
- telling a lunchtime supervisor
- telling the parent of a friend or an older relative

Staying Safe. Children can protect themselves in many ways.

- Avoid being alone by staying near others or an adult in charge.
- Avoid jealousy or theft by leaving expensive belongings at home.
- Choose a different route or time to travel to and from school.

WORKING WITH THE BULLIES

We should only continue behavior that is rewarding. What are the bullies gaining that causes them to repeat their behavior?

- Fun and entertainment
- Kudos
- Friends
- Possessions or money
- Power or dominance

Can we remove the rewards or match them with other rewards given for appropriate behavior? Specialists within the education system may be able to offer advice. The local police or community officers may speak to the aggressors but they usually prefer to do preventative work to avoid individual cases arising. In an extreme case, exclusion from school may be necessary if others are at risk.

A GRADED RESPONSE TO BULLYING

A move toward punishment should not be the first response as this may not be the most effective way forward.

- Sanctions are not always effective.
- Punishment may stop the bullying but not change the attitude of the bully.
- The culprits will need close supervision.

- The bullies may retaliate.
- Punishment is seen as the only response and does not extend the social repertoire of the culprits.

Many victims are reluctant to seek help because they fear reprisals from the bullies. One effective way of avoiding this is to address the bullying yet avoid punishing the bullies.

Avoiding punishment does not mean that bullying is ignored. To ignore the bullying is to condone it. If children see that the bullying goes unchallenged, they read this as adults condoning the bullying and agreeing with the negative evaluation of the bullies in considering their victims worthless. To do nothing gives a very complex and powerful message to the bullies and their targets.

There are many ways of tackling bullying without resorting to punishment. A graded response ensures that the culprits are able to make changes to their behavior without the risk of reprisals. If the victims know this approach will avoid reprisals, it is more likely that they will contribute more readily to the reparative process.

The response to bullying must be appropriate to the type of bullying behavior in evidence. As there is a spectrum of bullying behavior, in parallel there is a spectrum of responses. It is essential to start with a low-key approach giving the child a chance to change the behavior. At each stage, there must be consideration before moving on to a more punitive approach. Punitive responses should be made only after the child has shown reluctance to change. The responses form a spectrum approach with the strategies placed in order of severity to match the bullying actions (see Figure 7.1).

It is important that we *give every child a chance to change.*

Stage 1: Awareness Raising

Research suggests that gaining an awareness of the effect of their actions is effective in changing the behavior of bullying children. As most children respond to an awareness raising approach, this seems the best place to start.

- Assemblies, surveys, questionnaires, films, Web sites, and workshops for parents and governors are some of the numerous ways of raising awareness of bullying and highlighting the responsibilities of all members of the school community.
- Low-key class discussions can raise awareness. Topics that highlight the difference between leadership and dominance may help those who confuse the two styles of communication.
- It may be that the bully is bored and finds teasing and taunting others a fun way to pass the time.

Figure 7.1.
Spectrum of Bullying Behavior and Responses

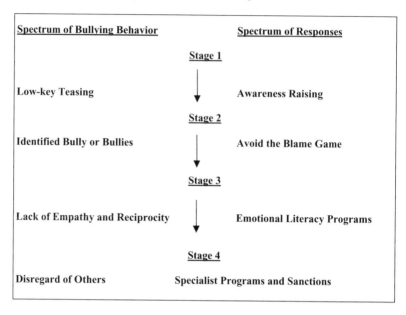

- Bullying often occurs when the children are unsupervised. For example, organized games, clubs, and other activities during free time can be effective in reducing aggression in any form, including bullying.

Stage 2: Avoid the Blame Game

It must be clear that the bullying behavior must stop immediately. It is necessary to begin with the culprits by using a low-key approach as they may have used a powerful mode of bullying without realizing the damage this could cause to the target. Discussion, persuasion, and negotiation may be the most appropriate response to some actions. A quiet word may be sufficient to bring about a realization of how their negative behavior has adversely affected others.

There are many reasons why a child may unintentionally cause distress to another.

- The child was immersed in the excitement of a game and disregarded the welfare of others in the group.
- The culprit considered the behavior as a game or joke not realizing it was causing hurt and offence.
- The child had not been taught to consider the welfare of others.
- The prize at stake overrode the empathic nature of the child.

Matt's Story. Matt was a physically strong boy with an exuberant personality. Each day he playfully pushed his way toward the front of the lunch line while keeping an eye on the adult supervisor as he knew he should wait quietly in line. The jostling would end with Matt moving position to the front of the queue. Sam was not as confident as the other boys so he was always left at the end of the line. By the time Sam reached the lunch counter, there was very little choice left. Matt had not noticed the effect of his behavior on the other boys in particular the effect on boys such as Sam. After a discussion with his teacher, Matt immediately changed his behavior as he realized the effect of his boisterous behavior on others.

Marie's Story. Marie was a girl of six who found it difficult to make friends. Her teacher and classmates thought she was shy and did not want to join in the games. Marie was not agile and had few games' skills so when she made tentative attempts to join in the games, the other girls shunned her. She was lonely and very unhappy in school. When her teacher noticed her watching the others playing together, day after day, she took a skipping rope and started a skipping game with Marie. Very soon, the other girls wanted to join in the game. After the game had ended, the teacher quietly pointed out to the group that it would have been kinder to encourage Marie to join in the games rather than exclude her. Marie is now happily taking part in all the playground games.

Bully or Leader? Many adults as well as children, confuse bullying behavior with leadership as the skills required for both are the same. A bully uses the skills in a dominant, egotistical manner incorporating coercion, domination, and threat to demand allegiance whereas an empathic leader uses a democratic, negotiated style of leadership.

A boy who is bullying another could be given the role of trainer to help younger boys develop computer or gaming skills. He would receive training in leadership skills from an adult based on the skills he already possesses. In this way he is now trained to use his skills in an empathic and democratic leadership role.

Group Responsibility. It will be necessary to challenge more than one child if a group has been involved in a bullying episode. In such cases, the group must take responsibility for the behavior and for bringing about change. One way of tackling this is for the adult to lead the bullies in a discussion about their behavior emphasizing the effect it has had on their victim.

Before tackling the group responsible for the bullying, it is essential for the adult dealing with the problem to discover what has happened. This is most effective if the adult watches and listens to the group unobserved. Bullying takes place out of sight of adults so it is beholden on the adult to go to places where it is likely to happen such as the school bus, the playground, the corridors, toilets, or a line. Older students trained as peer supporters can watch and listen to what is happening and give an impartial report for the teacher to follow up. It is far better for the adult approaching the bullying group to say that he or she has witnessed the bullying than to rely on the report of the victim.

The following is a process traditionally used in tackling inappropriate behavior. However, it is essential that the process is implemented in a structured manner. Close supervision and monitoring of both bullies and the victim is required to ensure the bullying has stopped. It is best to work with a mix of the bullies and a few of those in the class group who are likely to be strong supporters of the victim once they have understood the dynamics of what is happening. The victim may nominate those they wish to include.

- It is important to elicit the emotional effects of the bullying on the victim. Victims unable to talk about their feelings could choose a poem from several to describe their emotions or perhaps write a poem. With permission, this can be added to the poems shown to other victims in the future. They may prefer to describe their feelings using a tape recording or by drawing a picture or writing a story. Some may prefer to write a letter to the bullies.

- A meeting is arranged with the bullies where they are made aware of how their actions have adversely affected their victim as they need to know the effects of the bullying. The victim rarely wishes to be in such a meeting.

- In this meeting with the bullies, each child is asked in turn what they could do to take responsibility for their actions and to make amends.

- A review meeting is arranged where each child reports back about what they have done to change the situation.

It is important to stress that bullying is a behavior. Calling the child a bully or victim is not helpful as this locks them into a persona. If the focus is on the behavior it seems much easier to change.

Have a few suggestions ready for change in case the bullies cannot think of any. It is necessary to have several because

- not all will be suitable for each child to use;
- not all situations are suited to all responses;
- offering just one is giving advice that should be avoided;
- this gives the child choice; and
- this helps the child build up a repertoire of appropriate social behavior.

Garth's Story. Garth was being chased home by a group of boys in his class. This had been going on for several weeks. He did not want to tell his teacher as he thought she would punish the bullies who would then find ways of attacking him in revenge. He did not tell his parents as he thought the bullies would see the family car arrive at school. They would suspect his parents had come to complain about their behavior. The bullying caused Garth to have sleepless nights and he hated going to school.

Eventually, the parents of another boy in his class told Garth's parents that their son was so frightened by what he had witnessed that he, too, was now afraid to go to school. The teacher asked Garth how he wanted to let the bullies know that this was not a game to him. Garth chose to write a story about the attacks using a different name for his character.

The teacher called a meeting for the group and read out the story. The boys soon realized how badly they had treated Garth and were shocked to hear of the effect of their actions. They knew they had been unkind to Garth and had made fun of his distress, but they had not realized that things had gotten out of hand. When asked what they could do to make school a pleasant place for Garth, they all had suggestions. One boy asked him home to tea, another made sure he was included in their games, and another brought his new play station game for him to try. All six boys promised to make amends to Garth.

The teacher called a review meeting for all six boys a week later. First, she asked Garth's parents and teachers if he looked happier in school. All said he now had friends and seemed comfortable about going to school once more. The adults involved continued to monitor the situation until they were sure the bullies had genuinely changed their attitudes and behavior.

Monitoring the Situation. It is essential to closely monitor the situation. It is not sufficient to ask the victim if the bullying has stopped. Inevitably, the response will be that it has. Therefore, checks need to be made by observations of the group around school and by contacting the parents of the victim to ensure that things have improved at home. Faculty and school staff may be able to report on the concentration, standard of work, confidence, and the general demeanor of the victim around school. All are warning signs of bullying and lack of confidence. It will take time for the victim to recover from the bullying even once it has stopped, but a gradual improvement should be evident at home and at school.

The Method of Common Concern. Anatol Pikas has long advocated a method similar to the above for challenging the bullies and bringing about change. The main difference in the two approaches is that Pikas advocates that the bullies are seen individually starting with the group leader. Each student involved in the bullying is asked, in private, to take responsibility for changing the bullying behavior and, importantly, making the victim feel safe and comfortable in school. As with the previous method, a review meeting is held with each bully to repost on progress and a check is made that the victim is now more at ease in school.

Tips for Educators

✎ Have suggestions for change ready in case the child cannot give any. If the bully denies the behavior, say it is the responsibility of everyone to make others feel safe and comfortable in school and ask what they can do to help.

✎ If the bully blames someone else, say you will speak to that person later but you want their help even though they may not be to blame.

Tony's Story. Tony was no good at games. He had few games' skills such as catching, throwing, running, and balance. The other boys left him out of their activities, so he felt lonely in school. Soon, they began to taunt him and tease him about his lack of coordination. When any other boy had to partner with him, the ball would be thrown or kicked at Tony, not to him. The other boys started to trip him up and push him off his chair. No one boy did this more than once or twice a day so each thought it just a joke. However, there were several boys in the group attacking Tony so that he would have twenty or thirty attacks a day. Eventually, as the attacks escalated, he became so fearful he refused to go to school.

The teacher held a private meeting with each boy. None accepted responsibility for Tony's distress. Each boy said he had not attacked Tony as it had just been a bit of fun. In fact, each boy thought others should take the responsibility. The teacher told each boy he must accept responsibility for the seemingly small, infrequent actions that had developed into a barrage of attacks and take responsibility for changing his own behavior. Tony needed to feel safe and comfortable in school and it was the responsibility of each to make this change. Each boy was helped to suggest a way in which he could make amends.

The teacher held a review meeting with each boy after one week and Tony's parents and the teachers who had most contact with him were contacted to check on progress. After a short time, Tony settled happily in school once more and a situation that had escalated to cause such distress finally stopped. Some of the boys even became his close friends.

Mediation. Usually a brief discussion is held with the bully and the victim, separately, before the mediation meeting where they describe the dispute from their own point of view. The mediation procedure is explained to each of them as both need to be willing to attend the meeting.

Mediation is an effective mode of conflict resolution as it provides a safe setting where two disputants describe what they see as the issues causing the conflict. They express their views and state their feelings. In a dispute, each person often feels unable to explore fully the issue face-to-face with the other adversary. The participants are locked into their own positional stance. Believing they are in the right, they are unwilling to accept the position or viewpoint of their adversary. Mediation provides a safe forum for this change of positional stance to take place. Mediation is used throughout the judicial system in many countries with adults as well as young people and is used successfully in international disputes.

A boy who is fearful of his attacker should not be asked to sit beside him in a mediation meeting. Male bullies are usually physically stronger than their victims as the bullying is likely to have had some element of physical attack. Care must be taken that the victim is not cajoled into attending a meeting where he will feel intimidated. In the case of bullying among girls, this is not so common but neither girl should feel fearful of the other. If this is the case, a different approach may be more appropriate in the first instance.

Stage 3: Emotional Literacy—Empathy and Reciprocity

Many children have not had the advantage of years of family training regarding taking the feelings of others into account. An effective way to experience turn-taking, negotiating, and understanding the emotions of others is by playing games. Even the most "cool dude" will join in a game chosen with care. Young people will learn about sharing and negotiating, turn-taking and disappointment during the course of playing a game whereas they would dismiss "lecturing" from an adult.

The Egocentric Response. Some young people retain the egocentric attitudes of early childhood well into adulthood. The egocentric tracks that characterize their behavior are laid down in the early years. This may have been because they have a restricted repertoire of social skills and can only choose from the few available to them. Many children have not had the advantage of years of training in the family regarding taking the feelings of others into account when embarking on a course of action. Some young people are unable to respond appropriately to questions such as, "How do you think Angela feels being left out of things?" or, "How do you think Tom feels when you all chase him home?" They will not have any understanding of empathy and reciprocity if they have not been trained to consider routinely how others feel or react to their actions.

We cannot blame these young people if they have not had the advantage of training and exposure to appropriate social behavior and attitudes. Some children grow up in an environment where the first response to negative emotions such as aggravation, frustration, or jealousy, is to use violence to solve the issue and to gain their own way. Such children will readily resort to this mode of response when faced with difficulties. It may be that they would be responsive to exposure to other modes of tackling their problems if given the opportunity to learn.

By late childhood, most children have the ability to make a considered choice before taking action. They are able to look back on past actions and consider the result and effect of those actions. In addition, they are able to look to the future and consider the probable effect on others of any action chosen. They can then meld their experiences with possible outcomes to make a considered decision. They use past and future to decide on the option that will be best for them within the context of other people.

Unfortunately, some young people are unable to do this and react instantly to negative emotions such as provocation, anger, disappointment, rejection, or insult, real or imagined, with an aggressive response. These children receive sensations to the thalamus but these are not processed in the neocortex where past experiences and possible future outcomes meld to provide a sound base for appropriate choice. Instead of arriving at the thalamus, the sensations stimulate the primitive amygdala and the basic response of aggression emerges as an immediate response (see Figure 7.2).

Children who have a medical condition such as those with ADD (H) may act impulsively. They may not be able to take the time to contemplate the effect of their actions or to blend their experience with their options in order to make a considered choice and so often act impulsively and inappropriately.

Games as a Mode for Change. Playing games is an effective way to experience turn-taking, negotiation, and understanding the emotions of others. This must be under close tutoring and supervision by adults who must be able to bring this about in a planned and sensitive manner. Even the most challenging adolescent will consider joining an age-appropriate game or activity chosen with care. Young people will absorb the skills of negotiation and sharing instead of bullying during the course of playing a game with an adult participation whereas they would dismiss or forcibly reject "lecturing" from an adult. Table games, field games, sport, and a range of activities can be used as the vehicle for effective change.

Figure 7.2.
Brain Imaging Offers Explanations

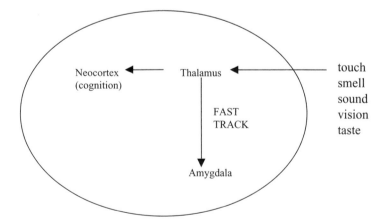

Unfortunately, a small number of bullies are unaffected by knowledge of the distress they cause to others. A smaller number may even enjoy hearing about the harm they have caused. Researchers found that some bullies have little remorse and may even enjoy watching the distress of their target. If we do identify this attitude and recognize it for what it is, and do not attempt to change it as soon as possible, we are giving these children permission to dominate the more vulnerable for their own need or gratification. They will see no reason to change and will continue to hold this belief into adult life. For most of these children, the immediate aggressive response is the easiest to make, and specialist programs and sactions are required (Stage 4).

WORKING WITH GROUPS AND GANGS

The Need for Expert Help

As some students enjoy giving a public display of their aggressive behavior, public sanctions could be counterproductive. Many highly aggressive young people suffer from mental health problems such as feelings of alienation, loss, helplessness, and depression. These powerful negative emotions lead them to employ challenging and deviant behaviors. Strategies that work with the majority will not necessarily be effective with those who have serious behavior or personality disorders.

Research now suggests that there are many young people who have the ability to meet challenges and achieve, but who simply do not want to meet the goals most adults set down for them. There are those who have serious behavior or personality disorders who will need support and advice from specialist services in the local community for example, dedicated education, social services, health organizations, and the police. It is essential that we support these students, either in schools or in specialist care, as the long-term prognosis for them is pessimistic with regard to their physical and mental health, their place in the community, and future parenting.

There has always been confusion about the use of sanctions when addressing antisocial behavior. There is no confusion about one aspect of the issue. It is human nature to continue to use behaviors that are rewarding and discontinue those that are not. We need to ensure that the bullies are not gaining in any way from their bullying.

The most effective and long-lasting way forward with such young people is to identify mechanisms that are equally rewarding as those gained from being in the group or gang. As rewards offered by the gang may be access to drugs, money, sex, and weapons, this can be a difficult thing to achieve. However, praise and achievement is one of the most powerful rewards if an acceptable manner of delivery can be found. If there are serious concerns regarding anyone involved, bully, victim, or witness, advice should be sought from the local police service or other public body.

Restorative Practices

One approach that uses sanctions in a sensitive manner and avoids reprisals against the complainant is the range of restorative practices. In these approaches, such as restorative justice, the perpetrator meets the victim in a safe environment to hear of the effects of the bullying and to seek some way of making a reparation. This is an expensive mode in terms of time and finance compared to most other methods of addressing individual cases involving bullying. Therefore it is mainly appropriate for the most complex and intractable cases. It is particularly useful in issues of community bullying where the complexity of the cases allows few approaches to be successful.

To proceed with a restorative justice approach, professional training is strongly advised. The procedure is similar in many ways to mediation. This process can resolve a wide range of disputes. The two antagonists, the bully and victim in a case of bullying, are approached before the meeting and given an outline of the procedure. Each is asked if they would like to invite to the meeting anyone else who has been affected by the dispute. They too are prepared for the meeting in the same way.

It is understood that all are willing to attend the meeting in the hope that a way forward, satisfactory to all, will be found.

There is a format to the meeting which in summary allows each party in turn to describe the incident, the effects, and their emotions about it.

Solutions are sought and a consensus regarding the way forward is identified. If this is not possible, hopefully having heard the stance of the opposing party in a safe and protected environment, the two parties will at least be able to part without antagonism. This is a system used very effectively in many parts of the world and is now in common use within the judicial system in Britain for adults and young people.

Peer Support Systems

Peer support systems are being increasingly used by schools as an effective component of their bullying policies. However, such systems must include accurate preparation, implementation, and training. These systems are useful as young people have more experience of their peers than staff. The input of peers is particularly useful in cases of bullying as adults do not see or hear what goes on outside the classroom.

WORKING WITH PARENTS

Most parents are highly motivated to react to their child being bullied. Parents have a strong ethological response to protect their offspring by attacking those they think may have put them at a disadvantage or harmed them in some way. Therefore, it is best not to react immediately to any suggestion of bullying but to take time to reflect, react in a rational rather than impulsive manner, and decide on the best plan of action.

Contact with School

It is important that the school discuss any concerns by phone or letter if the child is worried about the possibility of reprisals if parents are seen in school.

- Ask if the child can move seat, group, or class if necessary.
- Ask the school for ideas and help as it is rarely the sole responsibility of the parents.
- Ask if the school organizes parent workshops, if not ask if you can help to start one.
- Ask if there is a booklet for parents about bullying—if not ask if you can help design one.
- Look on the Web for information and advice.
- Ask about agencies in the community that can help.
- A different school may be the answer in extreme cases.
- It may be necessary to contact the police.

Once parents are certain the issue is seen as important by the school, and a date has been set for a review meeting to which they are invited, it is best to leave work in school to the school faculty and staff. It is not helpful to wait at the door for the child to arrive home from school and greet them with the daily inquisition, "What did they do to you today?"

The optimum way forward for parents is for them to concentrate on what they can do in the home situation.

- Lighten the load by finding new and interesting things to do—go out for the day, go to the beach or hills.
- Start a new hobby or activity outside the home and take the child—art, music, scuba diving, basketball, or golf.
- Go out to a cinema, a cafe for special coffee and cake, or a restaurant.
- Go away for a weekend.
- Make a fuss of the child, hugs and praise are good.
- Smile as much as is appropriate whenever you are with the child as smiles are catching and make you feel better.
- Try to see family and friends who get on well with the child.
- Home should be a place of comfort and safety, try not to make too many demands.
- Ask for special requests—a meal or favorite cake—get the whole family on board.

- Be positive rather than dwelling on the bullying.
- Look forward to the future and let the child know that things will get better.

SUMMARY

In dealing with bullying in schools, it is essential that every aspect of the issue is addressed. The needs of the victims need to be considered even after it appears that the bullying has stopped as continuing reparative work may still be required. Those who bully others may need an intensive program to help them to understand fully the concept of empathy with others. It is imperative that all in our schools are helped to make appropriate choices as this is a skill that will continue to impinge on all areas of their lives. Victims who remain fearful and lacking in confidence may not be able to secure jobs appropriate to their skill level, find suitable partners, or encourage confident behavior in their own children. Those who only draw upon aggressive responses are also at risk. In Norway, Olweus (1978) found a high proportion of children who bullied others had made appearances in court for offences by early adulthood. Being able to deal appropriately with bullying, as bully, victim, or witness may be one of the most useful and important skills we can teach children in our schools.

APPENDIX: THE OLWEUS BULLYING PREVENTION PROGRAM
(http://www.clemson.edu/olweus)

The program is implemented at the school, classroom, and individual levels as follows:

At School Level

- The formation of a coordinating committee to oversee the program implementation
- Distribution and analysis of an anonymous student survey on the nature and prevalence of bullying in the school
- Program of training events for committee members and school staff
- The development of a coordinated supervision system
- Adoption of an anti-bullying policy
- Implementation of guidance relating to positive and negative consequences relating to students' behavior
- Implementation of staff discussion groups to discuss the execution of the program
- Involvement of parents

At Classroom Level

- Teachers reinforce the school's anti-bullying policy.

- Teachers hold regular classroom meetings with students to further develop knowledge and demonstrate empathy.
- Implementation of meetings with parents to discuss information from staff-student consultations.

At the Individual Level

- Introduction of interventions for perpetrators of bullying behavior
- Introduction of interventions for victims of bullying behavior
- Meetings with the parents of students involved in bullying behavior

Further information on the Olweus Bullying Prevention Program can be obtained from Marlene Snyder, PhD, Research Associate, Institute on Family & Neighborhood Life, Clemson University, Phone: 864-710-4562, Fax: 406-862-8971, E-mail: nobully@clemson.edu.

REFERENCES

Besag, V. E. (2006). *Understanding Girls' Friendships, Fights and Feuds: A Practical Approach to Girls' Bullying*. Buckingham, UK: Open University Press.

De Shazer, S. (1985). *Keys to Solution in Brief Therapy*. New York, NY: Norton.

Olweus, D. (1978). *Aggression in Schools: Bullies and Whipping Boys*. Washington, DC: Hemisphere.

PART III

Advice for Parents

CHAPTER 8

Immediate and Long-Term Effects of Bullying

America's future will be determined by the home and the school. The child becomes largely what he is taught; hence we must watch what we teach, and how we live.

—Jane Addams (1860–1935), American Pacifist,
Social Worker, and Nobel Laureate

In their review of the research literature Hartup and Stevens (1997) found that adolescents who did not develop friendships during the early years were more likely to suffer from low self-esteem, and were less likely than their more popular peers to cope successfully with upheavals such as changing schools. Similarly, Haugaard and Tilly (1988) have argued that the absence of friendships during middle childhood will result in later difficulties in forming and maintaining romantic relationships in adolescence as a result of low self-esteem and a lack of social confidence.

EARLY RESEARCH

In a pivotal early study, Brian Gilmartin (1987) compared two groups of heterosexual men whom he described as "love-shy" (unable to form a lasting intimate relationship with a member of the opposite sex) to a sample of young men whom he described as being "socially successful with women and who engage in a great deal of informal heterosexual interaction including dating, partying, and lovemaking" (p. 475). Gilmartin argued that "love-shyness" in men was the result of inborn temperament, and that those with an "inhibition gene" were more likely to experience chronic bullying at school and had learned to associate feelings of "painful, anticipatory anxiety with the thought of informal, sociable interaction with male peers" (p. 471). He argued that both samples of "love-shy" men would compare less favorably than "nonlove-shys" on various measures including the number of friends they reported, their participation and enjoyment of contact sports, and the number of intimate relationships they had enjoyed. In addition, he believed that "love-shys" would recall a great deal more bullying at school than "nonlove-shys," and that they were more likely to agree with the statement, "Throughout most of my life I never had any friends" (p. 473). Gilmartin's results showed that not only had "love-shys" experienced a great deal more bullying at school than "nonlove-shys," but that they had disliked contact sports and "rough and tumble" play (horse play). Additionally, in terms of friendship, he found that 73 percent of older "love-shy" men (aged between thirty-five and fifty years) said that they had never had a friend as compared to 53 percent of the younger "love-shy" men (aged between nineteen and twenty-four years).

Bullying, Self-Esteem, and Depression: Cause or Effect?

Although various researchers have established a relationship between low self-esteem, depression, and bullying behavior among school-aged youth early on (Olweus, 1979, 1993a, 1993b; Kaplan, 1980; Rigby and Slee, 1993), it is unclear whether low self-esteem and depression are causes (i.e., provide an easy target for perpetrators) rather than consequences of bullying. For example, Kaplan (1980) argued that those boys who were likely to be victimized at school were also likely to exhibit behaviors that identified them as being timid or unwilling to retaliate when challenged. A similar view has been expressed by Olweus (1993a) following a series of detailed interviews with the parents of boys who were bullied at school. He found that introversion and a lack of assertiveness on the part of the boys seemed to cause the bullying they experienced, which resulted in high levels of anxiety and insecurity, and low levels of self-esteem if continued over a long time.

In a longitudinal study conducted in Norway, Olweus (1993b) considered the effects of repeated bullying at school (occurring over a period of three years) among a sample of seventy-one young men who were followed until the age of twenty-three. Using teachers' and peers' nominations collected seven years prior to the follow-up study, Olweus assessed the men on a number of measures of negative affect and social functioning to determine whether or not there was a relationship between current affective state (whether or not they showed symptoms of depression, anxiety etc.), and socialization skills, and teachers' and peers' estimates of the victimization. When he compared the data Olweus found that former victims of bullying differed significantly from their nonbullied peers on scores for depression and self-esteem—an outcome he related specifically to their experiences of school, rather than any current socialization deficits.

BULLYING IN ELEMENTARY SCHOOL

Research has shown that, in terms of frequency, most bullying occurs in elementary and middle schools. Bullying generally declines with age. For example, in the United Kingdom, Whitney and Smith (1993) found that approximately 27 percent of students report having been bullied at primary school (the equivalent to elementary and middle school in the United States), whereas only 10 percent reported being bullied in secondary school (middle, junior-high, and high school).

Early Signs of Behavioral or Emotional Difficulties at Home and at School

In the United States it is estimated that about 10 percent of students can be considered extreme victims of bullying, experiencing harassment daily or several times a week across an extended period of time. These students are often younger, or physically weaker than their aggressors, or have behavioral mannerisms or traits that distinguish them from their peers. Even within elementary schools, the establishment of the hegemonies of masculinity and femininity are present, and in the struggle to develop the unofficial pecking order within the school, those who do not conform (particularly in last two grades of elementary school) will find themselves ostracized by peers, and subject to physical assault and verbal taunt. Being labeled a "victim" can follow a student throughout her or his school career, and so the earlier bullying is addressed the better. Similarly, being labeled a "bully" can have devastating effects upon a student's academic progress as school reports rarely mention changes in students' behavior over time. The danger in being too prescriptive in the assessment of a child or young person's behavior is that the school administration may become "conditioned" to view that individual as a problem student, and one who is always the protagonist or perpetrator rather than an innocent bystander or victim. Such conditioning will ultimately alienate the student, resulting in further frustration, a lack of engagement, and ultimately, the rejection of school and the value of education.

Victims of Bullying in Elementary School: Indices for Parents. The emotional and behavioral indices that suggest a student may be the victim of bullying include the following:

- increased quietness
- withdrawal from family interaction
- visible sadness
- withdrawal from friends and from activities once enjoyed
- an increase in days off school (complaints of head- and stomachaches)
- poor school performance (drop in grades)

- loss of appetite
- sleep disturbance (including bed-wetting)
- only uses bathroom at home (school bathrooms are places where a lot of bullying takes place away from the view of teachers)
- torn clothes and/or unexplained cuts and bruises
- requests for extra money for lunch or additional allowance
- letters from school enquiring about homework that is reported lost, or reporting behavioral problems such as fights with other students.

The above indices do not occur in isolation as they are linked, and parents should be on the lookout for patterns that include more than one index.

Perpetrators of Bullying in Elementary School: Indices for Parents. By way of contrast, the emotional and behavioral indices that suggest a student may be the perpetrator of bullying are less well reported in the research literature but may include:

- changes in friendship groups (particularly the loss of a friendship group)
- expressing a dislike of school and teachers
- a desire to "show off"
- acquisition of items or goods that could not have been bought without parental knowledge
- unexplained outbursts of anger
- becoming easily frustrated
- an unwillingness to do homework
- hitting or trying to dominate younger brothers and sisters.

Just as with victims of bullying, the above indices do not usually occur in isolation, and are likely to be linked. Parents may feel that "suddenly" their child has become "a problem child" with more and more time being spent chastising or punishing her or him rather than offering encouragement or positive reinforcement.

Victims of Bullying in Elementary School: Indices for Educators. Educators who suspect that a student may be a victim of bullying should keep weekly records monitoring any changes in patterns of behavior, and provide opportunities for the student to discuss any difficulties she or he may be having. The chart provided in Chapter 5 (see Table 5.2) is useful in recording patterns of behavior in students. Key indices that a student is a victim of bullying in elementary school include:

- lack of eye contract and visible sadness
- the onset of uncontrollable outbursts of anger and frustration

- changes in friendship patterns and activities at recess
- a lack of engagement in class-based or group activities where previously there had been full engagement
- students make fun of him/her when he/she speaks?
- Less attention is paid to schoolwork and homework.

Comparable to the indices found at home, teachers should be on the lookout for patterns in student behavior that include more than one of the above.

Perpetrators of Bullying in Elementary School: Indices for Educators. Educators who suspect that a student may be engaged in bullying other students should look out for the following suggested indices:

- defiant eye contact when behavior is challenged by a teacher
- causing classroom disruption
- snatching, grabbing, or taking items that belong to or are being used by other students
- hitting and pushing other students out of the way
- ignoring a teacher's request to listen, or to stop talking
- an unwillingness to engage fully in class-based or group activities
- making fun of other students when they speak
- a lack of care in schoolwork and homework.

All of the above need to be considered with caution. Simply because a teacher witnesses an incident where a student pushes another out of the way, or grabs a pencil from the hand of another, does not mean that she/he is "a bully." Throughout elementary school, as well as the official curriculum, students are learning the unofficial curriculum governing the social rules of engagement and trying to find their own place within the peer group. As a result, in learning how to behave students will make mistakes, act inappropriately, and learn from the reactions of those around them (peers, teachers, and parents). A student's behavior should only be considered problematic if there is a perceived failure to learn or change behavior following repeated admonishments.

BULLYING IN MIDDLE, JUNIOR-HIGH, AND HIGH SCHOOL

In middle school, junior-high, and high school the nature of bullying changes dramatically: where once physical (hitting, kicking, and punching) and verbal (name-calling and labeling) bullying were the primary modes of delivery, during adolescence indirect or relational bullying (social isolation, rumor mongering, and selective attention) comes to the fore. In a recent report by the American Medical Association (AMA) of 15,000 sixth- to tenth-grade students, it was estimated that as many as 3.7 million students perpetrate bullying behavior and almost 3.2 million are victims of "moderate" or "serious" bullying (Nansel, Overpeck, Pilla, Ruan, Simons-Morton, and Scheidt, 2001). According to the National Association of School Psychologists (NASP), being a "bully" or a "victim" is associated with increased school dropout, poor psychosocial adjustment, an increased propensity to engage in criminal activity, as well as other long-term and negative psychological consequences (National Association of School Psychologists, 2007).

What are the Signs of Behavioral or Emotional Difficulties?

In the next chapter (Chapter 9), a detailed discussion is provided on what parents can do to support their children, who are accused of bullying or who have been victims of bullying, in light of the Federal Government's introduction of the *No Child Left Behind* Act. It is however important that both educators and parents be aware of the signs suggesting that bullying is taking place in a class or grade. Chapter 4 provides a useful overview of the issues that emerge during adolescence, and the role puberty and establishment of unofficial social hierarchies have upon the dynamics of the student group. The following pages identify some of the key behavioral and emotional indices of bullying and, similar to suggestions concerning indices of bullying in elementary schools, it is important that educators and parents look for patterns in the behavior of students.

Victims of Bullying in Middle, Junior-High, and High School: Indices for Parents. In middle, junior high, and high school, there will be a range of signs that include physical, behavioral, and emotional indices. These include:

- unspecified headaches, stomachaches (frequent requests to stay at home)
- outbursts of anger
- unexplained cuts and bruises, torn and mudsplattered clothing
- hitting out, flinching
- tiredness (often linked to sleep disturbance)
- loss of appetite
- unexplained crying
- unwillingness to walk or travel to school alone
- avoidance of students once classed as "friends"
- staying at home on evenings and at weekends
- stealing money
- staying late at school (to avoid encounters with students outside school)
- becoming introverted, sullen, and self-effacing

- expressing self-doubt
- greater uneasiness with expressing physical affection
- becoming easily distracted, forgetful (an indication that they are preoccupied with something else).

Perpetrators of Bullying in Middle, Junior-High, and High School: Indices for Parents. Signs that your child is a perpetrator of bullying may include some or all of the following:

- changes in friendship groups (particularly the loss of a friendship group)
- an unexplained but overall decline in grades
- expressions of disaffection with school
- the desire to "show off" especially in front of others
- ownership of items or goods that could not have been bought without your knowledge
- expressed anger or irritation with fellow students (including making disparaging comments about them or threatening to hit them)
- frustration with homework
- domination or subjugation of siblings.

Victims of Bullying in Middle, Junior-High, and High School: Indices for Educators. For educators, spotting bullying when it occurs, particularly indirect or relational bullying is not easy. It may be useful to undertake a short survey in the class to identify potential targets of bullying behavior. These will tend to be students with fewer friends and associates than others. A short survey questionnaire is proved in Chapter 5 (Table 5.3), which may be useful. Once you have identified potential targets of bullying, look for some of the following signs:

- visible tiredness
- a noticeable change in behavior (i.e., sudden and inappropriate outbursts of anger or frustration)
- lack of confidence
- social isolation and a lack of engagement with others at recess
- reticence in class-based or group activities where previously there had been full engagement
- other students make fun of him/her when he/she speaks?
- Changes in grades (in some cases this is not downward trend as students may spend more time alone studying and have few recreational outlets)

Perpetrators of Bullying in Middle, Junior-High, and High School: Indices for Educators. By middle, junior-high, and high school a pattern of behavior may have emerged with some students who bully others. It is always helpful to check student records, particularly those relating to elementary school, where concerns are raised about the behavior of a student suspected of bullying others. Also look for the following:

- defiant, rude, and challenging behavior when admonished by a teacher
- leading classroom disruption, particularly encouraging a small group of other students
- little or no regard for other students' property
- other students move out of their way in the hallways and at recess
- ignores a teacher's request to listen, or to stop talking
- an unwillingness to engage fully in class-based or group activities
- openly disparaging of other students' contributions to the class
- a lack of care in schoolwork and homework.

Some of the indices cited above are also indicative of many students' attempts to demonstrate their defiance of rules and regulations imposed by the school administration. For some students, such defiance is indicative of the emergence of an identity distinct from being the son or daughter of another person and her or his attempt to exert this new identity may be a challenge to school discipline but should not be construed as a propensity to be a bully. At this stage, testing the boundaries of acceptable or permissible behavior, whether at home or at school, is part of the process of growing up.

LONG-TERM EFFECTS FOR PERPETRATORS OF BULLYING

Very little research has focused specifically upon the long-term effects of bullying for perpetrators. What evidence there is suggests a link between criminal behavior in late adolescence and early adulthood and recollections of difficult or challenging behavior at school. For example, data from Norway and the United States suggests that, compared to their peers, perpetrators of bullying at school are more likely to be convicted of crimes in adulthood (Olweus, 1993c) and have a one in four chance of having a criminal record by age thirty (Eron, Huesmann, Dubrow, Romanoff, and Yarnel, 1987). Currently, we know very little about the long-term emotional effects bullying others have upon the perpetrator. It is likely that such behavior if left unchecked can lead to violent episodes in later life, or emotional coldness in relationships. Furthermore, where bullying has been sexualized in nature and perpetrated by one or more males against one or more females, those behaviors and the associated beliefs about women may manifest in later life as intimate partner violence.

There is some evidence to suggest that, for some students, bullying behavior is associated with Attention Deficit Hyper-Activity Disorder and Attention Deficit Disorder (ADHD/ADD). Where diagnosed, the appropriate medication and treatment will have a significant impact upon behavior. Having said that, the majority of students who bully others grow out of it as they develop their social skills, and understand the rules and customs governing social relationships, and it is perhaps in the teaching of these social skills that attention should be focused.

LONG-TERM EFFECTS FOR VICTIMS OF BULLYING

There is a considerable body of evidence to support the belief that bullying has long-term negative implications for the emotional well-being of victims. Such long-term effects include increased likelihood of suffering from depression, anxiety, low-self-esteem, and posttraumatic stress in adulthood. According to the American Academy of Child and Adolescent Psychiatry (AACAP), stressors such as bullying place students at an increased risk of depression. In extreme cases, bullying may result in students considering or attempting self-harming behavior or suicide.

Early Onset Depression

Students who are victims of persistent bullying may shown signs of early onset depression, which, if left unchecked, can lead to school failure (National Alliance on Mental Health, 2007). Signs of early onset depression include:

- persistent sadness
- expressions of hopelessness
- irritability
- increasing requests to stay at home
- drop in grades
- poor appetite
- sleep disturbance, fatigue
- poor concentration
- low self-esteem
- somatic complaints (e.g., headaches and stomachaches)
- lack of enthusiasm and engagement.

Later there may also be signs of the following:

- alcohol use
- drug use

- self-harming behavior (self-inflicted cuts on arms and thighs)
- thoughts of ending life.

Early onset depression has also been linked to youth running away from home, eating disorders, and the onset of bipolar disorder in later years. Therefore, it is imperative that support and guidance is sought by parents and educators as soon as symptoms appear. Early onset depression is treatable, and if the source of the stressor is removed, the prognosis is very good. Further guidance for parents on how to work collaboratively with the school to combat bullying is provided in the next chapter (Chapter 9).

Posttraumatic Stress Disorder

Until the early 1990s, it was presumed that posttraumatic stress disorder (PTSD) did not affect children, however, more recently researchers have demonstrated that PTSD can affect the lives of children and young people in school. Early studies of PTSD in children focused on the aftereffects of surviving natural or man-made disasters; however, more recently, it has been suggested that children are far more resilient than first believed in the face of such disasters, but that traumatic events initiated by people (i.e., physical or sexual assault) result in more severe symptoms. Within the general population of adolescents, PTSD occurs in about 5–10 percent of the population, and increases significantly among those who are drug and alcohol dependent. In one study, Rivers and Cowie (2006) reported that 17 percent of a sample of 116 former victims of homophobic bullying had symptoms associated with PTSD. PTSD is diagnosed when one or more of the following symptoms are reported, having lasted for one month or more:

- difficult or challenging behavior
- Avoiding school, classes, and people associated with bullying
- Easily frightened or startled
- Worries about death
- depression
- poor concentration
- emotional numbness, detachment, or disinterest
- feelings and expressions of guilt
- flashbacks (these may include images, sounds, smells, or feelings)
- irritability and easily angered
- loss of interest in people, pastimes previously enjoyed
- nightmares
- persistent and frightening memories of one or more events
- headaches, stomachaches

Not every student who is bullied develops PTSD. If a student experiences a particularly violent or emotionally hurtful episode she/he may experience some of the symptoms associated with PTSD, but these will generally disappear with time. Where parents or educators witness or are told about a particularly violent episode of bullying, or encounter a student who is visibly distressed, the National Association of School Psychologists (NASP) recommend that the student process and discuss their emotions within twenty-four to thirty-six hours following the incident to prevent PTSD.

RESILIENCY

What promotes resiliency? The International Resilience Project based at Dalhousie University in Canada provides a guide to resources and research materials detailing those factors that promote resiliency, particularly in the face of bullying, violence, and abuse (International Resilience Project, 2007). Research has shown that resilience is related to the following individual traits:

- assertiveness
- problem solving skills
- self-awareness
- perceived social support of others (family, friends, and teachers)
- positive outlook on life and future
- empathy
- having goals, aspirations, and ambition
- a responsible approach to the use of alcohol
- a sense of humor.

In terms of social support, resilient students also have a network of family and friends who provide:

- a positive mentor and role model
- meaningful relationships that have an emotional bond
- full integration into a peer group subculture.

In terms of the organization of the school, educators should ensure that all students have the following:

- opportunities to engage in age-appropriate work
- skills to avoid of exposure to violence
- career and skill guidance
- security

- equity for all students
- equitable and safe access to information, learning resources, and school facilities.

In addition to the above, resiliency has also been linked to cultural factors such as an affiliation with a church or religious organization and an appreciation of diversity and difference within the community.

SUMMARY

Research has shown that there are significant immediate and long-term effects associated with bullying in school. We know far more about the effects of bullying for victims than we do for perpetrators. Depression, anxiety, posttraumatic stress, self-harm, and suicide ideation have all been identified as consequences of bullying in schools, and without appropriate interventions students will continue to suffer at the hands of perpetrators.

Tips for Parents

- Don't be afraid to talk to the school principal or class teacher if you have concerns that your son/daughter is being bullied.
- Look out for telltale signs that indicate your child is a victim or a perpetrator of bullying.
- If your child exhibits symptoms of depression, anxiety or PTSD get help immediately, talk to a School Psychologist, or your family medical practitioner.

Tips for Educators

- Look out for signs that a student may be a victim or perpetrator of bullying.
- Use a record sheet to note down your observations (see Table 5.2).
- Discuss your concerns with colleagues.
- Don't be afraid to talk to parents, they may have similar concerns.
- Think about conducting a class survey to gauge student friendship networks (see Table 5.3).

REFERENCES

Eron, L. G., Huesmann, R. L., Dubow, E., Romanoff, R., and Yarnel, P. W. (1987). Aggression and its correlates over 22 years. In D. H. Crowell and I. M. Evans (Eds.), *Childhood Aggression and Violence: Sources of Influence, Prevention, and Control* (pp. 249–262). New York, NY: Plenum Press.

Gilmartin, B. G. (1987). Peer group antecedents of severe love-shyness in males. *Journal of Personality*, 55, 467–489.

Hartup, W. W., and Stevens, N. (1997). Friendships and adaptation in the life course. *Psycholological Bulletin*, 121, 355–370.

Haugaard, J. J., and Tilly, C. (1988). Characteristics predicitng children's responses to sexual encoutners with other children. *Child Abuse and Neglect*, 12, 209–218.

International Resilience Project. Last updated February 7, 2007 [online, February 2007], http://www.resilienceproject.org/cmp_text/?&strCompname=home.

Kaplan, H. (1980). *Deviant Behavior in Defense of Self*. New York, NY: Academic Press.

Nansel, T. R., Overpeck, M., Pilla, R. S., Ruan, W. J., Simons-Morton, B., and Scheidt, B. (2001). Bullying behaviors among U.S. youth: Prevalence and association with psychosocial adjustment. *Journal of the American Medical Association*, 285, 2094–2100.

National Alliance on Mental Health. Early onset depression. Last updated 2007 [online, February 2007], http://www.nami.org/Content/ContentGroups/Helpline1/Facts_About_Childhood_Depression.htm.

National Association of School Psychologists. Bullying: Facts for school and parents. Last updated October 7, 2003 [online, February 2007], http://www.baspcenter.org/factsheets/bullying_fs.html.

Olweus, D. (1979). Stability of aggressive reaction pattern in males: A review. *Psychological Bulletin*, 86, 852–875.

Olweus, D. (1993a). *Bullying at School: What We Know and What We Can Do*. Oxford, UK: Blackwell.

Olweus, D. (1993b). Victimization by peers: Antecedents and long-term outcomes. In K.H. Rubin and J.B. Asendorf (Eds.), *Social Withdrawal, Inhibition, and Shyness* (pp. 315–341). Hillsdale, NJ: Erlbaum.

Olweus, D. (1993c). Bully/victim problems among schoolchildren: Long-term consequences and an effective intervention program. In S. Hodgins (Ed.), *Mental Disorder and Crime* (pp. 317–349). Thousand Oaks, CA: Sage.

Rigby, K., and Slee, P. (1993). Dimensions of interpersonal relating among Australian secondary school children and their implications for psychological well-being. *Journal of Social Psychology*, 133, 33–42.

Rivers, I., and Cowie, H. (2006). Bullying and homophobia in U.K. schools: A perspective on factors affecting resilience and recovery. *Journal of Gay & Lesbian Issue in Education*, 3, 11–43.

Whitney, I., and Smith, P. K. (1993). A survey of nature and extent of bullying in junior/middle and secondary schools. *Educational Research*, 35, 3–25.

CHAPTER 9

Working with Schools: A Guide for Parents

States are required to establish a uniform management and reporting system to collect information on school safety and drug use among young people. The states must include incident reports by school officials and anonymous student and teacher surveys in the data they collect. This information is to be publicly reported so that parents, school officials, and others who are interested have information about any violence and drug use at their schools. They can then assess the problems at their schools and work toward finding solutions. Continual monitoring and reports will track progress over time.

—U.S. Department of Education (2004)

On January 8, 2002, President George W. Bush signed into law the *No Child Left Behind* Act that reauthorized Title IV of the *Elementary and Secondary Education Act* (EASA) Part A—the *Safe and Drug-Free School and Communities Act* (SDFSCA, 2006), which subsequently came into effect on July 1, 2002. The SDFSCA State Grants Program authorizes activities that have been designed to prevent school violence and drug use, and to assist in the development of safe, disciplined, and drug-free environments that will support student academic achievement. Key changes were made to the SDFSCA that included:

- A requirement that State and local prevention programs and activities meet the *Principles of Effectiveness* that can be summarized as follows:

  Funds must be used to support programs grounded in scientifically based research.

  States and local recipients have meaningful and ongoing consultation with, and input from, parents in the development and administration of programs/activities.

- Each State establishes uniform management information and reporting system to support decision-making.

- Local administrative costs are limited in the amount of the SDFSCA funds received via the grant made to the State.
- Funds can be used for the following activities only to the extent that funding for activities is not received from other agencies:

  purchase and installation of metal detectors, electronic locks, surveillance cameras, or other related equipment;

  reporting of criminal offenses committed at school;

  development and implementation of school security plans including the purchase of technical expertise to facilitate the execution of those plans;

  supporting activities that ensure students travel safely to and from school;

  the hiring and appropriate training of school security staff who enact the school's drug and violence prevention activities and who, by implication, will interact with students.

- A State cannot allocate a portion of their SDFSCA grant to local education authorities on the basis of perceived "greatest need."
- Local education authorities in receipt of SDFSCA funds must develop a plan to keep their schools safe and drug-free through the implementation of:

  appropriate and effective discipline policies;

  security procedures;

  prevention activities;

  student codes of conduct;

  the development of a crisis management plan in case of violent or traumatic incidents occurring on school property.

Parents are, therefore, entitled to participate in and be consulted about any activities undertaken by a school to challenge violence and drug use. Furthermore, it is incumbent upon State and local education authorities to report effectively on the actions they have taken to combat violence and drug use in schools, and parents have the right to question the efficacy of such programs based upon the monitoring data that each school, district, and State is required to collect, analyze, and publish.

For parents who believe their children are already attending "persistently dangerous schools" (as determined by the State), or who have been victims of violent crime, the State is required to offer an alternative choice of schools, and, where necessary, pay for transportation (although there is a funding cap). Under the SDFSCA, a school district is required to notify parents if their child is eligible for school choice because his or her school has been identified as needing improvement, corrective action, or restructuring as a result of failing to demonstrate yearly improvement in student achievement. The district must notify parents before or on the first day of the school year following identification of a school's need for improvement.

Each State is also required to ensure that a choice of schools is offered to parents in the event their child has been the victim of a violent crime that has taken place on school property (U.S. Department of Education, 2004).

YOU AND YOUR SCHOOL: LOOKING BEYOND THE SURFACE

Today, with the gradual increase in gun crime perpetrated by adults and by students, school safety is at the top of everyone's agenda. How safe will a child be in school during the day? Since the introduction of *No Child Left Behind* and the reauthorization of the SDFSCA no educator should feel that she or he has to act alone in challenging violent behavior in schools. The safety of each student rests not only with a teacher, but also with national and state legislators, members of state and local boards of education, commissioners of education, superintendents, principals, and, of course, parents. Federal law mandates that all schools take action in challenging violent behavior and drug use, and the provision of funding to undertake such action is a positive step forward. So, how do we promote safety at school for students?

Invariably, schools that are safest are those that acknowledge that violence and bullying behavior happens. Even with well-developed codes of conduct, disciplinary procedures, and restorative practices, some students will continue to bully others. It is therefore important that both parents and educators acknowledge that a school that recognizes that bullying takes place is not a failing school; it is a school on its way to becoming a safe and successful institution of education.

Research has shown that bullying is not always overt (involving hitting, kicking, and punching); it may involve name-calling, rumor mongering, or social isolation. It may be conducted using a cell phone, or e-mail. Regardless of its *modus operandi*, most educators readily acknowledge that any behavior that deliberately causes distress to another human being is a form of violence. *The Principles of Effectiveness* that underpin the SDFSCA clearly state that "Funds must be used to support programs grounded in scientifically based research." As we have demonstrated throughout this book, scientific research has shown that bullying is ever-changing, and with developments in technology come new ways of bullying others. Thus, teachers, administrators, and the school, local, and state boards will be constantly thinking about whether or not they have sufficient funds to maintain adequate vigilance, and parents can support their schools in ensuring that those funds are available through lobbying legislators and taking an active part developing programs that ensure that no child or young person is left behind, and that every child and young person matters.

YOU AND YOUR SCHOOL: ACTIVE PARTICIPATION

In Chapter 5, it was suggested that in order for parents to feel that their children will be safe at school, it is important to ask questions about student behavior policies, anti-bullying initiatives, and the nonpunitive interventions that are currently used in place of sanctions. We suggested that the most salient questions to ask include:

- How are students made aware of the procedure for reporting bullying to a teacher?
- Was the school's behavior policy drawn up in consultation with parents and students?
- Do staff actively demonstrate continued vigilance?
- How have staff been trained to deal with incidents of bullying, and what did that training cover?
- How are incidents of bullying addressed?
- What positive and nonpunitive interventions are used when bullying is found or suspected? How are these interventions delivered?
- How have recent incidents of bullying been addressed? What was the outcome?
- How does the school work with parents to tackle bullying?
- Are updates on bullying incidents regularly reported at school, district, and PTA/PTSA meetings?
- Who are the key people (by grade) to contact in the school when concerns about bullying arise?

A school that has taken its responsibilities seriously will include most of the answers to these questions in its handbooks for parents and students. If it does not, then suggest to the principal that a small working party should "parent-proof" the handbook on an annual basis and include a bullying FAQ (Frequently Asked Questions) providing clear answers to these questions.

Of course, school handbooks have to be backed up by actions and interventions, and parents need to know that their school is fulfilling its statutory requirements with respect to ensuring the safety and well-being of students, and working toward any recommendations that have been introduced at state level to ensure that bullying and violence is addressed effectively.

What Your School Should Be Doing

In addition to the requirements of the SDFSCA, parents should also be familiar with their own state laws (statutes and codes), requirements, rules and regulations, recommendations, and standards relating to bullying and violence prevention. Table 9.1 provides a quick guide indicating whether or not states currently have laws, requirements, rules and regulations, or have made recommendations, or set standards that address bullying and violence prevention. The table includes details of the grades to which any required or suggested course of action apply and we have provided the Web address of each state board of education where further information can be obtained.

Table 9.1.
Are Bullying, Harassment, Fighting, Health, and Well-Being Taken Seriously in Your State? An Overview of Each State's Activities

State	Where do I start? State Departments/Board of Education Web sites	Grades	Codes/Statutes	Requirements	Rules/Regulations	Recommendations	Standards
Alabama	http://www.alsde.edu/html/boe1.asp	4–7		✓			✓
Alaska	http://www.eed.state.ak.us/State_Board/	K–12					✓
Arizona	http://www.ade.az.gov/stateboard/	K–12					✓
Arkansas	http://arkansased.org/sbe/sbe.html	K–12	✓	✓			
California	http://www.cde.ca.gov/be/	2, 4, 6	✓				
Colorado	http://www.cde.state.co.us/index.sbe.htm	K–12	✓	✓			
Connecticut	http://www.state.ct.us/sde/board/index.htm	K–12	✓				✓
Delaware	http://www.doe.k12.de.us/info/sbe/	K–8				✓	✓
Florida	http://www.fldoe.org/board/	K–12					
Georgia	http://www.doe.k12.ga.us/doe/sboe/index.asp	K–12		✓		✓	✓
Hawaii	http://lilinote.k12.hi.us/STATE/BOE/HomePage.nsf?OpenDatabase	K–5				✓	
		3, 9–12				✓	
Idaho	http://www.boardofed.idaho.gov/	Not specifically required					
Illinois	http://www.isbe.state.il.us/	4–12	✓			✓	
Indiana	http://www.doe.state.in.us/stateboard/	K–10	✓			✓	
Iowa	http://www.iowa.gov/educate/content/view/322/245/	K–12	✓	✓			
Kansas	http://www3.ksde.org/commiss/board.html	K–12	✓	✓	No state policy		
Kentucky	http://www.education.ky.gov/KDE/Administrative+Resources/Kentucky+Board+of+Education/default.htm	K–12				✓	✓

Where do I start?

State	State Departments/Board of Education Web sites	Grades	Codes/Statutes	Requirements	Rules/Regulation	Recommendation	Standards
Louisiana	http://www.doe.state.la.us/lde/bese/home.html	K–12	✓	✓			✓
Maine	http://www.maine.gov/education/sb/homepage.htm	K–5	✓	✓			
Maryland	http://www.marylandpublicschools.org/MSDE/stateboard/	3–12		✓			
		Unspecified			Incorporated into health education		
Massachusetts	http://www.doe.mass.edu/boe/	K–12				✓	✓
Michigan	http://www.michigan.gov/mde/0,1607,7-140-5373—,00.html	K–12				✓	✓
Minnesota	http://www.education.state.mn.us/mde/index.html	K–12				✓	
Mississippi	http://www.mde.k12.ms.us/SBE.htm	2, 9–11	✓†			✓	
Missouri	http://dese.mo.gov/stateboard/	K–12		✓			
Montana	http://bpe.mt.gov/	4, 8			✓		
Nebraska	http://www.nde.state.ne.us/StateBoard.html	K–12		✓			✓
Nevada	http://www.doe.nv.gov/edteam/boardofed.html	3,5,8,12	✓	✓		✓	✓
New Hampshire	www.ed.state.nh.us/education/board/index.htm	K–12		✓			✓
New Jersey	http://www.state.nj.us/njded/sboe/	2 plus		✓			✓
New Mexico	http://www.nmsba.org/sbe.html	K–12		✓			✓
New York	http://www.emsc.nysed.gov/	Unspecified		✓			✓
North Carolina	http://www.ncpublicschools.org/state_board/	2–12				✓	
North Dakota	http://www.dpi.state.nd.us/	9–12	✓				
Ohio	http://www.ode.state.oh.us/GD/Templates/Pages/ODE/ODEPrimary.aspx?Page=2&TopicRelationID=574	K–6	✓	✓			✓
Oklahoma	http://www.sde.state.ok.us/home/defaultie.html	1–12				✓	✓
Oregon	http://www.ode.state.or.us/search/results/?id=144	K–12				✓	✓

(Continued)

Table 9.1. (Continued)

State	Where do I start? State Departments/Board of Education Web sites	Grades	Codes/Statutes	Requirements	Rules/Regulations	Recommendations	Standards
Pennsylvania	http://www.pde.state.pa.us/pde_internet/site/default.asp	3,6,9,12		✓			✓
Rhode Island	http://www.ridoe.net/regents/	K–12	✓	✓			✓
South Carolina	http://ed.sc.gov/agency/stateboard/	5,8,12		✓			✓
South Dakota	http://doe.sd.gov/secretary/board/	K–12		✓			✓
Tennessee	http://www.state.tn.us/sbe/	K–12		✓			✓
Texas	http://www.tea.state.tx.us/sboe/	3–12				✓	
Utah	http://www.schools.utah.gov/board/	2–12	✓	✓		✓	✓
Vermont	http://education.vermont.gov/new/html/mainboard.html	PreK–12		✓		✓	
Virginia	http://www.pen.k12.va.us/VDOE/VA_Board/home.shtml	2–10	✓	✓			✓
Washington	http://www.sbe.wa.gov/	Unspecified		✓			
West Virginia	http://wvde.state.wv.us/boe/	4–12	✓	✓			✓
Wisconsin	http://www.wisconsin.gov/state/core/education.html	K–12				✓	✓
Wyoming	http://www.k12.wy.us/sbe.asp	K–12				✓	✓

Codes/Statutes: Introduced via state legislature.
Requirements: Actions that must be taken.
Rules/Regulations: Administrative rules that set benchmarks for content of programs.
Recommendations: Suggestions that are positively supported.
Standards: Guidelines that determine the levels of achievement or understanding that should be attained by a certain grade.

Note: †Minnesota's Statute 120B.22 (2000) encourages districts to integrate programs of violence prevention, it does not require them.
Source: National Association of School Boards of Education (NASBE). State-by-state injury and violence prevention education. Last updated October 30, 2006 [online, November 2006], http://www.nasbe.org/HealthySchools/ States/Topics.asp?Category=A&Topic=8.

Apart from Idaho, Kansas, and Maryland, every other state has at the very least recommendations on how schools should tackle bullying, harassment, and violence. In the case of Maryland, these issues are incorporated into health education. Even though Idaho and Kansas do not have specific state policies, they are required to enact all aspects of the SDFSCA. In the Appendix to this chapter, further details are provided, state-by-state, of key statutes, regulations, and standards that require or recommend action to challenge bullying and violent behavior. This data is provided by the National Association of State Boards of Education (NASBE), which has regular updates of state initiatives on its Web site (http://www.nasbe.org), and provides hyperlinks to key pieces of state legislation, and programs, policies, and standards that have been implemented to address violence in schools.

WHAT IF MY CHILD IS A VICTIM OF BULLYING?

The SDFSCA requires the State to offer an alternative choice of schools, and, where necessary, pay for transportation where a student has been the victim of a violent crime. The onus upon parents is, in some degree, to demonstrate that the bullying their child suffered constitutes a violent crime. Currently twenty-four states have passed anti-bullying laws (Limber and Small, 2003), and in those states bullying is a crime. In other states where bullying per se is not a crime, legislation ensures that particular violent acts that occur on school property are brought to the attention of law enforcement officials. For example, in Alabama, although there is no specific policy on school bullying, Code 16-1-24.1 stipulates that physical harm or threatened physical harm is a violation of local policy. Furthermore, Criminal Code 13A-11-8(a) (1) (1996) defines harassment as a crime if the perpetrator was intent on harassing, annoying, or alarming another person that would cause a reasonable person to fear for his or her safety. In addition, Code 16-1-24.1 requires a school principal to notify law enforcement officials when policies concerning drugs, alcohol, or weapons are transgressed, or where physical harm is caused to a person, or is threatened (NASBE, 2006).

However, moving a victim to another school is all too often used as an inexpensive means of tackling bullying. Although it is just as inexpensive to move the student accused of bullying others, this option does not seem to occur with the same degree of frequency. In effect simply removing a student from a school offers only a limited solution to the problem of bullying, and it does not address the long-term problems associated with this form of antisocial behavior.

What Are the Telltale Signs of Bullying?

The telltale signs of bullying are common, and have been reported by various researchers around the world. Things to look out for if you think your child is being bullied fall into three categories: physical signs, behavioral signs, and emotional signs.

Physical Signs. In kindergarten and elementary school, physical signs may include bed-wetting, fear of the dark, night terrors, sleep walking, unspecified headaches, stomachaches, bruises and cuts, and torn or mud-splattered clothing. In middle, junior high, and high school, physical signs are likely to include unspecified headaches, stomachaches, outbursts of anger, cuts and bruises, torn and mud-splattered clothing, together with incidents of hitting out, flinching, tiredness (often linked to sleep disturbance), loss of appetite, and unexplained crying.

Behavioral Signs. Changes in behavior as a result of bullying often include things such as an unwillingness to walk or travel to school alone, school refusal, avoidance of students once classed as "friends," staying at home on evenings and at weekends, avoidance of specific classes on specific days (i.e., Physical Education), stealing money, staying late at school (to avoid encounters with students outside school), becoming introverted, sullen, and self-effacing.

Emotional Signs. Students who are the victims of bullying often doubt themselves, and believe that tasks in which they previously excelled are either worthless, or they are no longer any good at them. Such attitudes are linked with bouts of depression, a greater uneasiness with expressing physical affection, and a withdrawal from all social activity. In addition, victims also become easily distracted, forgetful (an indication that they are preoccupied with something else), intolerant of others (especially siblings), and become disillusioned with education (which may lead to underachievement and a desire to quit as early as possible).

Of course, many of the signs identified above may be symptomatic of other issues going on in a family (the arrival of a new baby, sibling rivalry, parental fighting, separation, and domestic violence) or in the neighborhood (recently moved in, gang warfare, social deprivation, and poverty). Nevertheless, where a child has moved up a grade early, been held back in a grade, moved to a new school, or has not developed those social bonds you see among other children and young people, then bullying is likely to be at the heart of the issue (Besag, 1989; Cósti, 2003).

What Do I Do?

Parents who believe their child is being bullied experience a range of feelings and emotions, often as a result of their perceived inability to help. These feeling and emotions often manifest in the form of beliefs that they have either failed or do not have the skills to help their child. Typical feelings include:

- A sense of failure in not spotting the bullying earlier.

- A sense of failure as a parent.
- Frustration.

For all parents, the sudden realization that their child has been bullied over a period of weeks, months, or even years without their knowledge will invariably undermine self-confidence, particularly in terms of parenting skills. But victims of bullying are very good at hiding the physical signs of bullying, and masking their inner pain. Similarly, children who are victims of bullying at school are not born that way; their victim status is the result of the social, academic, and sporting expectations institutions such as schools place upon young people. Parents should never feel inadequate, embarrassed, helpless, or a failure when they approach the school for support. Finally, parents have the right to feel frustrated if a school fails to take appropriate action. Therefore, when approaching the school and requesting a meeting with the principal and/or class teacher, be prepared. Have a series of questions ready. Be direct, and by the end of the meeting ensure that a plan of action has been agreed.

There are three steps in approaching the school. *Firstly*, find out as much as you can about the bullying that is going on. Do not be afraid to talk to other parents; they may have similar concerns, insights, or experiences. *Secondly*, find out what all schools in your state should be doing. Be familiar with state laws, regulations, rules, recommendations, and standards. For up-to-date information consult the NASBE Web site (http://www.nasbe.org). *Finally*, make sure that a record of the meeting is made, so take a notebook. We would recommend that parents ask to have a meeting with the school principal and the appropriate class teacher. A parent going into a meeting without a partner or spouse should take a close friend to provide support, as these meetings can be daunting. Use the notebook to write brief notes on the responses given by the principal and class teacher, and wherever possible get all the people in that meeting to sign and date that the notes you have made are true.

What Do I Ask? Earlier in this chapter, some questions were suggested about how the school tackles bullying behavior. Those questions are useful, and should be used to set the scene. Find out what the school policies and practice are, and how successful they have been. Next it is important to find out as much as possible from the class teacher. What has she or he seen, or knows? The following questions may be helpful in structuring the meeting:

Have you been aware of any changes in the behavior of my son/daughter?—If the answer is "yes," what were they?

Has there been a history of bullying in the class?

Have you had to address incidents of bullying recently?—If the answer is "yes," who were the perpetrators, and how was it resolved?

Who are my son's/daughter's friends in the class? Have these changed recently?

Does my son/daughter participate fully in class discussions?—If the answer is "no," why do you think this is so?

Have other children made fun of him/her when he/she speaks?

Have you noticed a change in the quality of his/her schoolwork?—If it is poorer than normal, how do you account for this?

The most important rule in conducting this meeting with the principal and class teacher is to remain calm. The principal will be all too aware of the legal requirements placed upon the school by the SDFSCA. The aim of this meeting is to develop an action plan to bring to an end any bullying that may be going on in a class. If a teacher is unaware of the dynamics of her or his classroom, and thus is unable to answer the questions posed to her/him fully, it may be helpful to suggest that she/he conducts a short survey (see Table 5.3).

What Could an Action Plan Include? In developing an action plan following an incident of bullying, it is important that it incorporates monitoring of individual students along with the implementation of wider school initiatives. For parents, the individual needs of their child must be met, and the action plan should include the following:

- Closer monitoring of the student's behavior at home and at school. Use the checklists provided in Tables 9.2 and 9.3.
- A commitment by the principal on the part of school to intervene when bullying and teasing takes place.
- A commitment by the school to talk to the parents of the perpetrators.
- Regular meetings between parents and teachers to monitor progress.

All of the above should be combined with those ongoing State and Federal programs that address bullying, harassment, and fighting in schools.

WHAT IF MY CHILD IS ACCUSED OF BEING "A BULLY"?

Bullying is a subjective term. It is as much defined by the effect a behavior has upon an individual as it is by the intention behind it. Students who bully come from a range of backgrounds; there are no social class distinctions associated with this form of behavior. Bullies can be confident, strong, feel personally secure, and popular when compared to peers. They can be anxious, academically weak, less popular, and have insecurities about the way they look, their abilities (as a result of school failure), or their status (few friends). Finally, the most unpopular students of all are bully victims: bullies in one situation and victims in another (Sullivan, 2000).

Various studies have suggested that students who bully come from particular backgrounds. Parents who are themselves aggressive and bullied others

Table 9.2.
Student Behavior Record for Teachers

Student Name: _____   Class: _____

Date observation commenced: ____/____/____   Grade: _____

Type of Observation	Day	Number of observations per day/week							
		Wk 1	Wk 2	Wk 3	Wk 4	Wk 5	Wk 6	Wk 7	Wk 8
Outbursts of anger, discipline problems, or lost or missing homework	Mon	—	—	—	—	—	—	—	—
	Tue	—	—	—	—	—	—	—	—
	Wed	—	—	—	—	—	—	—	—
	Thu	—	—	—	—	—	—	—	—
	Fri	—	—	—	—	—	—	—	—
Unexplained cuts and bruises, or torn and mud-splattered clothing	Mon	—	—	—	—	—	—	—	—
	Tue	—	—	—	—	—	—	—	—
	Wed	—	—	—	—	—	—	—	—
	Thu	—	—	—	—	—	—	—	—
	Fri	—	—	—	—	—	—	—	—
Absences, staying in at recess and lunch, or delaying going home	Mon	—	—	—	—	—	—	—	—
	Tue	—	—	—	—	—	—	—	—
	Wed	—	—	—	—	—	—	—	—
	Thu	—	—	—	—	—	—	—	—
	Fri	—	—	—	—	—	—	—	—
Withdrawal, tearfulness, forgetfulness, or easily distracted	Mon	—	—	—	—	—	—	—	—
	Tue	—	—	—	—	—	—	—	—
	Wed	—	—	—	—	—	—	—	—
	Thu	—	—	—	—	—	—	—	—
	Fri	—	—	—	—	—	—	—	—

Table 9.3.
Student Behavior Record for Parents

Name: _____ Date observation commenced: ____ / ____ / ____

Type of Observation	Day	Number of observations per day/week							
		Wk 1	Wk 2	Wk 3	Wk 4	Wk 5	Wk 6	Wk 7	Wk 8
Outbursts of anger, discipline problems, forgetfulness, easily distracted, flinches, tiredness, or loss of appetite.	Mon	—	—	—	—	—	—	—	—
	Tue	—	—	—	—	—	—	—	—
	Wed	—	—	—	—	—	—	—	—
	Thu	—	—	—	—	—	—	—	—
	Fri	—	—	—	—	—	—	—	—
	Sat	—	—	—	—	—	—	—	—
	Sun	—	—	—	—	—	—	—	—
Unexplained cuts and bruises, torn or mud-splattered clothing, or lost or missing homework.	Mon	—	—	—	—	—	—	—	—
	Tue	—	—	—	—	—	—	—	—
	Wed	—	—	—	—	—	—	—	—
	Thu	—	—	—	—	—	—	—	—
	Fri	—	—	—	—	—	—	—	—
	Sat	—	—	—	—	—	—	—	—
	Sun	—	—	—	—	—	—	—	—
Sudden headaches, stomachaches, or requests to stay at home rather than go to school. Also for younger children, bed-wetting, nightmares, or sleep walking	Mon	—	—	—	—	—	—	—	—
	Tue	—	—	—	—	—	—	—	—
	Wed	—	—	—	—	—	—	—	—
	Thu	—	—	—	—	—	—	—	—
	Fri	—	—	—	—	—	—	—	—
	Sat	—	—	—	—	—	—	—	—
	Sun	—	—	—	—	—	—	—	—

in school, use corporal punishment, and adhere to a strict hierarchical structure within the family may find that their children exhibit similar traits at school. Students who bully are sometimes from lower socioeconomic groups than their victims, though this is by no means the rule, and certainly, some researchers have found only very weak links between bullying and socioeconomic status (see, for example, Olweus, 1980). Bullying is sometimes the result of family breakups, the birth of a younger brother or sister, loss of a friendship group, or indeed high parental and school expectations (Besag, 1989). Whatever the reasons underlying a child's or young person's bullying behavior, it is impossible to identify the "type" of student who will bully in the future. Furthermore, it should not be assumed that a student who bullies others cannot change (Sullivan, 2000).

What Are the Telltale Signs My Child Is a Bully?

For parents, the key signs to look out for include changes in friendship groups (particularly the loss of a friendship group), a decline in grades and expressions of disaffection with school, a desire to "show off," ownership of items or goods that could not have been bought without your knowledge, low self-esteem, expressed anger or irritation with fellow students (including making disparaging comments about them or threatening to hit them), frustration with homework, or trying to dominate or otherwise subjugate siblings.

What Do I Need to Know?

It is important that parents understand their liability in situations where their son or daughter is accused of perpetrating an assault (which in twenty-four states includes bullying behavior). Basically, parents can be found directly negligent if they are aware of their child's wrongful behavior that is likely to cause harm to others. Whilst the majority of these statutes relate to gun crime, parental liability can include providing a child with access to a dangerous implement, and covers the intentional actions of a child in the perpetration of harm or injury to another. In determining negligence, courts take into account the following:

- In cases where a child or young person has a history of aggressive or violent behavior, have parents made a reasonable effort in trying to prevent its recurrence?
- Did parents respond appropriately to previous acts?
- Have their subsequent efforts to control the child's behavior been reasonable?
- Should and could they have prevented the incident that has brought them to the attention of the courts?
- Were there efforts in trying to prevent the specific incident reasonable?

The majority of states (excluding Delaware and Maryland) now have laws that clearly define parental liability for any and all damage caused by their children. These laws cover willful and malicious acts, property damage, property damage and personal injury in schools, hotels, and other specific community venues, and negligence while driving (Redding and Shalf, 2001). The financial impact of parental liability varies from state to state, ranging from $800–$25,000. The average is about $5,000 although three states do not impose any limit (Redding and Shalf, 2001).

The following table (Table 9.4), taken from New Jersey Care about Bullying, Office of Bias Crime, and Community Relations, gives an indication of the types of behaviors that might result in legal proceedings.

What Do I Do?

The first thing any parent needs to do is to ascertain whether or not the behavior of which their child is accused is, in fact, bullying. Therefore immediate contact with the school should be sought. If it is a one-off incident, then it is not necessarily bullying. It is generally agreed by those who have researched bullying over the past forty years that bullying is a persistent problem: it is repeatedly occurring over days, weeks, months, and even years. It is not bullying when two students of equal size and strength have a disagreement that turns into a fight. However, it is bullying where there is clearly an imbalance of power (it may be in terms of physical size or strength, or it may be in terms of the number of perpetrators). Any aggressive interaction between students should be dealt with quickly and effectively by a member of school staff, but it is important that those staff do not jump to conclusions about the nature of the behavior they have witnessed.

In cases where parents are contacted by a school for the first time about their child's bullying behavior, it is important that nonpunitive interventions feature at the top of the agenda. It is all too easy for a principal to suggest the suspension of a student, and most states recommend or require that schools work with students in developing nonviolent conflict resolution skills (see Appendix). It is also important that parents do not condone or reinforce such behavior by suggesting the fault lies elsewhere. An aggressive interaction has taken place, and whether one or both students acted inappropriately is not really important. What is important is the fact that the actions of one student have had a detrimental effect upon another. Thus parents should not trivialize such behavior or suggest that it will pass with time, or overemphasize self-protection. Similarly, it is important not to threaten corporal punishment as a response to bullying as it will only reinforce such behavior and send mixed messages.

In most cases, the school will have a range of options open to it, some of which might include family therapy, or counseling. Parents who are keen to work with a school in developing a program that will address their child's

Table 9.4.
Bullying Behavior Chart

Physical Bullying — Harm to someone's body or property		Emotional Bullying — Harm to someone's self-esteem or feeling of safety		Social Bullying — Harm to someone's group acceptance	
Verbal	*Nonverbal*	*Verbal*	*Nonverbal*	*Verbal*	*Nonverbal*
LEVEL ONE					
• Expressing physical superiority • Blaming the victim for starting the conflict	• Making threatening gestures • Defacing property • Pushing/shoving • Taking small items from others	• Insulting remarks • Calling names • Teasing about possessions, clothes, physical appearance	• Giving dirty looks • Holding nose or other insulting gestures	• Gossiping • Starting or spreading rumors • Teasing publicly about clothes, looks, relationships with boys/girls, etc.	• Ignoring someone and excluding them from a group
LEVEL TWO (some of these behaviors are against the law)					
• Threatening physical harm	• Damaging property • Stealing • Starting fights • Scratching or biting • Pushing, tripping, or causing a fall • Assaulting	• Insulting family • Harassing with phone calls • Insulting your size, intelligence, athletic ability, race, color, religion, ethnicity, gender, disability, or sexual orientation	• Defacing school work or other personal property, such as clothing, locker, or books • Saying someone is related to a person considered an enemy of this country (e.g., Osama bin Laden)	• Ostracizing using notes, Instant Messaging, e-mail, etc. • Posting slander in public places (such as writing derogatory comments about someone in the school bath room)	• Playing mean tricks to embarrass someone

(Continued)

Table 9.4. (Continued)

Physical Bullying Harm to someone's body or property		Emotional Bullying Harm to someone's self-esteem or feeling of safety		Social Bullying Harm to someone's group acceptance	
Verbal	Nonverbal	Verbal	Nonverbal	Verbal	Nonverbal
		LEVEL THREE (most of these behaviors are against the law)			
• Making repeated and/or graphic threats (harassing) • Practicing extortion (such as taking lunch money) • Threatening to keep someone silent: "If you tell, it will be a lot worse!"	• Destroying property • Setting fires • Physical cruelty • Repeatedly acting in a violent, threatening manner • Assaulting with a weapon	• Harassing you because of bias against your race, color, religion, ethnicity, gender, disability, or sexual orientation	• Destroying personal property, such as clothing, books, jewelry • Writing graffiti with bias against your race, color, religion, ethnicity, gender, disability, or sexual orientation	• Enforcing total group exclusion against someone by threatening others if they don't comply	• Arranging public humiliation

Source: New Jersey Cares About Bullying, Office of Bias Crime and Community Relations; Adapted from Atlantic Prevention Resources.

behavior problems need to be receptive to a suggested course of action. In addition, they should make a commitment to work with their children to help them understand the effect their behavior has upon others.

In elementary school, it is sometimes the case that larger and more boisterous students may not be aware that their playful behavior can hurt others, and so it is helpful if parents talk to their children and try to deflect their boisterousness by supporting them in the pursuit of activities and pastimes that allow them to use up excess energy. Quite often we also find that students do not realize that name-calling and social isolation are forms of bullying. In some cases, students may have resorted to such behavior in place of hitting out, and it is a useful exercise to talk through other ways in which they could have responded (walking away initially and then trying to talk to the individual one-on-one, or through the mediation of a teacher or parent). (This type of response requires a certain degree of maturity, and many statewide conflict resolution initiatives include skills such as this.)

Sometimes students who are accused of bullying do not realize that the behavior they have modeled has been taken up by others when they are not there. It is helpful to provide students with an opportunity to reflect upon their actions and consider how others would have viewed what they have done. Students can also confuse leadership with dominance, and they need to understand the difference between the two and be provided with alternative models of leadership. In secondary school, it may be possible for a student to visit workplaces or attend talks by state legislators to see how leadership is demonstrated in other contexts. It is also helpful if parents monitor their children's television viewing habits. Where do their models of human interaction come from? Are they from the television? Sometimes they may be from within the home environment (as a result of changes in family circumstances, relationship breakup, or even moving house). Try to give the school as much information as possible, and try not to be embarrassed or circumspect about family difficulties. The more insights and information that a parent can offer about the origins of a student's behavior, the more likely it is that the principal, teachers, and counselors can offer solutions, and the less likely it is that they will recommend suspension.

SUMMARY

Schools are partners in the raising of children and young people to become responsible citizens, and as such always try to work in the best interests of their students. With the active cooperation of parents, and the support of state and national legislators, bullying can become a thing of the past. Perpetrators and victims of bullying are not born, they are made, and it is only through education that we can eradicate this form of behavior for good. Work with your local school to make it safe for all young people.

Tips for Parents

✎ Don't be afraid to talk to the school principal or class teacher if you have concerns that your son/daughter is being bullied.

✎ Talk to other parents.

✎ Check what your school should be doing to tackle bullying.

✎ Be prepared for any meeting you have at school.

✎ If you think your child is a perpetrator or victim of bullying, watch his/her behavior—use the checklist provided in Table 9.3.

✎ If bullying is not addressed in your school, find out about SDFSCA funding.

✎ If your child is accused of bullying others, consider the possibility that it may be true, and work with the school to find a solution that does not involve a school change or suspension.

Tips for Educators

✎ Listen to parents concerns about bullying in the school.

✎ Make sure you are familiar with the mandatory requirements of *No Child Left Behind* and the SDFSCA.

✎ If you have not done so already, try applying for SDFSCA funds through the local education authority and ensure that parents are advisors and collaborators in the bid.

✎ Don't prejudge students whom you perceive to be "bullies."

APPENDIX: STATE GUIDANCE ON ADDRESSING BULLYING, HARASSMENT, AND FIGHTING IN SCHOOLS

Edited and reproduced with permission from the National Association of State Boards of Education. Readers are recommended to check the NASBE website regularly for updates at http://www.nasbe.org/.

Alabama

The Alabama Course of Study: Health Education (2003) sets the minimum required content standard for teaching students about bullying and harassment. In grade 4, students discuss non-violent solutions to conflicts among youth in schools and communities by reporting bullying and weapons brought to school. In grade 7, students are taught to apply assertiveness, negotiation, and refusal skills to situations involving health risks, including objecting to bullying. Students in grades 6–7 study ways to protect oneself and others from sexual harassment and how to respond appropriately to such situations.

Alaska

Bullying is not specifically addressed, however the State Board has adopted content standards in Skills for a Healthy Life (1999) that recommend students learn conflict resolution skills. The Board has also adopted content standards in Skills for a Healthy Life recommend students learn how to "recognize patterns of abuse directed at self or others and understand how to break these patterns."

Arizona

Bullying is not specifically addressed, however, Standard 5 of the Comprehensive Health Education Standards (1997) requires students in grades K–12 be taught non-violent conflict resolution skills.

Arkansas

Code 6-18-514 (2003) requires all local school boards to adopt policies to prevent pupil harassment (bullying). The policies must clearly define conduct that constitutes bullying; prohibit bullying on school property, at school-sponsored activities, and on school buses; state the consequences of bullying; require school employees to report any incidents to the principal; require bullying notices to be posted in every classroom, cafeteria, restroom, gymnasium, auditorium, and school bus in the district; and provide copies of the notice to parents, students, school volunteers, and all employees. This statute also expands Code 6-18-1005(5)(c) (2003) by requiring student services program to include programs to prevent bullying as part of its group conflict resolution service.

California

Bullying is not specifically addressed, however, Education Code §51266 calls for the Office of Criminal Justice Planning, in collaboration with the California Department of Education, to develop a model gang violence suppression and substance abuse prevention curriculum for grades 2, 4, and 6. The Office of Criminal Justice Planning is further asked to develop an independent evaluation of pupil outcomes of the model gang violence suppression and substance abuse prevention curricular program.

Colorado

Statute 22-32-109.1 (2005) requires district boards of education to adopt a specific policy concerning bullying education. This statute also encourages school districts to develop "a comprehensive, age-appropriate curriculum that teaches safety in working and interacting on the Internet," which addresses "recognition and avoidance of on-line bullying." Statute 22-25-104.5 (2000) creates the prevention initiatives unit within the Department of Education, aimed at reducing the incidence of gangs in public schools through education. Districts are urged to implement age appropriate law-related educational programs to specifically address antisocial gang behavior. If implemented, such programs must meet certain topic requirements and guidelines stated within this statute. The Statute also urges districts to implement law-related educational programs, which may include instruction in mediation and conflict resolution.

Connecticut

Standard 2 of the Health and Safety Education Curriculum Framework (1998) recommends students in grades K–12 learn how to avoid and reduce any form of sexual harassment. Standard 2 of the Health and Safety Education Curriculum Framework recommends students in grades K–12 learn non-violent conflict resolution skills. Students in grades 5–12 should learn strategies to reduce and avoid abuse and assault. Statute Chapter 164 Sec. 10-6b (1997) requires public schools to provide instruction in safety education, which may include the dangers of gang membership.

Delaware

The Delaware Health Education Curriculum Framework (2001) provides content standards, which include teaching students in grades K–12 how to deal with and avoid bullies. The frameworks also include teaching middle school students how to handle and identify sexual harassment. The Framework provides content standards, which include teaching conflict resolution and violence prevention in grades K–12.

Florida

Bullying is not specifically addressed, however, H.E.B. 1.1.6, 1.2.5, and 1.3.5 of the Sunshine State Standards for Health and Physical Education (1996) call for instruction not only strategies to avoid threatening situations but also how to seek help when needed in grades K–8. In addition, H.E.B. 3.1.7, 3.2.6, 3.2.7, 3.3.6, 3.3.7, 3.4.6, and 3.4.7 require students in K–12 receive instruction on knowing various ways to resolve conflict using non-violent, positive behavior, and understanding the possible causes of conflict among youth in schools and communities. Statute 1006.07(6) (2004) requires district school boards to provide for the welfare of students by using the Safety and Security Best Practices to conduct a self-assessment of the district's current safety and security practices. The self-assessment includes indicators for districts to adopt violence and drug prevention, safety and health curricula and programs and to teach students at each grade level violence prevention, conflict resolution, and communication/decision making skills.

Georgia

The Quality Core Curriculum Standards and Resources recommend resources and curricula for teaching, as required, bullying prevention in grades K–12 and sexual harassment in grades 9–12. The Quality Core Curriculum Standards and Resources recommend curricula and resources for teaching students, as required, about abuse in grades K–7, conflict resolution skills in grades K–12, and the causes of conflict and strategies on how to handle them, including gangs, in grade 8.

Hawaii

Standard 5 of Hawaii's Health Content Standards (2005) recommends students in grades K–5 are taught strategies to avoid inappropriate communications. Standard 5 of Hawaii's Health Content Standards recommends students in grades K–3 and 9–12 are taught non-violent conflict resolution strategies, such as collaboration and negotiation.

Idaho

Bullying is not specifically addressed.

Illinois

ILCS 5/27-23.7 (2006) requires school districts "to make suitable provisions for instruction in bullying prevention in all grades." "Bullying prevention" includes instruction in intimidation, student victimization, sexual harassment, sexual violence and strategies for student-centered problem solving regarding bullying. Violence prevention and conflict resolution education are mandated for students in grades 4–12 under 105 ILCS 5/27-23.4 (1995). Public schools may incorporate anti-bias education and inter-group conflict resolution under 105 ILCS 5/27-23.6 (2000). Goal 24 of the Illinois Learning Standards for Physical Development and Health recommends late elementary aged students learn the causes and consequences of conflict among youth and which situations refusal skills are necessary, such as instances of physical abuse or when approached to join a gang. Middle school and junior high aged students should learn the possible causes and consequences of conflict and violence among youth. Early high school aged students should learn the effects of conflict and violence on individual, family, and community health and strategies for conflict resolution and prevention. Late high school aged students should learn different strategies for preventing conflict and resolving differences.

Indiana

Standard 3 of the Indiana Academic Standards for Health Education (2002) recommends students in grade 1 be taught how to avoid fights with bullies and recommends students in grades 5 and 9 be taught how to handle unwanted sexual attention and sexual assault. Standard 5 of the Indiana Academic Standards for Health Education recommends students in grades K–10 be taught conflict resolution skills. Standard 3 recommends students in grades 1 and 8–10 be taught how to avoid fights and similar threatening situations, how to avoid and report weapons in grade 4, and how to report and handle physical, emotional, and mental abuse in grade 7.

Iowa

Bullying is not specifically addressed, however, Code 280.9B (2005) requires the department of education to contract with a law-related education agency that serves the state and provides a comprehensive plan to develop violence prevention program based on law-related education for grades K–12, provide training for teachers and administrators, and develop school-community partnerships.

Kansas

No state policy.

Kentucky

Bullying is not specifically addressed. The Program of Studies requires students in grades K–12 be taught conflict and anger resolution strategies. Students in high school are required to be taught the different definitions of abuse and strategies for prevention.

Louisiana

Upon approval of its governing authority, RS 17:416.17 (2001) authorizes elementary schools to develop and offer youth development and assistance programs for students in kindergarten and elementary grades. The statute further allows the programs to include the services of behavioral training and intervention techniques for conflict resolution skills, peer mediation, anger management, and bullying prevention. Standard 5 of the Health Education Content Standards requires students to receive instruction in non-violent conflict resolution. RS 17:13.1 (1992) requires the State Department of Education to develop and implement minimum guidelines for a program on prevention of crime and disruptive behavior in public schools, which includes coordination of school safety programs and any other existing programs that address gang membership and violence.

Maine

Standard 3 of Education Rule Chapter 131 (1997) requires students in grades 3–12 be taught how to deal with and avoid threatening situations, such as physical, emotional, and sexual abuse. Standard 5 requires students in grades 3–12 be taught conflict resolution skills and other non-violent strategies to resolve conflicts.

Maryland

Not specifically required but incorporated into health education and guidance lessons.

Massachusetts

Standard 9 of the Massachusetts Comprehensive Health Framework recommends students are taught how to deal with bullying through role-play in grades K–5. Standard 11 recommends students in grades 6–8 learn about bullying and its effects through videos and discussion. The Standard also recommends students be taught how to define harassment based on gender, race, national origin, sexual orientation, religion, or handicap in grades 9–12. Standard 11 recommends students in grades 6–12 are taught the social, mental, emotional, and legal consequences of harassment. Standards 9 and 11 recommend students in grades 6–12 be taught how to recognize and get help for the various types of abuse. Standard 11 recommends students in grades K–12 are taught the factors leading to violence, conflict resolution skills, and how to identify helpful resources concerning violence and reasons why people join gangs and how gangs undermine the community and lead to violence.

Michigan

The Policy on Quality Character Education (2004) recommends that schools adopt a secular character education program focused on developing positive relationships and prosocial norms to decrease negative behaviors such as bullying. The Michigan Model for Comprehensive School Health Education, specifically referenced as a guide for schools to meet the State Board's recommendation, contains violence prevention modules with bullying and harassment specific lessons for grades K–12. The Health Education Content Standards and Benchmarks (1998) recommend minimum content standards for teaching avoidance and reduction of conflicts and threatening situations in grades K–12, non-violent strategies to resolve conflicts in grades K–12, and how to solve interpersonal problems without harming others in grades 9–12.

Minnesota

Statute 120B.22 (2000) encourages each district to integrate a program for violence prevention into its existing curriculum that includes: a comprehensive, accurate, and age appropriate curriculum on sexual, racial, and cultural harassment, and student hazing; planning materials, guidelines, and other accurate information on prevention sexual, racial, and cultural harassment. Statute 120B.22 encourages each district to integrate a program for violence prevention into its existing curriculum that includes a curriculum on non-violent conflict resolution.

Mississippi

Code §37-11-54 (2003) calls the State Board of Education to develop a list of recommended conflict resolution and mediation materials, models, and curricula that addresses causes and effects of school violence, harassment, and non-violent methods for resolving conflicts. The Comprehensive Health Framework (2006) provides guidelines for instruction in conflict resolution in grades 2 and 9–12. Code §37-11-54 calls for the State Board of Education to develop a list of recommended conflict resolution and mediation materials, models, and curricula that addresses causes and effects of school violence, harassment, and non-violent methods for resolving conflicts.

Missouri

The Missouri Violence Prevention Curriculum Framework recommends strategies to prevent students from becoming abusers of others by bullying and harassment. The Framework recommends conflict resolution be taught in district schools and for the use of community resources, such as DARE officer, for gang awareness education in district schools. Rule 5 CSR 50-350.030 (1999) requires the department of elementary and secondary education to identify and, if necessary, adopt a program regarding violence prevention that includes instruction for students on the negative consequences of membership and/or participation in criminal gang activity. Revised Statute 161.650 requires the department of elementary and secondary education to identify and adopt programs to be administered by public school districts regarding violence prevention. The program should include instructing students on the negative consequences of membership in or association with criminal street gangs or participation in a criminal street gang activity. Revised Statute 170.046 (1995) requires the department of health and senior services, in consultation with the department of elementary and secondary education, to develop program materials known as "School-Based Nonviolent Conflict Resolution" for use by school districts. The Statute allows the program to be presented to students in grades K–12 at least once each school year; however, academic credit cannot be received for participation in this program.

Montana

No state policy that specifically addresses bullying. However, the teaching of the causes of interpersonal conflict and conflict resolution are addressed in Administrative Rules 10.54.7087 (1999) for grade 4 and 10.54.7092 (1999) for grade 8. Administrative Rules 10.54.7061 (1999), 10.54.7062 (1999), and 10.54.7063 (1999) establish grade level benchmarks for Health Enhancement Program content, which includes for all grades the teaching of non-violent strategies to resolve conflicts. The teaching of the causes of interpersonal conflict and conflict resolution are also addressed in Administrative Rules 10.54.7087 for grade 4 and 10.54.7092 for grade 8.

Nebraska

Bullying is not specifically addressed. Principle 5 of the Nebraska Health Education Frameworks (1998) recommends students be taught conflict resolution skills in grades K–12. Principle 3 recommends students be taught how to avoid fighting and violence in grades 3–12. Principle 1 recommends students in grades 6–8 be taught conflict management.

Nevada

NAC 389.2423 (2000) and Standard 3 of the Health Content Standards (2000) require students by the end of grade 2 to learn about the characteristics of bullies and by the end of grade 5 to learn the consequences of harassment. NAC 389.281, 389.2944, 389.381, and 389.455 requires students by the end of grades 3, 5, 9, and 12 to learn how to identify and report abusive behavior, about sources of help for protection from neglect and physical, emotional, or sexual abuse, and the causes and effects of child abuse. Standard 1 of the Health Content Standards requires students by the end of grade 5 to learn procedures to protect oneself from violence. Standard 3 requires students by the end of grades 5 and 8 to learn the consequences of fighting, anger management, and applicable conflict resolution skills. Standard 5 requires students by the end of grades 3, 5, 8, and 12 to learn the causes, associated behaviors, and ways to manage and resolve conflict.

New Hampshire

The Health Education Curriculum Guidelines (2003) recommend students learn how to avoid and deal with bullying in elementary and middle school and recognize sexual harassment in high school. Standards 4 and 5 of the K–12 Career Development Framework (2000) require students learn conflict resolution skills. The Health Education Curriculum Guidelines (2003) recommend students learn the causes of conflict, conflict resolution techniques, avoidance, and non-violent ways to calm charged situations in grades K–12. Recognition of abuse is also recommended for learning in elementary school.

New Jersey

N.J.S.A. 18A: 37-15 requires each school district to adopt a policy prohibiting harassment, intimidation and bullying, which includes consequences and remedial actions for offenders. N.J.S.A. 18A: 37-17 (2002) encourages schools to establish bullying prevention programs and other initiative involving school staff, students, administrators, volunteers, parents, law enforcement and community members. Standard 2.1 of the CCCS for Comprehensive Health and Physical Education (2004) requires students learn social and emotional health skills, including strategies to recognize and deal with bullying and harassment. Standard 2.2 requires students learn how to seek help when bullied by the end of grade 2. Standard 2.1 of the CCCS for Comprehensive Health and Physical Education requires students to learn social and emotional health skills, including conflict resolution and prevention.

New Mexico

New Mexico has no specific policy for bullying or harassment education. However, Content Standard 3 in 6.30.2.19 NMAC and Content Standard 5 of the Health Education Standards set required benchmarks for teaching students in grades K–12 ways to avoid and reduce threatening situations. 6.30.2.19 NMAC details the Health Education Standards content standards with benchmarks and performance standards for health education, which include safe schools and conflict resolution prevention education for grades K–12. Local schools are required to align health education curriculum to the performance standards. The Health Education Standards sets required benchmarks for teaching students in grades K–12 non-violent conflict resolution strategies, the difference between positive and negative behaviors in conflict situations, and the causes of conflict according to Content Standard 5.

New York

Bullying in not specifically addressed. Standard 2 of the Learning Standards for Health, Physical Education, and Family and Consumer Sciences (1996) requires students learn how to reduce and avoid threatening situations at the elementary level, conflict management and negotiation skills, the causes of conflict in school, and ways to reduce and avoid threatening peer situations at the intermediate level, and strategies to avoid or cope with potentially dangerous situations such as assault at the commencement level.

North Carolina

Competency Goal 4 of the Healthful Living Education (2001) requires students learn how to respond to teasing and bullying in grade 2. Competency Goal 4 of the Healthful Living Education requires students in grades 1, 5, and 9–12 learn how to resolve conflicts without fighting. Goal 2 requires students learn anger management in grades 2–3 and 5.

North Dakota

Standard 5 of the North Dakota Health Content Standards (2000) recommends content standards and gives examples of specific knowledge and activities for teaching students possible causes of conflicts in schools, families, and communities and strategies to prevent conflicts in these situations in grades 9–12, which includes bullying. Standard 5 recommends content standards and gives examples of specific knowledge and activities for teaching students possible causes of conflicts in schools, families, and communities and strategies to prevent conflicts in these situations in grades 9–12, which includes gangs.

Ohio

Bullying is not specifically addressed. As part of the health education requirements under ORC §3313.60 (2001), students in grades K–6 must receive instruction in "personal safety and assault prevention."

Oklahoma

The PASS Integrated Curriculum: Health, Safety and Physical Education (2002) recommends students be taught how to identify bullying, how to diffuse and avoid bullies, how to report bullying, and the difference between teasing and bullying, and how to identify different types of harassment in grades 1–4 (Standards 4 & 5). The Curriculum also recommends students be taught anger management (Standards 3–5), how to avoid threatening situations (Standard 3), violence prevention (Standards 1 & 3), non-violent conflict resolution (Standards 3–5), how to report violence (Standard 3), and abuse protection strategies (Standard 1) in grades 1–12.

Oregon

The Health Education Standards recommend students in grades K–12 be taught how to identify, handle, and report bullying and harassment and about its effect on health and safety. The Health Education Standards recommend students in grades K–12 be taught non-violent conflict management skills, anger management, and how to avoid physical violence.

Pennsylvania

Standard 10.3 of the Academic Standards for Health, Safety, and Physical Education (2003) requires that students be taught how to recognize unsafe practices, such as bullying, by the end of grade 3 and requires students be taught personal safety practices, such as how to handle and avoid harassment, by the end of grade 6. Fighting/Gangs: Standard 10.3 of the Academic Standards for Health, Safety, and Physical Education requires students be taught how to recognize, analyze, avoid, and resolve conflicts and violence by the end of grades 3, 6, 9, and 12. Such strategies include anger management, peer mediation, reflective listening, negotiation, refusal skills, adult intervention, walking away, and assertive behavior. The standard also requires students be taught violence prevention practices, such as avoiding gangs, by the end of grade 6.

Rhode Island

General Law §16-21-26 (2003) requires district school boards to adopt a policy prohibiting bullying and harassment, and recommends the policy address education about such behavior. Standard 5 of Rhode Island's Health Education Framework (1996) requires students in grades K–12 to learn non-violent conflict resolution strategies, the difference between positive and negative responses in conflicts, the causes of conflict, and conflict prevention. Standard 3 requires students in grades K–10 to be taught how to reduce and avoid threatening situations.

South Carolina

No state policy on bullying. Content Areas 3 and 4 of the Health and Safety Standards (2000) require students to be taught non-violent strategies for resolving and managing conflicts, the causes of conflict amongst youth, the causes and effects of violence, media and cultural effects on violent behaviors, and resources for helping to deal with violent and abusive behavior by the end of grades 5, 8, and 12.

South Dakota

Bullying is not specifically addressed. The state does not require students to receive instruction on this subject. However, the South Dakota Health Education Standards (2000) recommends students in grades K–12 be taught conflict resolution techniques such as negotiation skills.

Tennessee

Standard 9 of the School Counseling & Career Guidance Standards (2001) recommends students learn the consequences of bullying and harassment in grades 3–5 and techniques for handling overt and subtle bullying in grades K–12. Lifetime Wellness: Grades 9–12 (2000) requires students learn socially acceptable ways of resolving interpersonal conflict by practicing non-abusive behavior. Standard 9 of the School Counseling & Career Guidance Standards recommends students learn how to recognize physical and sexual abuse in grades 3–5 and conflict management and the emotional effects of abuse in grades 6–8.

Texas

The Texas Essential Knowledge and Skills for Health Education the ethical and legal ramifications of harassment are taught in grades 9–10. It recommends personal and interpersonal skills is taught, including conflict resolution, in grades 1, 3–4, 6–8, & 11–12. It is also recommended that students be taught how to identify and respond to/prevent the various forms of abuse (physical, emotional, sexual) in grades 3–10. Gang prevention measures are also recommended to be taught in grades 3–8.

Utah

The Health Education Core sets standards for students in grades 7–12 to be taught how to identify those behaviors that may lead to sexual harassment and how to manage sexual harassment. The Core requires students in grades 2, 4, and 7–12 be taught the causes of conflict and conflict resolution/management skills. Students in grades 3 and 6–8 are also to be taught abuse prevention strategies, how to identify abuse, and how to manage abusive situations. R277–436 (1999) recommends gang prevention instruction by establishing rules and procedures for distributing funds for gang prevention and intervention programs.

Vermont

Standard 1 of the Vermont Standards and Learning Expectations requires students in grades 5–6 be taught how to avoid or change situations that threaten personal safety, such as bullying and harassment. Students in grades 7–8 must also learn the difference between hazing, bullying, harassment, and respectful interactions/relationships. Health content to be integrated into these GEs is to include how bullying, hazing, and harassment affects others and strategies to deal with this issue. Standard 1 also requires students in grades 5–6 be taught how to avoid or change situations that threaten personal safety, such as abuse. Standard 5 requires students in grades 1–12 be taught diverse non-violent methods for resolving conflict, such as negotiation and refusal skills. Health content to be integrated into these GEs is to include safety practices for unsafe or abusive situations for students in grades PreK–4, signs of emotional, physical, and sexual abuse in grades 5–8.

Virginia

The Health Education Standards of Learning (2001) requires students to be taught how to identify bullying behaviors in grade 4. Code §22.1-208.01 (2005) requires local school boards to establish character education programs, which must address the inappropriateness of bullying. The Health Education Standards of Learning also requires students be taught the relationship between self-image and gang-related behaviors in grade 6. Students are also taught resistance skills to avoid violence, gangs, weapons, and drugs in grade 6 and 10. Alternatives to gang-related behavior are taught in grade 7 and 8. Students are to be taught about the risks associated with gang-related activities. The standards also require students to be taught the conflict resolution and non-violent/peaceful strategies, the impact of verbal and nonverbal aggressive, and the consequences of acts of violence in grades 2–10.

Washington

The Health and Fitness Essential Academic Learning Requirements (2002) mandate students learn how to identify risky situations, such as bullying and harassment, and safe behaviors to prevent injury to self and others.

West Virginia

Standard 3 of Board Policy 2520.5 requires students to receive instruction in potentially dangerous situations, such as bullying and how to obtain help appropriately in grades 5–6 and 9–12. Standard 3 of Board Policy 2520.5 also requires students to receive instruction in protective behaviors used to avoid and reduce threatening situations, such as harassment, in grades 4–6 and 9–12. Standard 4 requires students to learn the types of harassment and their impact on health in grades 7–8. Standard 7 requires students to learn the ramifications of bullying and how to identify resources advocating against bullying and harassment in grade 8. Code §18-2C-5 (no date available) requires each district to develop a process for educating student on the harassment, intimidation, or bullying policy to the extent fund are appropriated. Standard 5 in Board Policy 2520.5 requires students to receive instruction in conflict management and resolution in grades 3, 5–6, and 8. Standard 3 requires students learn anger management and protective behaviors in grades 5–6 and 9–12 and recognize and report self-destructive behaviors, such as gang membership, in grade 8. Standard 7 requires students learn how to identify resources advocating against violence in grade 8. Code §18-2-7b (no date available) requires the State Board prescribe programs for training students in conflict resolution skills.

Wisconsin

Wisconsin's Sticks and Stones Bully Prevention Curriculum (2002) can be a stand-alone or integrated set of curricula which teaches students in grades K–12 anti-bullying and anti-harassment lessons and skills Standard F of Wisconsin's Model Academic Standards for Health Education (1997) recommends students by the end of grades 4, 8, and 12 be taught how to identify the possible causes of conflict and strategies to prevent and resolve them without harming self or others. Standard B recommends students by the end of grades 4, 8, and 12 be taught ways to avoid and reduce threatening situations.

Wyoming

Bullying is not specifically addressed. Standards 3 and 5 of the Wyoming Health Content and Performance Standards (2003) recommend students in grades K–12 be taught conflict resolution skills.

REFERENCES

Besag, V. E. (1989). *Bullies and Victims in Schools*. Milton Keynes, UK: Open University Press.

Cósti, M. (2003). *School Phobia, Panic Attacks and Anxiety in Children*. London, UK: Jessica Kingsley.

Limber, S. P., and Small, M. A. (2003). State laws and policies to address bullying in schools. *School Psychology Review*, 32, 445–455.

Office of Safe and Drug-Free Schools [Online, November 2006]. http://www.ed.gov/about/offices/list/osdfs/index.html.

Olweus, D. (1980). Familial and temperamental determinants of aggressive behavior in adolescent boys: A causal analysis. *Developmental Psychology*, 16, 644–660.

Redding, R. E., and Shalf, S. M. (2001). The legal context of school violence: The effectiveness of federal, state, and local law enforcement efforts to reduce gun violence in schools. *Law & Policy*, 23, 297–343.

Sullivan, K. (2000). *The Anti-Bullying Handbook*. Auckland, New Zealand: Oxford University Press.

U.S. Department of Education. Choice and Supplemental Educational Services. Last updated September 14, 2004 [Online, November 2006]. http://www.ed.gov/parents/schools/choice/choice.html.

U.S. Department of Education. Questions and Answers on *No Child Left Behind*. Last updated November 27, 2004 [Online, November 2006]. http://www.ed.gov/nclb/freedom/safety/creating.html.

PART IV

The Way Ahead

CHAPTER 10

Beyond Childish Antics

Bullying remains a perennial problem in public schools. Despite the implementation of various initiatives since the early 1990s, it continues to thrive. It would seem that those factors that impact upon the continued presence of bullying in student subculture include our failure as adults to engage early enough with the potential of new technologies, and the persistence of belief systems and practices that value one student above another. Studies have already shown the significant impact our failure to tackle bullying has upon student achievement. Schwartz and colleagues (2005) found that, among elementary school students, depression arising from peer group victimization has a significant impact upon scores for SAT-9 Math, SAT-9 Reading, and overall grade point average (GPA). Disrupting a student's learning at one or more critical points in development is likely to result in the crystallization of antischool sentiments, and the further erosion of learning potential. Gazelle and Ladd (2002) have suggested that it is only through the introduction of specialized educational assistance as well as anti-bullying interventions that students who have been the victims of persistent bullying can recover lost learning potential. Such specialized educational assistance may involve one-on-one tuition or additional classes to recover lost ground, and this comes at considerable financial cost to a district and to parents. In essence, it is far easier to address all forms of bullying at an early age and regularly address them through annual audits or surveys, and regular refresher courses or programs for teachers. Indeed, Wilson, Lipsey, and Derzon (2003) have shown that programs that tackle behavioral change and provide counseling services have the greatest effect upon reported levels of school-based aggression. Keeping anti-bullying initiatives alive and positively reinforcing prosocial behavior would seem to be the key to making schools safe. The challenge we face as parents and educators is to consistently model those behaviors we wish to instill in those we raise and those we teach. As we have discussed in Chapters 2 and 3, there may be elements of our own behavior or language upon which we may be forced to reflect and address. For example, do we value each student equally? Do we value individuality? Are there students in our classes today that we perhaps dismiss, or would find it easy to give up on? These are difficult and challenging questions, but they are questions we need to consider in order to ensure that no one student is left behind, and that every student matters.

WHAT HAVE WE LEARNED ABOUT BULLYING?

We have learned that bullying has been a facet of the social interactions of human beings for several hundreds of years, if not thousands. References to willful acts of violence visited upon the innocent can be found in the artifacts of many societies and cultures. Thanks to the early work of Peter-Paul Heinemann and Dan Olweus, we now not only question the acceptability of bullying occurring in our schools, but also actively challenge it. Researchers have shown us that, quite often, the perpetrators of bullying behavior do not acknowledge their own individual responsibility for their actions because of their belief in the shared culpability of the group. The notion of "diffusion of responsibility" arises from our understanding of mob culture and the fact that while identifiable individuals may have been brought to book for their incitement of violence, rarely are each and every member of the mob challenged for their part in an atrocity. History has shown us that mob behavior is all too easily forgiven, and that we have all turned a blind eye to the neighbor who once took the law into her or his own hands. In a world of violence and at times of war we are learning it is imperative that we do not imbue those with historical, cultural, or faith-based links to our nations' enemies with the same traits as those who make war against us. Schools are charged with the protection of all students and there are no exceptions.

We have discussed the need to understand the perpetrator of bullying and the victim. We have also discussed the need to consider the reasons why some students feel compelled to assert their authority through physical, verbal, or emotional violence, and why others are the targets of their animosity. While bullying should never be condoned, understanding the motivation behind an act of aggression can be the starting point to finding a solution. For the educator there should be no fear in considering whether rules, regulations, the ethos, or long held practices of a school are contributing factors in the maintenance of bullying behavior. Do one or more of those factors promote views or attitudes that discriminate against those who have in the past held less power, been subjugated, or perhaps vilified because of their differences? Are there ways in which individual and institutional practices can be altered so that respect for one another sits at the very core of the work of the school?

In considering ways to address bullying, not only have we looked at the needs of victims, and the skills they will need to overcome bullying, but we have also considered those interventions that actively seek to address the behavior of perpetrators. All young people have a right to an education— even bullies—and it is important that when challenging bullying behavior we look at restorative practices, and not solely those that are punitive. In Chapter 8, we have focused particularly upon the immediate and long-term effects of bullying behavior for both perpetrators and victims. It is imperative that we never underestimate the long-term damage bullying can cause to a young person's future potential. Educators and parents need to be aware of the danger signs, and act upon them. For parents the knowledge that their son or daughter is a victim or perpetrator of bullying can be devastating, and it is important that educators consider how this information is transmitted. We have discussed the fact that parents of victims often do not know that their child has been suffering harassment at the hands of peers for months and, perhaps, even years after it first started. Such knowledge when finally revealed can bring with it a sense of failure, and educators need to be able to support and comfort parents, and help them understand how victims of bullying become skilled in the art of hiding outward signs of distress. For the parents of perpetrators too there is a role for educators in providing support. Issues at home, issues relating to disability, relocation, or academic frustration and anxiety can be at the root of outbursts of anger. While it is important that parents understand their legal responsibilities when their child is accused of bullying another, quite often they will be unaware of such behavior until it is brought to their attention. Thus, a measured approach is required, and it is always best to presume a lack of knowledge in the first instance.

THE FUTURE: TOWARD SAFE SCHOOLS

Ultimately, this chapter leaves us with the question, "What needs to de done to make schools safe?" We would argue that the answer is, "Education." Students need to be educated, educators need to be trained, and parents need to be informed. Students, educators, and parents need the knowledge and skills to tackle bullying effectively. A student needs to be able to remove herself or himself from a bullying situation safely. An educator needs to able to deal with an incident of bullying immediately, identify its cause, offer a solution, and implement it soon thereafter. Parents need to feel confident in working collaboratively with a school to address their child's involvement in bullying if it arises, and to ensure that the school provides an environment that facilitates learning.

As we have noted in the previous chapter, with the gradual increase in gun crime perpetrated by students, school safety is at the top of everyone's agenda. The safety of each student rests not only with teachers, but also with national and state legislators, members of state and local boards of education, commissioners of education, superintendents, principals, and, of course, parents. Federal law requires that all schools challenge violent behavior and drug use, and provide evidence of their achievements in doing so. We believe that the safest schools are those that acknowledge that bullying occurs. Even with well-developed codes of conduct, disciplinary procedures, and restorative practices, some students will continue to bully others, and it is only by acknowledging the presence of bullying that educators can begin to openly work with parents and change student behavior.

A Model of Joint Parent-Teacher Education about Bullying

On the following pages we provide an outline of an introductory training program for educators and parents covering the issues we have raised in this book. The training is broken down into eight sessions. In planning the content of these sessions we considered flexibility in parents', teachers', and administrators' schedules, and recommend that the program is delivered over a four-week period, one evening per week. This will allow both parents and teachers to come together and discuss issues raised in the sessions, offering mutual support and providing each with insights into the perspective of the other. This program very much represents a starting point for a school community exploring bullying behavior for the first time. We believe that anyone can deliver this training program as long as they use the book as a guide. We have included brief notes for facilitators that are cross-referenced with key sections from each of the chapters, and information sheets that can be reproduced for the audience. We recommend that the full program is delivered, and recognize that issues such as bullying on the grounds of sexual orientation may result in heated debate, therefore it is important that state board regulations governing such issues are consulted beforehand (see http://www.nasbe.org).

Recommended Structure of this Introductory Training Program. Figure 10.1 provides an outline of our program and includes suggestions on the length of presentations, and how much time should be allocated to questions or comments. Invariably some topics more than others will generate conversation and strong views. Everyone has the right to be heard, but it may be helpful to set parameters of acceptable behavior and language.

Useful Tips on Structuring Presentations

Delivering a presentation is not an easy task; it is not so much about skill but about confidence. We hope that this book will provide the facilitator with the necessary information to feel confident about delivering an introductory program for educators and parents. We have identified some key issues and skills necessary for a successful presentation and training event.

Figure 10.1.
Suggested Format for the Introductory Training Progrm on Bullying (Four Weeks Duration)

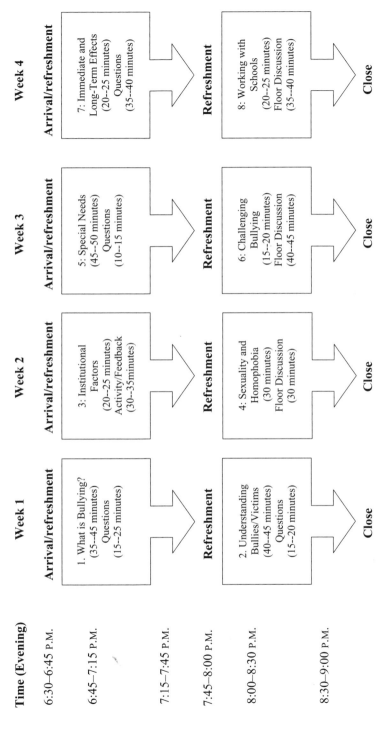

Note: Floor Discussion—encourage comments and a discussion from members of the audience using their own insights/experiences.

Preparing the Presentation. In preparing your presentation, always identify the aims or objectives of the session, and what your key goals are for that session. So, consider the following:

- What are the objectives of your session?
- What are the main points you want to make?

If there is anything that you find difficult to express, or feel uncomfortable about presenting (e.g., bullying and sexual orientation), think about beginning your presentation with the legal standpoint, and ask your audience the following questions:

- What does the law require us to do?
- How can we achieve this?

You may find it useful to prepare cue cards with key words and phrases, or quotes that enhance visual aids, or clarify points. A helpful tip is to mark on your cue cards when visual aids should be revealed, so that what you say and what you visually present correspond.

Always rehearse your presentation. Think about the words you are using, think about alternative definitions for words, phrases, or concepts that the audience may find difficult to understand (e.g., hegemony).

Delivering the Presentation. It is generally agreed that a good presentation follows a pattern that can be summarized as follows:

- tell the audience what you are going to say;
- then say it;
- and then summarize what you have said.

Always keep presentations short; visual aids should be succinct (see below), and never left up for more than five minutes. Try not to digress too much, but personal anecdotes will be helpful in making concrete ideas and concepts you have introduced.

Speaking to an Audience. Always try to speak clearly. Before the session begins try out the acoustics of the room. Are there any points in the room where you cannot be heard? Most experts agree a good presentation has a relaxed pace, so take your time. When you want to stress a key point, pause immediately after it, not a long pause, but a few seconds to allow the audience to understand the importance of the point you have made.

Try to maintain eye contact with your audience, do not focus on one person, but look around the room. If the audience is sitting in rows, try the four corners and center approach. With each new point you make, look toward the people sitting at the front left, back left, back right, front right, and then center. In large rooms or with large audiences, it is best to pitch your presentation toward the back.

Visual Aids. In the following pages we have provided some suggested content for overhead transparencies, power point, and flipchart presentations. These contain the minimum information necessary to stimulate thought. We have tried to stick to three or four key points per slide, and important information presented on its own. Always ensure that your visual aids are readable from a distance of six feet without using projectors.

You should consider how the venue for your training session is lit. If there is too much light near the projector screen or flipchart the contents of your presentation will be difficult to see.

Managing Your Audience and Questions. Perhaps the most difficult aspect of any presentation is managing an audience. If you are not confident that you can manage a question and answer session, ask a colleague or friend whom you trust to chair the session for you. The chair's role is to introduce the speaker, manage the time (giving appropriate prompts when time is nearly up), and manage the questions from the audience, identifying questioners in order, and ensuring that one questioner does not monopolize the event.

Since some of the topics raised will be challenging or controversial, it is worth suggesting guidelines for audience participation. For example, the anti-bullying intervention, Circle Time, provides a venue in which all members of a class can come together and talk about their feelings in a non-judgmental environment. The principles associated with this intervention are that everyone is listened too, everyone's views are respected, and that personal issues raised in the session are not disclosed to others. These three rules provide a useful framework for proactive discussion, and the means to gain a full understanding of the issues that face the whole school community.

If members of your audience begin to talk among themselves, there is a judgment call to make. Are they perhaps discussing a quick point with their neighbor, or are they trying to disrupt your presentation. Some experts suggest silently staring at the individual talking will have the desired effect. However, you may have said something that resonates with that member of the audience, and so you may wish to suggest that an opportunity to make comments or raise discussion points will follow soon. If an audience member is being disruptive, or challenging points you raise, it is entirely appropriate for you to ask them to keep their observations until the question and answer session. Remember, disruptive behavior such as talking over a presentation is a form of bullying too.

If there is one piece of advice we can offer to you as a facilitator of a presentation it is: do not be afraid to acknowledge that you may not be able to answer all the questions put to you. You can offer to find out and report back at a subsequent session, or even ask the questioner if she or he has any ideas how such information could be gathered and disseminated.

Ending the Session. End the session by reiterating the key points you wish to make, and thank the audience for their attention and participation.

APPENDIX

Session 1: What Is Bullying?

Suggested content of overhead. transparencies, powerpoint, or flip chart presentations.

Facilitator's Notes

In this session it is important to introduce bullying as one that affects *all* schools. Remember to stress that current definitions of bullying relate to repeated actions and not one-off incidents. You may wish to initiate a conversation about whether one-off incidents should count as bullying.

Stress the importance of understanding the dynamic nature of bullying behavior and that it takes many forms. A history of research on bullying can be found in Chapter 1 (pp. 3–6). Although it is not mentioned here, bullying incorporates actions resulting from hate/bias whether it is on the grounds of religion, race or color, sex, culture, disability, or sexual orientation.

What Is Bullying?

Bullying includes behaviors that constitute harassment, intimidation, taunting, and ridicule. Bullying can be motivated by hate or bias, ignorance or fear; it can be instilled through cultural norms, and peer pressure. Initiation rituals are a form of bullying.

National Conference of State Legislatures

1

Types of Bullying

- **Direct-physical bullying**
  - Hitting, kicking, punching, tripping up, or theft
- **Direct-verbal bullying**
  - Name-calling, labeling, or singing derogatory songs
- **Indirect or relational bullying**
  - Social isolation, rumor mongering
- **Cyberbullying**
  - Sending threatening text messages, e-mails, or posting hurtful comments on Web sites

2

Understanding Bullying

- **Ingroups and outgroups**
  - Categories/traits/people who are socially acceptable; belonging; social status
- **Diffusion of responsibility**
  - Larger the group, the less responsibility individuals take for their actions
- **Status**
  - Historically some groups are imbued with higher status than others.

3

Facilitator's Notes

Chapter 1 (pp. 6–8) provides a brief resume of social science research that underpins our understanding of why bullying exists. Examples of racial bullying and islamophobia as are provided on pages 8–10 that may lead to discussions about how we discuss 9/11 and the War in Iraq.

Session 2: Understanding Bullies and Victims

Suggested content of overhead transparencies, powerpoint, or flip chart presentations.

Bullies and Victims

- **Who are bullies?**
  - Boys who are physically stronger than others
  - Boys and girls who are more socially skilled, and can demonstrate leadership skills (although often in an aggressive way).
- **Who are victims?**
  - Boys and girls who are unable to defend themselves when challenged
  - High and low achievers
  - Those with poor social skills.

4

Facilitator's Notes

In this session it is important to explain that bullying can be very subjective. It is defined by either the intentions of the perpetrator, or by the way in which an action or behavior is perceived by the victim. Where it is repeated, there may be little doubt, and you should stress that there are key signs to look out for, which are summarized in *Information Sheets 1 & 2.*

Facilitator's Notes

Not all bullying involves a clear cut "victim" and perpetrator, Chapter 2 (pp. 19–21) provides some useful examples of the different types of "bully" that have been found. You may wish to initiative a discussion around how to identify the different types of "bully" and the reasons underpinning why particular students will engage in bullying behavior.

Some Different Types of "Bully"

- **The bully/victim**
  - A bully in one situation and a victim in another.

- **The provocative bully**
  - Provokes others as a means of retaliating through fighting.

- **The anxious bully**
  - Feelings of failure lead to the victimization of students perceived to be more successful.

5

Building upon a discussion of the different types of "bully," you may wish to discuss the fact that there are also different types of victim. How do we deal with the victim who is the target of jokes, who engages in attention-seeking behavior, or who is the willing target, and differentiate her/him from other victims?

Some Different Types of Victim

- **The target of jokes**
  - A student who is constantly made fun of, and who is often accused of not having a "sense of humor" by the aggressor; don't be fooled often the joker is acting deliberately.

- **The false victim**
  - Attention seeking behavior.

- **The colluding victim**
  - A student who willingly becomes the group's target to win "friends."

6

Session 3: Institutional Factors in Bullying

Suggested content of overhead transparencies, powerpoint, or flip chart presentations.

Socio-Cultural Perspective

The characteristics and systems within a school and their expression by faculty and staff will have an impact upon behavior in terms of the way in which students:
- determine those personal characteristics that are valued, and those that are not;
  - develop their own unofficial rules relating to success, and methods of competition.

7

Facilitator's Notes

Chapter 3 introduces a new way of looking at bullying. In this session, focus on the ethos of the school and how students learn and demonstrate those values, personal characteristics that are valued and those that are not. What are the values of the school? What attributes do (a) parents and (b) teachers value? Are they the same? We would advise reading Chapter 3 (pp. 36–41) before this session.

Group Activity

What student attributes does our school value?

- **What are those attributes?**
  - e.g., academic success, sporting achievement
- **How do we reward them?**
  - e.g., medals, prizes, cups, and certificates
- **How do we honor student achievements?**
  - e.g., do we make examples of them?
- **What sorts of attributes do students value?**
  - academic success, sporting achievement?

8

You may wish to break attendees into groups, and ask them to consider the questions posed on *Slide 8*. A second useful group activity is to get groups to consider the case study of *Prize-Giving Day at Westway High School* (page 42). Are there any problems with Mrs. Lopez's speech? In what other way might she have inspired students to value achievement? Is Mrs. Lopez's speech divisive?

Facilitator's Notes

This particular slide (*Slide 9*) challenges some of the core thinking behind SATs, and the way in which we look at students. It is important that educators can demonstrate to parents the ways in which they do value all students equally, and encourage skills beyond those that are purely academic. It is also important to consider language and how we use it in relation to some students (see pp. 45–46).

Have We Created a Climate Where Bullying Thrives?

- **Do we value all students equally?**
  - i.e., do we value some more than others?
- **Do we talk about students differently?**
  - i.e., do we dismiss some students as lost causes?
- **Do we value conformity above individuality?**
  - i.e., do we encourage each student to develop skills beyond the classroom and do we value them?

9

Session 4: Sexuality, Homophobia, and Bullying in Schools

Suggested content of overhead transparencies, powerpoint, or flip chart presentations.

Facilitator's Notes

Chapters 4 and 5 introduce aspects of bullying that rarely appear in mainstream literature. It is important to stress that physical, verbal, or indirect bullying that involves sexual content or is based upon a person's sexual orientation is likely to constitute criminal behavior (see *Information Sheet 3*).

Sexual Bullying

- **What is the purpose of "sexualized" language?**
  - Is it to sexually objectify a person and/or demean her or him?
- **Do we values female and male students equally?**
  - How can we demonstrate this?
- **How do we ensure that students value each other regardless of sex?**
  - What examples do we have of good practice?

10

Homophobic Bullying

- Do we recognize that alternative lifestyles exist that are not heterosexual?
  - How would we deal with a lesbian/gay student in our school?
- Do we ensure that our published literature acknowledges that all forms of bullying will not be tolerated?
  - Do we specifically mention sexual orientation?
- What can we do to ensure that homophobic bullying does not occur?

11

Facilitator's Notes

Addressing homophobia in schools is a particularly sensitive topic as it challenges some people's fundamental beliefs about that which is "natural." There are also issues relating to the appropriate age at which to discuss homophobia. In this session it would be useful to hear teachers' stories of their experiences of working with gay students, or indeed of views parents have on how this issue can be addressed effectively.

Things to Do

- Include sexual bullying and homophobic bullying in our nondiscrimination policy.
- Check the state board's regulations on sexual orientation discrimination.
- Where you suspect homophobic bullying, use the checklist provided.

12

Consider taking a secret vote to establish how many attendees agree with the inclusion of sexual bullying and homophobic bullying in the school's nondiscrimination policy. After the vote, provide guidance on the state's boards regulations governing discrimination on the grounds of sex or sexual orientation (check http://www.nasbe.org/ or the Web link provided in Table 9.1 (pp. 146–148).

Session 5: Special Needs and Bullying

Suggested content of overhead transparencies, powerpoint, or flip chart presentations.

Facilitator's Notes

For this session, it is important to consider bullying behavior in terms of disability harassment. Disability harassment is illegal under S. 504 of the Rehabilitation Act (1973), and Title II of the Americans with Disabilities Act (1999). Provide examples of disability harassment (see page 96).

Disability Harassment

Disability harassment is:

Intimidation or abusive behavior toward a student based on disability that creates a hostile environment by interfering with or denying a student's participation in or receipt of services, or opportunities in the institution's program.

U.S. Department of Education (2000)

13

When discussing IDEA it may be useful to refer to Schwartz's book in this series *"Including Children with Special Needs: A Handbook for Educators and Parents."* Reproduce the quick guide for school administrators on Title II of IDEA (see p. 97 and *Slide 15*), and discuss the 2004 reauthorization of IDEA and the requirements to consult with educators and parents where school conduct codes are broken (see pp. 98–99).

Title II of IDEA

Individuals with Disabilities Education Act 1997
- **State and school districts are responsible for:**
  - Ensuring the a free appropriate public education (FAPE) is made available to eligible students with disabilities; and
  - Ensuring that state and local civil rights, child abuse and criminal law is not violated by failure to act when disability harassment occurs.

14

District and School Liability

- Harassment based upon a student's disability

- Harassment denied student educational benefit

- Personnel with authority to stop the harassment had knowledge of it

- Personnel failed to act or acted with "deliberate indifference" to the harassment of a student.

15

Facilitator's Notes

A legal claim under federal antiharassment laws may be made where standards have been developed that establish district liability where one student harms another. Claims may be pursued if the one or more of the criteria identified in *Slide 15* can be established. Summaries of state laws, directive and standards are provided in appendix of Chapter 9 (pp. 160–172).

Lessons Learned by Parents

Suggestions:

- Always talk about bullying, define it, and make sure your child knows how to report it
  - Don't make your child a fashion victim
  - Suggest exit strategies such and teach them key phrases
  - Help your child build friendships outside school
  - Work with the school to stop bullying.

16

Slide 16 provides attendees with some suggestions from parents of children with special needs who have been bullied at school.

Facilitator's Notes

Slide 17 provides educators with an opportunity to consider some suggestions from the parents of children with special needs. Ensure that some of the discussion focuses upon the reauthorization of IDEA and the need to consult and consider individual circumstances where a school's conduct code is broken by a student with special needs. See Chapter 6 (pp. 98–99).

Suggestions from Parents

- Remember that not all disabilities are "seen," think before speaking!

- Introduce social skills training into the curriculum for all students

- Rethink zero-tolerance policies (IDEA requires that you consider individual circumstances in deciding whether to remove a student from school)

- Make sure unstructured time at school is adequately monitored and staffed.

17

Further information can be obtained from the Department of Education's Web site for IDEA.

Where Do I Go for Further Information?

http://www.idea.ed.gov/

18

Session 6: Challenging Bullying Behavior in School

Suggested content of overhead transparencies, powerpoint, or flip chart presentations.

Supporting Victims: Quick Tips

- Ignoring techniques
- Fogging
- Broken record
- Concentration techniques
- Desensitization

19

Facilitator's Notes

Chapter 7 provides an overview of the various interventions that have been used to challenge bullying behavior at individual, class, and school level. Here we provide Val Besag's quick fix when working with victims to help them cope with the bullying they are experiencing (pp. 106–112). These are not an alternative to group and curriculum-based interventions, and do not stop bullying.

Working with "Bullies": A Graded Response

- **Stage one:** Raise awareness of what constitutes unacceptable behavior

- **Stage two:** Avoid the blame game. Give the perpetrator an opportunity to explain what she/he thought she/he was doing

- **Stage three:** Try teaching empathy and reciprocity skills (e.g., turn-taking, debating rather than arguing)

- **Stage four:** Consider specialist programs/ sanctions.

20

Not all bullying behavior is deliberate, and in Chapter 7 (pp. 112–121) we discuss the fact that it is important *to give every student a chance to change*. Provide copies of Figure 7.1. Spectrum of Bullying Behavior and Responses.

Facilitator's Notes

How much bullying goes on in the school, and how has this been measured? The appendix of Chapter 7 provides an outline of *The Olweus Bullying Prevention Program* provided by Clemson University with contact details for further information. On a class-by-class basis educators might also want to use the short questionnaire provided in Table 5.3 of Chapter 5 (page 80).

How Much Bullying Is There in Our School?

- Do we know?
- If "yes," how do we know?
- Should we consider conducting a schoolwide survey?
  http://www.clemson.edu/olweus.

21

Session 7: Immediate and Long-Term Effects

Suggested content of overhead transparencies, powerpoint, or flip chart presentations.

Facilitator's Notes

In this session refer attendees to *Information Sheets 1 & 2.* Familiarity with the early signs of bullying and prompt action will mean that many of these long-term effects never take hold. Provide a brief overview of the signs of early onset depression and posttraumatic stress disorder (Chapter 8, pp. 137–138).

Long-Term Effects: Victims

- Depression
- Anxiety
- Latent aggression/expressed frustration
- Thoughts of ending life
- Posttraumatic stress disorder.

22

Long-Term Effects: Bullies

- Violent or abusive behavior in adulthood
- Broken or unsuccessful relationships
- Poor social skills
- Criminality.

23

Facilitator's Notes

For students who are perpetrators of bullying behavior, there remains a great deal of contention about the existence of long-term effects. *Slide 23* provides an overview of long-term effects for bullies that have some foundation in research literature.

Resilience

- **Individual factors include:**
  - assertiveness, problem-solving skills, self-awareness, positive outlook on life, empathy, having goals, aspirations and ambition, responsible alcohol use, a sense of humor.
- **Social support factors include:**
  - mentor or role model, meaningful relationships with others, integration into a peer-group.
- **Organizational/school factors include:**
  - equality, social-skills training, security.

24

The final slide for this session deals with the issue of resilience. It may be useful to ask attendees to consider what they currently do to facilitate resilience (i.e., offer assertiveness training) and what they could do following this training program. For example, linked to issues raised in Session 3 (*Institutional Factors in Bullying*) how can educators foster ambition in all students.

Session 8: Working with Schools: A Guide for Parents

Suggested content of overhead transparencies, powerpoint, or flip chart presentations.

Facilitator's Notes

In this session refer attendees to *Information Sheets 1 and 2* that provide much more detailed information on indices of bullying where students are both victims and perpetrators. Provide attendees with a summary of the implications of the reauthorization of the SDFSCA and *No Child Left Behind*. See *Information Sheet 4*.

Is My Child a Victim?

• **Physical signs**
  • cuts, bruises, torn or muddy clothes, and unspecified ailments such as headaches and stomach aches.

• **Behavioral signs**
  • unwillingness to travel to school alone, school refusal, avoidance of "friends," avoidance of specific classes, or stays in on evenings/ weekends.

• **Emotional signs**
  • sadness, distracted, forgetful, withdrawn, or intolerant of others.

25

In Chapter 9 (pp. 149–159) practical guidance is given to parents on what to ask if their child is suspected or accused of being a bully. Reinforce the fact that schools should adopt the graded response to bullying, and only consider punitive sanctions if the student has been brought to the attention of teachers and parents on a number of occasions (see *Slide 20*).

Is My Child a Bully?

• **Do any of these seem familiar:**
  • Changes in friendship patterns
  • A decline in grades
  • Expressions of disaffection with school
  • A desire to "show off"
  • The "purchase" of new items
  • Expression of low-self-esteem
  • Expressions of anger/irritation with others
  • Frustration with homework
  • Domination of siblings.

26

What Should I Do?

- **Talk to the teacher and/or principal**
  - try to confirm your suspicions.

- **Arrange a meeting with the teacher and/or principal**
  - Find out what s/he or they recommend(s).

- **Know your rights and responsibilities**
  - if your child is a victim, do you have sufficient grounds to ask the district to pay for a change of schools? If your child is a bully, will the school work with you to change the behavior?

27

Facilitator's Notes

Chapter 9 provides useful tips on questions to ask in meetings with parents and educators. It is important that educators find a solution that parents can support. If the student in question is a victim, SDFSCA may be required to pay for relocation expenses if a student has been the victim of a violent crime (see ***Information Sheets 3 & 4***). If the student in question is a perpetrator, make sure that parents are aware of their legal responsibilities (see page 155).

Information Sheet 1 for Educators and Parents
TELLTALE SIGNS OF BULLYING: ELEMENTARY SCHOOL

Parents

*If you think your child is a **victim** of bullying look out for the following:*

- increased quietness
- withdrawal from family interaction
- visible sadness
- withdrawal from friends and from activities once enjoyed
- an increase in days off school (complaints of head- and stomachaches)
- poor school performance (drop in grades)
- loss of appetite
- sleep disturbance (including bedwetting)
- only uses bathroom at home (school bathrooms are places where a lot of bullying takes place away from the view of teachers)
- torn clothes and/or unexplained cuts and bruises
- requests for extra money for lunch or additional allowance
- letters from school enquiring about homework that is reported lost, or reporting behavioral problems such as fights with other students

Educators

*If you think a student is a **victim** of bullying look out for the following:*

- lack of eye contract and visible sadness
- the onset of uncontrollable outburst of anger and frustration
- changes in friendship patterns and activities at recess
- a lack of engagement in class-based or group activities where previously there had been full engagement
- students make fun of him/her when he/she speaks
- Less attention is paid to school work and homework

*If you think your child is a **bully**, look out for the following:*

- defiant eye contact when behavior is challenged by a teacher
- causing classroom disruption
- snatching, grabbing, or taking items that belong to or are being used by others
- hitting and pushing other students out of the way
- ignoring a teacher's request to listen, or to stop talking
- an unwillingness to engage fully in class-based or group activities
- making fun of other students when they speak
- a lack of care in schoolwork and homework

*If you think a student is a **bully** look out for the following:*

- defiant eye contact when behavior is challenged by a teacher
- causing classroom disruption
- snatching, grabbing, or taking items that belong to or are being used by other students
- hitting and pushing other students out of the way
- ignoring a teacher's request to listen, or to stop talking
- an unwillingness to engage fully in class-based or group activities
- making fun of other students when they speak
- a lack of care in schoolwork and homework

Information Sheet 2 for Educators and Parents

TELLTALE SIGNS OF BULLYING: MIDDLE AND HIGH SCHOOL

Parents

*If you think your child is a **victim** of bullying look out for the following:*

- unspecified headaches, stomach aches (frequent requests to stay at home)
- outbursts of anger
- unexplained cuts and bruises, torn and mudsplattered clothing
- hitting out, flinching
- tiredness (linked to sleep disturbance)
- loss of appetite
- unexplained crying
- unwillingness to walk/travel to school alone
- avoidance of students once classed as "friends"
- staying at home on evenings and at weekends
- stealing money
- staying late at school (to avoid other students outside school)
- becoming introverted, sullen, and self-effacing, and/or expressing self-doubt
- greater uneasiness with expressing physical affection
- becoming easily distracted, forgetful (an indication that they are preoccupied with something else).

*If you think your child is a **bully**, look out for the following:*

- changes in friendship groups (e.g., the (loss of a friendship group)
- an unexplained decline in grades
- expressions of disaffection with school
- the desire to "show off" especially in front of others
- ownership of items or goods that could not have been bought without your knowledge
- expressed anger or irritation with fellow students (including making disparaging comments about them or threatening to hit them)
- frustration with homework
- domination or subjugation of siblings

Educators

*If you think a student is a **victim** of bullying look out for the following:*

- visible tiredness
- a noticeable change in behavior (i.e., sudden and inappropriate outbursts of anger or frustration)
- lack of confidence
- social isolation and a lack of engagement with others at recess
- reticence in class-based or group activities where previously there had been full engagement
- other students make fun of him/her when he/she speaks
- Changes in grades (in some cases this is not a downward trend as students may spend more time alone studying and have few recreational outlets)

*If you think a student is a **bully** look out for the following:*

- defiant, rude, and challenging behavior when admonished by a teacher
- leading classroom disruption, particularly encouraging a small group of other students
- little or no regard for other students' property
- other students move out of their way in the hallways and at recess
- ignores a teacher's request to listen, or to stop talking
- an unwillingness to engage fully in class-based or group activities
- openly disparaging of other students' contributions to the class
- lack of care in schoolwork/homework

Information Sheet 3 for Educators and Parents

THE SLIDING SCALE OF BEHAVIOR

Actions that should be challenged but may not constitute criminal behavior

Direct-Physical Bullying	Direct-Verbal Bullying	Indirect/Relational Bullying	Cyberbullying
• Damaging property • Pushing/ shoving	• Making threats • Trying to demean or embarrass another • Gossiping, teasing, calling names • Making fun of a student's clothes or possessions	• giving dirty looks • ignoring someone • excluding someone from the group • spreading rumors	• Currently some state legislators are attempting to pass laws specifically addressing cyberbullying

Actions that should be challenged, some of which constitute criminal behavior under state/federal law

Direct-Physical Bullying	Direct-Verbal Bullying	Indirect/Relational Bullying	Cyberbullying
• Causing physical harm • Damaging property • Initiates fighting • Defacing personal or school property (e.g., graffiti)	• Threatening physical harm • Insulting family • Insults about weight, size, body shape, race or color, religion, culture, sex, disability, or sexual orientation • Making threatening or harassing telephone calls	• Playing tricks with the aim of embarrassing a person	• Sending derogatory e-mails, text-messages • Posting derogatory comments about or inappropriate pictures of a person on Web site

Actions that should be challenged, and that constitute criminal behavior under state/federal law

Direct-Physical Bullying	Direct-Verbal Bullying	Indirect/Relational Bullying	Cyberbullying
• Causing physical harm • Physical cruelty • Violent assault • Assault with weapon • Arson • Repeated threatening behavior/gestures • Destroying personal property • Writing graffiti that makes comments about weight, size, body shape, race or color, religion, culture, sex, disability, or sexual orientation	• Making repeated threats • Extorting money through threats of violence • Blackmail • Insults about weight, size, body shape, race or color, religion, culture, sex, disability, or sexual orientation	• Enforcing group exclusion of an individual by means of threats against personal safety • Organizing meetings or events with the intention of publicly humiliating a student	• Sending threatening e-mails and text-messages • Posting derogatory comments about or inappropriate pictures of a person on Web site • Making threats in chatrooms

Information Sheet 4 for Educators and Parents

SAFE AND DRUG-FREE SCHOOL AND COMMUNITIES ACT

On January 8, 2002, President George W. Bush signed into law the *No Child Left Behind* Act that reauthorized Title IV of the *Elementary and Secondary Education Act* (EASA) Part A—the *Safe and Drug-Free School and Communities Act* (SDFSCA). The SDFSCA State Grants Program authorizes activities designed to prevent school violence and drug use, and to assist in the development of safe, disciplined, and drug-free environments that will support student academic achievement. Key changes include:

- State and local prevention programs and activities are required to meet the *Principles of Effectiveness*, which are:
  - Funds must be used to support programs grounded in scientifically based research.
  - States and local recipients have meaningful and ongoing consultation with, and input from, parents in the development and administration of programs/activities.
- Each State establishes a uniform management information and reporting system to support decision making.
- Funds can be used for the following activities if funding for activities is not received from other agencies:
  - purchase and installation of metal detectors, electronic locks, surveillance cameras, or other related equipment;
  - reporting of criminal offenses committed at school;
  - development and implementation of school security plans including the purchase of technical expertise to enact those plans;
  - supporting activities that ensure students travel safely to and from school;
  - the hiring and appropriate training of school security staff who enact the school's drug and violence prevention activities.
- Local education authorities in receipt of SDFSCA funds must develop a plan to keep their schools safe and drug-free through:
  - appropriate and effective discipline policies;
  - security procedures;
  - prevention activities;
  - student codes of conduct;
  - development of a crisis management plan in case of violent or traumatic incidents occurring on school property.

Parents are entitled to participate in and be consulted about any activities undertaken by a school to challenge violence and drug use. It is incumbent upon State and local education authorities to report effectively on the actions they have taken to combat violence and drug use in schools, and parents have the right to question the efficacy of such programs based upon the monitoring data that each school, district, and State is required to collect, analyze, and publish. For parents who believe their children are already attending *"persistently dangerous schools"* (as determined by the State), or who have been victims of violent crime, the State is required to offer an alternative choice of schools, and, where necessary, pay for transportation (although there is a funding cap).

Questions for Parents

🖎 Do I model appropriate behavior?

🖎 Do I know the danger signs of bullying?

🖎 Do I know how to approach the school when my child is being bullied, or accused of bullying another student?

🖎 Am I confident in talking to teachers or the school principal about my child's behavior?

Questions for Educators

🖎 How can I keep anti-bullying initiatives alive?

🖎 Do I model appropriate behavior?

🖎 Do I dismiss some students, or value one more than another?

🖎 Do the rules, regulations, ethos, and practices of the school effect bullying behavior?

🖎 Do I know the danger signs of bullying?

🖎 Do I know how to deal with an incident of bullying effectively?

🖎 Do I know what alternatives courses of action I can take to stop bullying behavior?

REFERENCES

Gazelle, H., and Ladd, G. W. (2002). Interventions for children victimized by peers. In P. A. Schewe (Ed.), *Preventing Violence in Relationships: Interventions Across the Life Span* (pp. 57–78). Washington, DC: American Psychological Association.

Schwartz, D., Forman, A. H., Nakamoto, J., and Toblin, R. L. (2005). Victimization in the peer group and children's academic functioning. *Journal of Educational Psychology, 97,* 425–435.

Wilson, S. J., Lipsey, M. W., and Derzon, J. H. (2003). The effects of school-based intervention programs on aggressive behavior: A meta-analysis. *Journal of Consulting and Clinical Psychology, 71,* 136–149.

Glossary

Direct-physical bullying. A form of bullying behavior characterized by actions such as hitting, kicking, punching, or tripping up another individual. Some researchers include the destruction of homework and theft of personal belongings as forms of direct-physical bullying.

Direct-verbal bullying. A form of bullying behavior characterized by actions such as name-calling, labeling, or singing songs about another individual.

Early onset depression. A form of depression beginning in childhood. Symptoms include persistent sadness, expressions of hopelessness, irritability, increasing requests to stay at home, drop in grades, poor appetite, sleep disturbance, fatigue, poor concentration, poor self-esteem, somatic complaints (e.g., headaches and stomach pains), and a lack of enthusiasm and engagement.

EASA. *The Elementary and Secondary Education Act* which was reauthorized in 2002 as part of the *No Child Left Behind Act.*

FAPE. Free and appropriate education. *See* IDEA

Fogging. Fogging is a technique whereby a victim of bullying deflects insults by saying well-rehearsed phrases.

Hegemony. The way a society or community maintains the belief that there is no alternative to the status quo.

Heteronormativity. The presumption that everyone is or will grow up to be heterosexual.

Homophobic bullying. A genre of bullying behavior that includes behaviors that are direct-physical, direct-verbal, or indirect/relational, but which are aimed at an individual who is victimized because of her or his actual or perceived sexual orientation.

Hypermasculinity. Excessive portrayal of masculinity as strong, virile, and powerful.

IDEA. The Individuals with Disabilities Education Act 1997 is a federal law which ensures that all students with disabilities have access to free and appropriate public education.

IEP. The individualized education plan is a student-centered learning plan developed by a multidisciplinary team to meet the short- and long-term special educational needs of students.

Indirect bullying. A form of bullying behavior characterized by actions such as rumor mongering, or by the social isolation of an individual by one or more peers.

Relational bullying. *See* Indirect bullying

SDFSCA. The *Safe and Drug-Free School and Communities Act* which was reauthorized and came into effect on July 1, 2002. The SDFSCA State Grants Program authorizes activities that have been designed to prevent school violence and drug use, and to assist in the development of safe, disciplined, and drug-free environments that will support students' academic achievements.

Self-Esteem. The value an individual places upon her or his own perceived attributes and status.

Sexual bullying. Sexual bullying is not only manifest in inappropriate touching or crude remarks, it is also systemic and psychologically invasive with its driver being the attainment of social power through acquiring a high-status reputation.

Social-esteem. The value others place upon an individual's perceived attributes and status.

Special needs. Special needs include students with physical disabilities, learning difficulties, or any form of physical, behavioral, emotional difficulty. Increasingly researchers are including children who suffer from clinical obesity under this term, recognizing the impact it has upon physical and emotional health and well-being.

Index

About the Authors

VALERIE E. BESAG is an educational psychologist and former teacher who is an international expert on school bullying prevention. She is the author of *Bullies and Victims in Schools* (1989) and *Understanding Girls' Friendships, Fights, and Feuds* (2006). Besag has been the recipient of the prestigious Churchill Fellowship which allowed her to travel overseas to further understand and explore the phenomenon of bullying and peer support in schools.

NEIL DUNCAN is Senior Lecturer in Education at the University of Wolverhampton in the United Kingdom. He is the author of *Sexual Bullying* (1999), considered by practitioners and academics alike to be one of the most significant texts on the nature and expression of verbal bullying among boys and girls.

IAN RIVERS is Professor and Head of Psychology at Queen Margaret University in Edinburgh, Scotland. He is the author of over 70 articles and book chapters on bullying and homophobia in schools. He is the recipient of the British Psychological Society's 2001 award for Promoting Equality of Opportunity in the United Kingdom through his work as a researcher and psychologist.